The Women Incendiaries

The Women Incendiaries

Edith Thomas

Translated from the French by
James and Starr Atkinson

Haymarket Books
Chicago, Illinois

Originally published as *Les Pétroleuses*
© 1963 by Editions Gallimard
First published in English in 1966
Translation © 1966 George Braziller, Inc.

This edition published in 2007 by Haymarket Books
P.O. Box 180165, Chicago, IL 60618
773-583-7884
www.haymarketbooks.org

ISBN-13: 978-1931859-46-2

Trade distribution:
In the U.S. through Consortium Book Sales, www.cbsd.com
In the UK, Turnaround Publisher Services, www.turnaround-psl.com.
In Australia, Palgrave MacMillan, www.palgravemacmillan.com.au.

Cover design by Josh On

This book was published with the generous support of the
Wallace Global Fund.

Printed in Canada by union labor on recycled paper
containing 50 percent post-consumer waste in accordance
with the guidelines of the Green Press Initiative,
www.greenpressinitiative.org

Library of Congress Cataloging-in-Publication Data
is available

2 4 6 8 10 9 7 5 3 1

CONTENTS

	Introduction	vii
ONE	Women during the Second Empire	3
TWO	The Debate over Women	21
THREE	The Siege of Paris	37
FOUR	The 18th of March	52
FIVE	The *Union des Femmes*	70
SIX	The Clubs	88
SEVEN	Opinion and Action	104
EIGHT	Education	112
NINE	A Great Journalist	119
TEN	Ambulance Nurses, Canteen Workers, Soldiers	133
ELEVEN	Bloody Week	150
TWELVE	Were There Any *Pétroleuses?*	165
THIRTEEN	The Execution of Hostages	189
FOURTEEN	The Major Trials	197
FIFTEEN	From Auberive to New Caledonia	217
	Appendix—Further Sentences	231
	Notes	245
	Manuscript Sources	262
	Newspapers Consulted	263
	Bibliography	264
	Index	270

INTRODUCTION

THIS STUDY CONCERNING the women of the Commune does not arise from arbitrary choice; it grows out of the nature of things.

Unquestionably, there is only one history: that by which the entire human species is swept along. But this history is almost exclusively the work of men—which, to judge by the results, is no compliment to them. In any case, women almost never figure in it, except in minor roles or as victims.

The fact that "feminism"—or rather "feminine humanism," of which feminism is merely the nineteenth-century avatar—is thought today to be outmoded is a means of conjuring away the problems it posed, problems that are still very far from being solved. To confirm this one need only look at the composition of the committees that run political parties, ministerial councils, and meetings of the United Nations. Despite declarations concerning the political and social equality of men and women, this equality more often than not remains illusory. But that the principle has been accepted is already a considerable achievement; a century ago, it would have seemed foolish and outrageous.

The history of half the human species, then, which has almost always been enacted on the fringes of History, raises its own questions, peculiar to itself. In France, from Christine de Pisan to Louise Labé, from Marguerite de Valois to Marie de Gournay, from Mme. du Châtelet to Mme. de Coicy, from Olympe de Gouges to Mme. de Staël, we never lose sight of its secret thread: all of them demand that women be considered as human beings. From 1830 on, Saint-Simon and his followers, Fourier and his

adherents, Cabet, and Marx posed the question simultaneously with that of the proletariat: what was involved
was the liberation of all of humanity, whatever be the
form of servitude by which it had hitherto been fettered.
Claire Demar, Flora Tristan, Pauline Roland, Jeanne
Deroin, Daniel Stern, George Sand, and many others
passionately discussed the conditions of this liberation:
education, career, marriage, position under the law, political rights, and so on.

If women had participated in the great battles of the
1789 Revolution, they were even more caught up in the
1848 Revolution, from which they hoped for recognition
of their rights. But the men of 1848 did not seem disposed
to grant them these rights, any more than did their "great
forefathers" of 1789. The battle lines were drawn again in
1871, on the occasion of the Commune.

The history of women, considered as a branch of social
history, is generally held to be insignificant. For "serious"
historians, it deserves to be taken no more seriously than
any other "lady's work." An historian of the Commune
has recently written: "There will inevitably be feminine
demonstrations, and they will be enacted by the petty
bourgeoisie. They may be the rowdiest of all, but the
essential point does not lie in that; it lies in the fact that
the working women of the Commune shattered the illusion according to which the emancipation of their sex was
to occur as a side effect of the class struggle." Now this
emancipation is by no means an illusion. The women who
today have access to intellectual professions (university
professors, doctors, engineers), in the capitalist countries
as well as in the socialist ones; who earn a living without
a protector, either lover or husband; who are directly
engaged in society—these women are infinitely more
"free" than their grandmothers would have dared to
dream. The liberation of woman, then, is not necessarily
fused with that of the proletariat. The two do not move

at the same rate. The fact that Marxist historians and bourgeois historians are in accordance on this issue proves merely that the former are as bogged down in masculine prejudice as their colleagues, although for them it is more a question of political tactics.

Other people have traditionally believed that the problem no longer exists. Women hold no interest for them except in their amatory relations—that is, they matter only as objects. Bedroom histories will always be bestsellers. Mme. de Pompadour and Mme. du Barry still draw attention to themselves, and re-emerge periodically, accommodating themselves to the tastes of the day. Mme. de Staël is more interesting for her lovers than for the struggle she waged against Napoleon. Flora Tristan and Pauline Roland interest no one.

Therefore, it must be agreed that the history of women's movements flows against the tide, and unites everyone against it. Also, even more than in other fields, large vague syntheses have preceded the precise, necessarily limited, studies which would have allowed the former to be compiled with some degree of accuracy. My ambition is solely to do a little clearing of a terrain that is still covered with brush, to pursue a task of analysis so that there can be a subsequent attempt at a real synthesis—which is impossible given the present state of our knowledge. In short, I seek to establish a few modest truths. The studies I made about the women of 1848, Pauline Roland, and George Sand, led me logically to the Commune.

Contemporaries were struck by the importance of women's participation in the 1871 Revolution. I shall summon a few before the jury, to justify my having taken on this task.

Maxime du Camp: "The weaker sex drew attention to itself during those deplorable days, and, as a sequel to *Mérite des Femmes,* one might write a quaint book called *On the Role of Women During the Commune.* The story of their folly ought to titillate the talents of a moralist or alienist. They tossed much more than their caps over windmills; not stopping at this minor detail, all the rest of their clothing followed. They bared their souls, and the amount of natural perversity revealed there was stupefying. Those who gave themselves to the Commune—and there were many—had but a single ambition: to raise themselves above the level of man by exaggerating his vices. There they found an ideal they could achieve. They were venomous and cowardly. . . . They were all there, agitating and squawking: the vacationing boarders of Saint-Lazare; the natives of little Poland and greater Bohemia; the vendors of *modes à la tripe de Caen*; the gentlemen's seamstresses; the gentlemen's shirtmakers; the teachers of grown-up schoolboys; the maids-of-all-work; the vestals of the Temple of Mercury, and the Virgins of Lourcine. What was profoundly comic was that these welfare-clinic escapees unfailingly invoked Joan of Arc, and were not above comparing themselves to her. . . . During the final days, all of these bellicose viragos held out longer than the men did behind the barricades. . . . Many of them were arrested, with powder-blackened hands and shoulders bruised by the recoil of their rifles; they were still palpitating from the overstimulation of battle. . . ."[1]

And from Dauban, also an extreme reactionary: "The women were like the men: ardent, implacable, frenzied. Never had they turned out in such great number, braving peril and defying death. They dressed the horrible wounds made by *mitrailleuses,* shells, and cylindrical bullets; they ran to the side of those who, under the pressure of unheard-of tortures, were howling, sobbing, and bellowing with pain and rage; then, their eyes filled with blood, their ears full of those cries torn from the last living shreds of flesh, they resolutely took the chassepot and ran toward the same wounds and the same agony. And what dauntlessness at the barricades, what ferocity in combat, what presence of mind, against the wall, before the firing squad. . . ."[2]

From Dumas *fils*, this final word: "We shall say nothing about their females, out of respect for women—whom these resemble once they are dead."[3]

On the other side is Benoît Malon: "Above all, one important fact that the Paris revolution brought to light is the entry of women into politics. Under the pressure of circumstances, and through the spread of socialist ideas and the propaganda of the Clubs . . . they felt that the cooperation of women was indispensable to the triumph of the Social Revolution which had reached the fighting stage; that woman and the proletariat, those ultimate victims of the old order, could not hope for their emancipation except by forming a strong union against all the forces of the past. Then again, they recalled that the women of Paris had been responsible for the 5th and 6th of October, one of the finest chapters of the Revolution of 1789, as well as for many others. They passionately put themselves at the service of the Commune's Revolution. . . . Impressive numbers were always to be found in group activities, and many of them gave their lives for the revolutionary cause. A number of these heroines were daringly, yet modestly shooting at the advanced posts, some in the uniforms of the National Guard. One could no longer keep track of the canteen workers who distinguished themselves. Ten or more had been killed, and the survivors were no less brave."[4]

From Lissagaray: "That woman who greets and accompanies you is the valiant, the true Parisian woman. The androgynous scum risen out of the filth of the Empire has followed her clientele to Versailles, or is working the Prussian army at Saint-Denis. The woman who comes forward now in the streets is strong, loyal, tragic; she knows how to die as she loves, because of that pure and generous vein which, since 1789, has run richly through the heart of the people. The companion of work also wants to be associated with death. 'If the French Nation were composed of nothing but women, what a terrible nation it would be,' wrote the correspondent of *The* [London] *Times.* . . . She does not hold her man back; on the contrary, she thrusts him into battle, bringing soup and linen to him in the trenches as she did when he was on the job. Many women did not want to go back, but took up a rifle. . . ."[5]

Finally, from Marx: "The tarts had again picked up the scent of their protectors who had gone to ground—those men of family, of religion, and especially of property. In their stead, the real Parisian women had come to the surface: heroic, noble, and devoted, like the women of Antiquity." And again: "The women of Paris joyfully give up their lives on the barricades and execution grounds. What does this prove? It proves that the daemon of the Commune changed them into Megaeras and Hecates."[6]

I could go on amassing evidence but this would be useless. It is not very important that the critics of the Commune called the women who participated in it "females" and "viragos," and that the supporters of the Commune exalted those "pure heroines." From these contradictory opinions one certain fact can be extrapolated: the massive, extraordinary, momentous participation of women in the Commune. The parliamentary inquiry into the insurrection of March 18th, moreover, confirms this officially: 1,051 women were called before the Councils of War. Others—how many will never be known—were killed at the barricades and in the great slaughter during Bloody Week.

Who were these women? What did they do? What did they want? What did they think? Were the *"pétroleuses"** a myth or a reality? All of these questions demand the historian's attention.

* See note, p. xiv.—*Trans.*

The documents that allow history to be retraced—here, apart from newspapers and memoirs, the dossiers of the Councils of War in the Archives of the Ministry of War, and the reprieve dossiers in the National Archives—remain so much dead and meaningless paper, unless they be selected, criticized, interpreted, and organized by the historian who uses them. In this confrontation the historian's personality must necessarily be apparent. Historical method is a science, surely, and a rigorous one. But objectivity is a decoy, particularly when we are concerned with periods that are near to us and touch upon problems that are still burning issues. One's view of the Commune varies depending upon whether one considers it as the revolt of a people rightfully inflamed by defeat and social injustice, or as an undertaking of criminal subversion against the established order. In the former instance, one will tend to consider the women and men of the Commune as pure, sympathetic heroes; in the latter, as common criminals.

We shall endeavor to escape this naïve Manichaeism. Despite its mistakes and shortcomings, the Commune embodies a significant moment in revolutionary history, in the progress of justice. But the cause of justice is not upheld by choirboys and Girl Scouts.

Nor do I believe that an historian can speak about things which he has not himself experienced, can understand actions that are utterly alien to him. There is no question that one must not trust analogies in history: nothing ever repeats itself exactly. But Mathiez stated that what had made him able to understand the legality of the revolutionary tribunals was having served on military tribunals during the First World War. This "bourgeois" historian, brought up during a period of relative social calm, could not have understood the imperatives of exceptional justice without this experience.

What allows me, perhaps, to understand the woman of the Commune is that during the Resistance, I took part in the coordinating committee of the Union des Femmes Françaises, edited their tracts, and helped them to plan the women's demonstrations against the Vichy government and the Nazi occupation; the barricades of 1944 replied to the barricades of 1871.

But if the historian has the right to be impassioned, and to be—whether as man or as woman—committed to his time, this passion should under no circumstances entitle him to pass in silence over awkward documents, nor to conceal truth, which, like Janus, always has two faces.

A final word about the title.* The term *"pétroleuses"*[7] was coined in 1871 to designate the women who were accused of having set fire to Paris. I am using it in a much wider sense: it applies to all the women who were involved in the revolutionary movement of 1871. In no way is its use pejorative.

* The original French title is *Les Pétroleuses,* here rendered as *The Women Incendiaries.—Trans.*

THE WOMEN INCENDIARIES

CHAPTER ONE

WOMEN DURING THE SECOND EMPIRE

A T THE OPERA BALL, the most fashionable courtesans—Marguerite Bellanger, Blanche d'Antigny,
Cora Pearl, La Païva, and others of lesser renown—were
waltzing with the men of the hour. Dressed in silk, em-
broideries, lace, and furs, the *dames aux camélias* were in
their glory. The crinoline had come into style, and was
becoming a symbol. A gown called *à la Béguine*, of Chan-
tilly lace and Indian cashmere, was made of 250 yards of
fabric and cost 10,000 francs.[1] On the Market, fortunes
accumulated one day and were gobbled up the next. A
new-moneyed luxury, a petty depravity, a certain bad taste,
characterized the zenith of a class whose motto remained,
more than ever, Guizot's saying: "Get rich." But the full

advice, it seems, was "Get rich by work and by thrift."
Amen: in this case it was still other people's work. Never
had money been so fashionable, never did it so take the
place of everything else.

Two distinct classes, then: the rich and the poor. This
was carved into the very stones and asphalt of the city, for
everyone to see. Reconstructing the old Paris, Baron
Haussmann had drawn new thoroughfares which could
easily be swept by cavalry charges from north to south,
west to east. Thus no more barricades. No more would
you see those citadels of the poor which caused the authorities so much bother in 1830, in 1848, in 1851. No longer
were the houses divided perpendicularly, as in the eighteenth century, between bourgeois and artisans. The workers were pushed back toward the north and east of Paris,
to Belleville, Ménilmontant, and, beyond the fortifications, toward the suburbs that were emerging into the
ugliness of industrial anarchy (called "freedom").

All along the new streets sprung up the expensive
houses of the eminent banking and business families.
Two different worlds, with hatred and fear—or at best,
ignorance—of one another.

For the condition of the workers had scarcely improved
at all since 1830. Wages were still beneath the level that
would allow a man to live like a human being. Yet within
the proletariat itself, a distinction must be made: women
were the more exploited. At Lyon and in the Nord,
women worked in factories, where their wages were rela-
tively high: 3.5 francs for a weaver, 3 or 4 francs for a
warper.* But most women could earn a living only doing
the needlework which had given Paris an international

* A rough approximation of contemporary (1871) comparative
money values: a franc, consisting of 100 centimes, equaled $.20
or 9½ pence. Thus there were 5 francs to the dollar and 25
francs to the pound. For prices during the siege of Paris, see p.
38.—*Trans.*

reputation, even if these masterpieces provided them with little more than a starvation wage. Certain working women (tailor's seamstresses, for example) might manage to make 4.5 francs, but others got no more than 50 centimes. Seamstresses earned, on the average, 1.70 francs; embroiderers, 1.71 francs; dressmakers, 1.98. A deluxe linen-draper might get 5 or 6 francs, but most received barely 2 or 2.50 for an eleven-hour working day. Out of 112,000 working women, 60,000 were employed in needlework, and 6,000 made the artificial flowers that were so much in fashion during the Empire: "The most skillful are veritable artists, who study natural flowers lovingly and reproduce them more faithfully than do the best painters."[2]

I still have paper boxes of those fuchsias, roses, and ivy leaves which my great-grandmother made during the Second Empire, and which are masterpieces of their kind. The "veritable artists" earned 3 francs for 11 hours of this work.

Le Journal des Demoiselles called the attention of young bourgeois ladies to the lot of their unfortunate sisters: "Among the poor girls who ply the needle, there is a wage-scale which goes from 5 francs down to 15 centimes per day. The average comes to 2 francs earned for a thirteen-hour day . . . and still the thread or silk used by the worker must be deducted from this sum."[3]

The highly paternalistic Jules Simon subsequently figured out the budget of a working woman living alone on the streets of Paris: if she was very skillful, she earned 2 francs per day, not counting Sundays, holidays, and the off season, which was very important in the fashion industry. The earnings of a working woman added up, then, to about 500 francs per year, if she was not sick a single day. First, she must have a place to live. When Haussmann's thoroughfares were opened, numerous workers' dwellings were destroyed. For a tiny seventh-floor garret, one had to allow 100 to 120 francs on the left bank, 150 francs on the right; for an actual room, 20, 30, or 40 francs more. In 1851, inspectors reported a woman "buried rather than dwelling in a hole five feet deep and three feet wide"; another who, in order to breathe, had to break a pane of her attic window. Jules Simon figured 115.50 francs for clothing. As for heat, a coalman would fill the foot-warmer with charcoal and ashes for 5 centimes. Light was a wick steeped in oil, counting on 10 centimes' worth of oil for three hours. Thirty-six francs, then, for light and heat. Thirty-six francs for laundry. Assuming the rent to be the minimum of 100 francs, that's a total of 287.50 francs; 212.50 francs were left for food—that is, 60 centimes a day, enough not to die of hunger. Many working women ate only bread and milk. If one chanced to become ill, there was no way of paying for a doctor and medicine. And of course many did not earn even 2 francs a day.[4]

The convents gave the linen-drapers and dressmakers great competition, for the handiwork of the convent sewing-rooms did not cost much. A nun, "who is not rushed by anything, works slowly and works well." Thus the religious orders could supply excellent work at prices 25 per cent lower than those of working women.[5] This competition was not, perhaps, irrelevant to the anticlericalism of the Commune women.

Therefore it was almost impossible for a working woman to live off her wages alone. She found a mate, legal or not. A shoe-stitcher, Victorine Brochon, whose evidence we shall come upon again and again, describes the life of a working-class family in these terms:

I have seen poor women who work 12 or 14 hours a day for ludicrous wages, forced to leave aged parents and children and to shut themselves up for long hours in unhealthy workrooms, beyond the reach of either air or light or sunshine—for they are lit by gas.

Droves of women are crammed into factories to earn the modest sum of 2 francs a day, or even less, and nothing on Sundays and holidays. Saturday night, having finished their day's work, they spend half the night mending the family clothing; they also go to the washhouse to soak their clothing, so that they can wash it on Sunday morning.[6]

Her husband escaped the hovel where they lived by passing his free time in bars; there he spent three-quarters of his pay. Sometimes he beat his wife, and she would have to protect the children from his blows. She had to ask for credit from the butcher, coalman, and grocer; to pawn her old clothes at the Mont-de-Piété,* that poor man's bank. For the woman, there was no rest: she went to work and kept house. For the man, there was the bar. This description bears out Villermé's inquiries, or Michelet's *Le Peuple*.

What good was it, among such poverty, to invoke traditional morality? "The words honor, virtue, faith, ring false in the ears of these outcasts. For them, they are hollow phrases, void of meaning."[7]

Prostitution, then, appeared as a normal, and often indispensable, means of supplementing one's wages, or of earning a living when regular employment was unobtainable. In 1867, the Lyon Academy proposed the following subject, suggested by a former Saint-Simonian, Arlès-Dufour: "How to raise women's wages to the same level as men's, when the work they do is equal, and to make new careers available for women." A girl named Julie Daubié won the prize with her study *The Poor Woman in the Nineteenth Century*. She, like Jules Simon, emphasized the economic character of this prostitution:

* The Mont-de-Piété was a sort of city-owned pawnshop where those who needed to, could pledge their goods or part of their salaries against a cash loan.—*Trans.*

The inadequate pay of the urban working-woman sometimes drives her, even during a period of industrial prosperity, into meeting her budget by selling her body; this is called the fifth quarter of the day. During periods of unemployment, this kind of right to work fills the entire day. In various cities, according to the testimony of the inspectors of the Morals Bureau, women who have decidedly not lost all sentiment of honor are forced into ignominy because they lack means of subsistence. . . . Generally the poverty of women is such that among 6,000 registered in Paris, only 2,000 had any resources. One woman can be mentioned who struggled three days against the tortures of hunger, before giving in. . . .[8]

In any case, marriage in the eyes of the law and of God was not the rule in the working-class family. But these irregular unions were often of long duration, and displayed a much greater fidelity than many legitimate marriages.[9] This "concubinage," which outraged the chaste Councils of War and seemed to them one more charge against the *Communards,* was indeed considered scandalous by all right-minded people. The Catholic Association of Saint-François-Régis made it its business, although in vain, to facilitate the marriage of women. Generally, people were a good deal more indulgent toward courtesans who had succeeded in climbing up into the demimonde than toward the poor girls of the Rue Quincampoix and the Faubourgs.

Thus the morality of the working class was not, as a rule, that which reigned among the bourgeoisie. It had other laws: the foremost virtue was that of solidarity; the ideal to be pursued blindly was that of justice.

In 1864 the International Working Men's Association was founded in London; its inaugural address was drafted by Marx, and its French section organized by Tolain,

Fribourg, and Charles Limousin. These men were Proudhonians, and it is known that Proudhon, who adjusted so
well to the Empire, was resolutely hostile to women
working. Consequently, the French section of the International drew up a statement against the participation of
women in industry. This stand did not keep women from
belonging to the International. Victorine Brochon took
part in the meetings and brought her husband to them.
She wrote: "Even though Frankel was a Hungarian, he
was as much a compatriot of ours as if he came from
Montmartre."[10] She helped set up a cooperative butcher
shop in the quarter of La Chapelle.[11] One-third of the
profits went to the members of the cooperative, one-third
made up the reserve fund, and the final third was lent
without interest to establish another cooperative. But in
1867, the bread problem became so acute that they could
not deny workers credit; that was the ruin of the undertaking.

Nathalie Lemel, a bookbinder, started another food
cooperative, *La Marmite*, with the worker Varlin. Born in
Brest in 1826 of a well-to-do family—her parents owned a
café—the carefully raised Nathalie Lemel was highly respected in the town. At first, she ran a bookstore with her
husband in Quimper. But their business became rather
shaky, and the Lemels went to live in Paris, where she
worked in several binderies. She belonged to one of those
mutual societies which the police kept under constant
surveillance because they could easily turn into societies
of resistance. In 1866, Nathalie Lemel became a member
of the First International. She was a militant who read
"evil newspapers" aloud. By virtue of her intelligence and
"the luminous clarity of her mind," she exercised an
undeniable influence over her fellow workers. But her
independence and her political opinions separated her
from her husband who, moreover, had started to drink.

La Marmite, whose aim was to "furnish workers with

food at a low price," was a cooperative authorized by the government. Thanks to the activity of Nathalie Lemel, who was its treasurer, the society developed rapidly. Taking up Jeanne Deroin's former project for federating the trade unions, they created an organizing committee which was to consolidate the various food, consumer, and production cooperatives. There too, Nathalie Lemel, who took on its secretarial duties, played an important role. This banding together for solidarity had two goals, political education and propaganda for the International,[12] which were what separated the cooperatives of working-class origin from similar efforts established by the charitable segment of the bourgeoisie. The former societies were only stopgaps which were moving toward social revolution; charity was an end in itself.

Yet another consumer cooperative, with the strange name of the *Société des équitables de Paris*, was set up by another woman, Marguerite Tinayre. She belonged to a middle-class family from Issoire, where she was born in 1831. She was a good student and in 1856 received her qualifying certificate at Lyon as an elementary school teacher. She married a notary clerk, and first ran a private school in Issoire. Then, "giving vent to her reckless imagination and having always professed advanced ideas" (so reads a police report in the inimitable style of documents of this type), she "went up" to Paris and ran private and "protestant" schools in Neuilly, Bondy, Noisy-le-Sec, and Gentilly. She was a woman "of unusual energy and quickness" who, alas, was irreproachable from the viewpoint of "morality"—except for the fact that she shared her family's subversive ideas: those of her brother Antoine Guerrier and her brother-in-law Jules Babick, a slightly crazy adherent of the Fusionist religion. Along with some former Saint-Simonians who, unlike most, remained faithful to the ideals of their youth, Marguerite Tinayre then organized *Les Équitables de Paris*. The meetings were held on the Rue des Vieilles-Haudriettes, at the home of a shoe-maker, Henry, who was its president. Marguerite Tinayre, a member of the Control Committee, allied the coopera-tive with the International and the *Fédération des Sociétés Ouvrières*. She took the floor at political meetings, organized as of 1868, to defend "socialist and antireligious ideas." A dangerous woman, in short, and one who would bear watching.[13]

But Marguerite Tinayre was also a novelist who put herself under the patronage of George Sand, to whom she dedicated her first work, *La Marguerite*, in 1864. Natur-ally, like George Sand and Daniel Stern, she took a mascu-line pseudonym, and her novels may be found in the Bibliothèque Nationale under the name of Jules Paty. These ill-starred novels have not had a single reader in the course of a century; I had to cut their pages.[14] Their fault lies in their being long-drawn-out and full of pathos. But, good or bad, a novelist never conceals himself in his works: even if he believes that he is objective, traces of his personality can be found there. This is why I would have felt I was remiss had I not tried to know Marguerite Tinayre a little better through the novels of Jules Paty. The Council of War that made me aware of this identifi-cation was right. Jules Paty took as setting the Auvergne and Issoire, where Marguerite Tinayre was born. His novels are dated from Noisy-le-Sec, where Marguerite Tinayre once ran a school. Jules Paty cites as an epigraph a sentence from a certain Jean Guerrier (*Oeuvres In-édites*), who must have been some distinguished member of her family, since Marguerite Tinayre's maiden name was Guerrier. These little games of internal criticism are diverting for the researcher; the reader will forgive me if they bore him.

In her first work, *La Marguerite*,[15] the edifying story of a sister's devotion to her nephews, Marguerite Tinayre describes for us some peasants from the Allier who came to Paris to try to make their fortune. The coalman of the Rue des Amandiers manages to earn a decent living, but the laundress of the Rue des Blancs-Manteaux wears herself out in bringing up her four young nephews. Disease is a catastrophe which throws budgets so precarious as hers into confusion. There is no meat in the pot even on Sundays, and they take their old clothes to the Mont-de-Piété. In Paris, "being poor is a hundred times worse than anywhere else."[16] All these common people are described precisely and lovingly. They are the ones we shall meet again among the participants in the Commune. In this novel, the Sisters of Saint Vincent-de-Paul appear as good angels, showing that Marguerite Tinayre was not at this time at all anticlerical—or rather, that her anticlericalism admitted of careful nuances. Everything ends happily, as in the novels of George Sand: the uprooted peasants, unable to adjust to Paris, return to their village—a conclusion that obviously contains nothing subversive.

But in her second novel, *Un Rêve de femme,*[17] Marguerite Tinayre frees herself from the influence of George Sand. She displays a disabused skepticism that is hardly present in her mentor's work, and that seems rather surprising coming from a revolutionary temperament. Marguerite Tinayre must have been a woman without illusions—which still did not keep her from participating in a revolution. In literature, she wished to be neither classical (she acknowledged only the rule of common sense) nor romantic (she did not dream of the Middle Ages, "that monstrous abuse of force against justice, which delivered the nation's masses, like vile matter, over to the iron gears of feudalism"), nor eclectic ("the rule of choice is still a rule"). A realist, then? Yes, "if realism consists in seeking the ideal of art in the sincere imitation of nature, particularly if this inquiry into the physical order should lead to the discovery of harmonies and world balances of which religion and morality are merely formulas brought within the scope of a human understanding obscured by ignorance, tainted by passion, or atrophied by poverty."[18]

Marguerite Tinayre, then, was a moralist above all else, but a moralist who distrusted current morality and religion: it is in this that she was revolutionary. She adds that her book is not for the eyes of young people. An advocate of absolute liberty in art, she wants art to be no more chaste than nature. Yet be reassured: despite its stereotypes, *Un Rêve de femme* seems today very decorous. What Marguerite Tinayre wanted was to put women on their guard against "their pointless aspirations, their groundless worries," and to draw their attention to the necessity of "physical harmony" in marriage, a delicate subject that was scarcely spoken of in 1860. A pure young girl, Valentine de Rochebrune, whose father is a ruined nobleman, marries a wealthy young marquis, Gustave de Bergonne. Under the influence of his wife and his secretary Artona, a poor country youth, Gustave sets up a factory which gives work to the peasants, and creates a model city with houses for the workers, a day nursery, a school, and a hospital. But alas, with the couple Valentine and Gustave, "the laws of nature were reversed," "the natural protector was the protected," the woman superior to the man. One day, Valentine gives herself to Artona, who, unlike the finer-bred Gustave, is handsome, strong, stalwart, and so forth. This mistake brings terrible ills upon all these equally noble and generous beings. Gustave goes mad, abandons the factory and village, refuses to recognize his son, and shuts up his wife, who finally commits suicide.

Marguerite Tinayre introduces a loathsome businessman, the typical newly-rich bourgeois, whom she despises. But she does not, on the other hand, show herself as the dupe of revolutionary phraseology. The Clubs of 1848 in Issoire seemed to her "political pasquinades," and she cannot have too much sarcasm for the bands of imbeciles who overrun the tribune. "In this second dawn of liberty illuminating the rights of the common people, showing them the duties attached to universal emancipation, the peasants, brutalized by fifty years of ignorance, hoped for no progress but the repeal of the tax on drinks, and knew only one political duty: the abolition of that fee by force or otherwise."[19] The women, massed outside, listened to the orators and exchanged stupid remarks about the "tarts of the harsh Rollin (Ledru-Rollin), la Mennais (Lamennais), and la Martine (Lamartine)." But this description, which seems to accord with that of the scorners of the Revolution of 1848, is still not a right-wing criticism. Artona, the author's spokesman, explains, in fact: "The folly of individual interests possesses this mass . . . But let the light shine into all darkened minds, and you will see to what heights man can rise."[20]

Thus, for Marguerite Tinayre, there had to be, first and foremost, a task of education among the masses. The mutual benefit societies and the consumers' cooperatives, in which she participated actively, were the means of this education.

The "political" activity of women, then, appeared first in these various consumers' cooperatives; and this follows tradition. Women are much closer to everyday realities than men are. Feeding the family is a part of their age-old role. The price of bread has been their business for centuries. Thus, before seeking to involve themselves in truly political activity, they tried to attend to "the administration of things," upon which they could act directly. It is from this angle that the most aware women among them thought to have a hold on the social reality.

But that was obviously only one aspect of the question.

It was not just the working women who had complaints to make of an order that excluded women from society.

A century ago, a woman could scarcely exist socially without a protector, either husband or lover. The education she received was mediocre or nonexistent. The Law of 1850 had indeed ordered the creation of a girls' school for every commune with a concentrated population of more than 800. But the law lay dead on the books. Out of 48,496 public schools, 18,732 schools were for boys, 11,836 schools were for girls, and the others were coeducational. It is true that the private schools re-established the balance to some extent. But, generally, one child in five never went to any school, because he was in rags and was dying of hunger. Those men and women who taught in elementary schools constituted a decently-dressed proletariat. More than 4,000 schoolmistresses earned less than 400 francs annually. Almost 2,000 earned 100 to 200 francs.[21] We have seen that the minimum budget of a Parisian working woman was fixed at about 500 francs.

The liberal professions were virtually closed to girls of the bourgeoisie. When Julie Daubié sat for her baccalaureate, despite the opposition of the rector of Lyon, and passed that examination, the Minister of Public Education refused in his turn to give her her diploma, for fear of "forever holding up his ministry to ridicule." This incident marks the starting-point of a revolution, and one forgets today that this revolution is the outcome of a patient, daily, and colorless struggle.

This demand for equal education, which the old Christine de Pisan had already made in the fifteenth century, this passion for culture, this feeling of frustration—we meet them all during the Empire, among those poor schoolmistresses, who "went up" to Paris to escape being swallowed by the provinces, to initiate themselves into the culture that the provinces refused them, to transcend the destiny that was imposed upon them by tradition. Marguerite Tinayre had come from Issoire; Louise Michel came from Audeloncourt. Let us pause a moment over this girl, who became a symbol.

On May 28, 1830, at the Château de Vroncourt in the Haute-Marne, a young servant, Marianne Michel, gave birth to a little girl whom she named Louise. Who was her father? Perhaps the owner of the château, Charles-Étienne Demahis; more likely his son Laurent, who, some days later, left the castle and settled down at a nearby farm. The servant remained at the Château de Vroncourt with her little Louise. The latter was brought up by Charles-Étienne Demahis and his wife, whom she called "grandfather" and "grandmother," with an unfailing care and tenderness. On the paternal side of her family were members of the legal profession who had been brought up on Voltaire and Rousseau, and who welcomed the 1789 Revolution sympathetically. On her mother's side were decent and upstanding peasants who had taught themselves how to read. Louise Michel was raised within the confines of the Voltairian rationalism of her Demahis grandparents, and the popular Catholic mysticism of her mother's family. She went to the village school, where she attracted attention because of her gaiety and her unmalicious pranks. She read all the books her cousin brought home from the *collège,* and also read, under her grandfather's guidance, Corneille, Lamartine, and Lamennais, who had a decisive influence upon her. During the long winter evenings, her grandmother sang, and her grandfather read or recounted the legends and epic struggles of the First Republic. But she also loved the rough games of boys, and long walks when the wind was blowing. She knew of the poverty of the peasants, and tried to assuage it. She gave out fruit from the garden and money she stole from her grandfather; he offered to give her a small amount every week for her charities. "I refused," she says, "thinking that I lost too much by doing so." No sense of property, the giving of all she had—she retained these character traits all her life. But she also learned that charity was not enough: "I understood," she says, "the agrarian revolts of ancient Rome." Her pity extended even to animals mistreated by the peasants.

Her sensibility and her intelligence were apparent in her early poetry, which she sent to Victor Hugo. The poet answered, and encouraged her. Later, in 1870, they met, and Louise Michel figures briefly in the *Carnets intimes*.[22]

Although—despite her stunning eyes and forehead—she was not pretty, the girl who was called "Mlle. Demahis" in the country was twice asked for in marriage by substantial country bourgeois. She turned them away by laughing at them. She did not accept the condition of women, any more than she could bear the misery of animals or the poverty of peasants. Chrysale's* theories exasperated her. She wanted to find a love based on admiration, a Saint-Just and not an Arnolphe, a man whom she could admire, whose ideal she could share, with whom she could devote herself to the same cause. But a Saint-Just cannot be found every day, at Vroncourt or elsewhere.

Twice, then, Louise Michel rejected the classic destiny of women. Her grandfather died in 1845, her grandmother in 1850. Laurent Demahis' wife turned her out of the château as a "bastard"—the first time this word had been hurled at her—and forbade her to use the name of Demahis. Her grandfather had arranged a small dowry for her, but Louise had turned down the option of marriage. It was necessary, therefore, for her to earn a living. Today, a girl like Louise Michel would enroll at a university; in 1850, she had no solution but that of becoming a schoolteacher. She got her diploma at Chaumont and took a job at Audeloncourt, so as not to be separated from her mother.

The December 2nd coup d'état threw her onto the side

* A character of well-intentioned, but dull and plodding common sense in Molière's comedy *Les Femmes Savantes.—Trans.*

of the opposition. Her students sang *La Marseillaise* and left church when prayers were said for Napoleon III. The schoolteacher was denounced. She had to go to Chaumont to give an explanation to the inspector who, as an old liberal, admonished her paternally and asked her to promise to be more prudent. But Louise Michel backslid; she published a violent article in one of the newspapers of the *département*.

> Domitian reigned. He had banished the philosophers and the wise men from Rome, raised the praetorians' pay, reinstated the Capitoline games; people were admiring the merciful emperor while they waited for his assassination. The finale comes earlier for some and later for others; that's the only difference. We are in Rome, in A.D. 95.

This time she had gone too far. The prefect threatened to send her to Cayenne. She insolently replied that she would go willingly, at the government's expense, to establish a school there.

The case stopped at that for the time being. But Louise Michel was suffocating in provincial conformity. She wanted to find a community of thought and action. Paris lured her, as it does so many provincials from Julien Sorel to Rastignac. But Louise Michel did not leave as they did, impelled by a will to power. She wanted, not to "arrive," but to fulfill her destiny.

We find her first as assistant headmistress in the school of Madame Vollier, at 14 Rue de Château-d'Eau; then—because schoolteachers in the State-run system had to swear an oath to the Empire—she directed a private school at 24 Rue Oudot. She used remarkably bold methods, which presaged the methods of the new education a century later. She put children into touch with concrete objects, flowers and stones, and got them to know and to love animals. Later she declared before the Council of War: "The morality I was teaching was this: to develop a conscience so great that there could exist no reward or punishment apart from the feeling of having done one's duty, or having acted badly. As for religion, that was left to the will of the parents."[23]

She taught herself at the same time she was teaching the children. She eagerly attended the night courses at the Rue Hautefeuille, run by Jules Favre, Eugène Pelletan, etc.

The women who, during the Empire, were young schoolteachers or were preparing to be, were greedy for this knowledge, in which women can share only insofar as they snatch out at it with both hands; they came to the Rue Hautefeuille to quench their thirst for knowledge and liberty. A passion for knowledge possessed us. I believe that more often than not we seemed like students, not like schoolteachers.[24]

She learned physics, chemistry, and natural history. In Darwin's *Origin of Species,* in Claude Bernard's *Introduction à la Médecine Expérimentale,* she discovered the foundations of the scientific method and of determinism. Louise Michel declared herself an atheist and a materialist. But "although the individual does not survive in a personal form, he still remains, to whatever extent he has been able to devote himself to the human community." In politics, she joined the International.[25]

This education of women, however mediocre it may have been, was carried on in the professional schools founded by Élisa Lemonnier. At the Rue Thévenot school, Louise Michel taught literature and ancient geography.[26] She also turned her attention to the immediate relief of working women's poverty, by founding *La Société Démocratique de Moralisation,* whose goal was to help women live by, or return to, work done "in duty." The declaration specifies that what mattered was not theoretical problems, but furnishing workers with bread and jobs.[27]

None of that went very far. It was the condition of women itself that had to be transformed; and, at the same time, the whole of society.

CHAPTER TWO

THE DEBATE OVER WOMEN

THIS SECOND-RATE position which transformed women into objects was justified by the "thinkers" of the period: Auguste Comte, Michelet, Émile de Girardin, and particularly Proudhon.

Whereas most socialist theorists—Saint-Simon and his followers, Fourier and his adherents, Cabet, and Marx— were proclaiming that women, like the proletariat, had the right to be considered as free and equal human beings, Proudhon fell into step with the most reactionary theorists, in this realm as in others. His influence on the French working class was too profound, at that time, for us not to linger a little over his lucubrations.

In *Amour et Mariage*, Proudhon sets out to demonstrate

woman's triple inferiority from the physical, intellectual, and moral points of view. Physically, woman is an instrument of reproduction and nothing more. Therefore she cannot exist in society without a "protector"—father, brother, husband, or lover. With pseudo-scientific pedantry, he declares that if man's physical strength be given the factor 3, that of women will have the factor 2. It is not known upon what investigations Proudhon based these mathematical conclusions, but no matter.

From the intellectual viewpoint, woman cannot, he says, sustain man's "cerebral tension." Her intellectual frailty affects not only the quality, but also the duration and intensity of her activity. Woman has a mind that is essentially erroneous, and the error is irremediable. Her mind is neither critical nor synthesizing. Without man, she would be incapable of transcending the state of bestiality. For intelligence is a function of strength, from the intellectual viewpoint as well as from the physical. In this realm also, man therefore has the right to the factor 3, and woman 2.

One might at least hope that woman would recover ground on the moral plane. Even many misogynists have acknowledged this. But Proudhon, lucid spirit, sees what no one else has perceived: virtue, too, is proportional to strength. Thus the conscience of woman, insofar as it concerns justice, is inferior to that of man. She is aware only of charity. In politics, woman is reactionary; for her, the aristocracy represents the true social order. Her character is weak and inconsistent: she whines, weeps, and wails. These facts, expounds the latter-day Chrysale, are generally observable. Moreover, woman is immodest, for chastity is a corollary of justice.

From these irrefutable observations are derived precise measurements. Woman = 2 x 2 x 2, man = 3 x 3 x 3. Q.E.D.

According to these eminently scientific revelations, the

subordination of women is therefore inevitable, and entirely justified. Woman has not the choice between "housewife or courtesan": marriage alone can keep her from falling into evil ways. Moreover, it is obvious that in marriage the authority and power of command revert to man. Divorce, of course, is prohibited. In *La Pornocratie*, Proudhon confirms the preceding observations. Woman does not know how to walk; she is meant for dancing or for the solemn gait of a procession. A philosophizing woman becomes ugly. If, by ill luck, it should happen that he, Proudhon, marry a lady author, he would offer her this heartfelt address:

> Madame, you have appeared against my will at the meeting of the Academy. You are smothered in vanity, and it will be the downfall of us both. But I shall not drink the cup to the dregs. At the first act of disobedience, wherever you may run for refuge, I shall reduce you to such a helpless state that you can never bounce back and get yourself talked about.

A pity that Proudhon did not write for the Boulevard; he would have been a hit. He advises a young man thus: "If you want to get married, understand at the outset that man's primary condition is to dominate his wife and to be the master." And this other advice, unparalleled in baseness: "If she brings you money and you have none yourself, you must be four times stronger than she is." And that is what passes for socialist parlance.

If it serves any purpose to pause a moment over these idiocies, it is because Proudhon was, during the Empire, the principal thinker of the French proletariat. Therefore it is no wonder that in 1866 the French section of the International presented a memorandum against work for women. Nor, under these circumstances, is it any wonder that women did not always join forces with the proletariat, as Flora Tristan once did, nor that they waged war on their own ground—even those who, from the political point of view, claimed kinship with the Republic, socialism, and democracy. When it came to the problem of women, reactionaries and progressives often fell into agreement about keeping them subservient.

Jenny d'Héricourt, in *La Femme Affranchie* (1860), led the attack, with violence but with wit. She had no wish to reply to those who claimed that, because woman had been the first to sin, God had willed that she be submissive; instead, she answered the others—Michelet, Proudhon, Émile de Girardin, Auguste Comte—who carried on the debate at the level of reason and justice. Malicious jokes, slander, and insults were lavished upon women who defended their rights. "Vain hopes. The time when we could be intimidated is no more." Woman, it was said, cannot have the same rights as man, because her intellectual faculties are inferior to his. This means that "you consider yourselves all to be equal in ability, and each as intelligent as any of the others." How absurd! Yet men considered themselves all to be equal before the law; the law, then, is not based on ability. The proof is the same as far as function is concerned: woman performs only inferior functions. "Then you have to prove that the functions each of you performs individually are equal; that Cuvier, Geoffroy Saint-Hilaire, Arago, Fulton, and Jacquard did no more for civilization than an equal number of pinhead-manufacturers." It remains to be proven that the jobs of motherhood and housekeeping are not as useful to humanity as those "of jewelsmiths or manufacturers of children's toys." It also remains to be proven that schoolmistresses, dressmakers, and milliners did not perform functions equal to those of schoolmasters, tailors, or hatmakers. If the law is not based upon function, why speak of the value of function when women are concerned?

Woman could not be man's equal before the law, it was said, because she was temperamentally unsuited to enter

certain careers. A man unfit for bearing arms, then, would
be excluded by the law. "If a woman had written anything
so silly, she would be trumpeted as a fool from one end
of the world to the other." Woman could not be man's
equal before the law because he protected and fed her.
"Then acknowledge the rights of grown-up daughters and
of widows whom you do not feed or protect." It was also
said that woman laid no claim to their rights. But "was it
necessary to wait for the whole male population to lay
claim to the vote before it was given them?"

Today this whole debate seems founded upon truisms.
But it took almost a century for these common-sense assertions to be no longer shocking, or not to seem like ludicrous paradoxes. Jenny d'Héricourt warned the democrats
of the consequences of their ostracism of women. If women
drifted away from the Revolution of 1789, it was because
they saw that the Declaration of the Rights of Man had
nothing to do with them. History repeated itself in 1848.
"I tell you this in all sincerity: all your struggles are in
vain, if women do not march with you." Indeed, it was
women who inculcated children with their earliest ideas:
"You are blind not to understand that if woman is on the
one side and man on the other, humanity is doomed to do
the task of Penelope." And, in a last appeal to the democrats who were condemning women to eternal subordination, she cried:

> Woman is ripe for civic liberty, and we declare to you
> that, from this time on, we shall regard as an enemy
> of progress and of the Revolution anyone who comes
> out against our legitimate claim, just as we shall rank
> among the friends of progress and of the Revolution
> those who speak out for our civic emancipation—even
> if they be your enemies.

The challenge had been flung down. A young friend
of George Sand, Juliette Lamber (Mme. Edmond Adam),

had it in for Proudhon in particular; witness her *Idées anti-proudhoniennes sur l'amour, la femme et le mariage* (1861). The tone was calmer, but the criticism was as far-reaching.

Proudhon's theories on love were too backward to awaken the slightest response. But his opinions on women were much more dangerous, "for they express the general feeling of men who, whatever party they belong to, progressive or reactionary, monarchist or republican, Christian or pagan, atheist or deist, will be delighted to have found a means of soothing their ego and their conscience at the same time." Proudhon's crime was having tried to prove that man's superiority to woman was at once necessary and legitimate. Juliette Lamber then reconsidered Proudhon's pseudo-arguments in order to refute them. She insisted upon the necessity of giving women an education which would enable them to earn a living. They had to become "producers," for work alone could establish their freedom. She recognized the importance of motherhood; but maternal concerns did not occupy all of a mother's time, and, besides, many women had no children. Women's wages were often indispensable to the livelihood of the family, and indispensable, too, if prostitution was to be kept within bounds. "Giving women access to careers with free and decently paid work is the same as shutting the brothel doors. Do you want that, men?" And that was of course the most important aspect of the problem. Men's attitude to prostitution was, in general, ambiguous. They pretended to be outraged by it, expressing their scorn for the prostitutes who would not exist without the use to which men put them. Concerning marriage, Juliette Lamber proclaimed women's rights to divorce, and to the possibility of marriage contracts allowing them the administration of their own property. These aspirations, shocking a century ago, are today written into the law.

Louise Michel attacked Michelet: "The great man

makes woman into an idol—and a poor idol, for her husband, a pretty puny specimen, has had to create her in his image."[1]

But women were not content with writing. In answer to Barbey d'Aurevilly, who in an article on *Les bas-bleus* had insulted "smart women," a well-brought-up young girl, Maria Deraismes, decided to overcome the timidity that an excessively good education had given her. At the request of two editors of *L'Opinion Nationale*, she agreed to participate in the Conferences of the Grand Orient (1865). Even though the reporter on Émile de Girardin's newspaper was very hostile to the preferment of women, he wrote: "I was very much surprised when I saw a girl of twenty-four or twenty-five walk in, with a rather pale face, great distinction of form and bearing, a simple elegance; neither foolishly timid nor insolently poised." Maria Deraismes was famous overnight.

From 1866 to 1870, before an increasingly large audience, she spoke of women's emancipation and of free thought. Wisely and knowledgeably, she examined the historical, legal, and familial condition of women. "The inferiority of women is not a fact of nature; it is a human invention and a social fiction." In downgrading women, people lower the potential of the entire society. And after September 4, 1870, when the Republic was proclaimed, she warned the republicans: "If the democrats do not have women on their side, their triumphs will be merely superficial and transitory." The education of children would pass out of their hands, and women would constantly be preparing for reaction.[2]

In 1868, the Empire granted freedom of assembly. The people, who had been silent for so long, awakened. The conferences at Vaux-Hall were directed at a public much more of the working-class than that of the Grand Orient. The cycle of conferences began with "Work for Women." Women's wages, always lower than those of men, had decreased with a "terrifying rapidity," and would end up "permitting no other alternative but prostitution or suicide to women who have only work to live by," stated a great number of orators.[3] But a strong Proudhonian current existed in the International. For these followers of Proudhon, woman, as we have seen, was mere "receptivity" and consequently incapable of creating anything by herself, "a housewife or a courtesan," etc., etc. The discussions started out on these premises.

Maria Deraismes, Paule Minck, and André Léo came to defend the political rights of women. Much notice was taken of Paule Minck, founder of the *Société Fraternelle de l'Ouvrière,* and editor of a little paper called *Les Mouches et les Araignées.* Her father, Jean Népomucène Mekarski, former aide-de-camp in the Polish army, had emigrated to France in 1831. Her mother, Jeanne Blanche Cornelly de la Perrière, belonged to the lesser nobility. Their children, Paulina Mekarska (Paule Minck) and her brother Jules, a quantity-surveyor, caught the attention of the police because of their "dangerous and harebrained opinions." (Jules Mekarski was to become commissioner of police during the Commune.[4]) Paule Minck was "a little, very dark woman, somewhat sarcastic, who spoke with great energy." A language teacher, linen-draper, and sometime journalist (for none of these occupations gave her enough to live on), it was said that she was "as skillful at plying the needle as at giving lessons."[5]

André Léo, too, was one of the more prominent orators. She was already known for her novels; *Un mariage scandaleux* had attracted critical attention. "This novel is one of the most noteworthy works that has come to light during recent years," we read in *Le Siècle* for September 4, 1863. And in *Le Constitutionnel* for July 28, 1863: "There are passages that are as beautiful as the best of George Sand: the same strength, the same scope and the same simplicity; less idealism and lyricism, perhaps, but a better conceived plot and a more exact observation."

Un mariage scandaleux is, indeed, as interesting as George Sand's best novels (which, in my opinion, is a compliment). The story is well constructed and well handled. The descriptions of the countryside are pleasant, and one feels that the sensibility behind them is very much attuned to trees, earth, the sky, and the seasons. Peasants and bourgeois appear, delineated with a sharp, sometimes almost cruel, pen—one that is, in any case, without illusions. The subject-matter itself—the marriage of a poor girl of the bourgeoisie to an intelligent young peasant—comes directly from George Sand. Love overthrows social barriers; happiness is possible when it is removed from considerations of rank and money.

In *La Vieille Fille,* André Léo returned to the theme of the girl who prefers celibacy to a second-rate marriage. But in the end, it is the obstacle of age which she has to surmount; the marriage will be happy, even though the thirty-five-year-old girl is wed to a boy of twenty-five.

In *Un Divorce,* André Léo studies the consequences of divorce with great objectivity. One might believe that this bold woman was defending a right which did not yet exist in France at the time, and which was proclaimed by the socialists and the republicans. Not a bit of it. With great clarity she shows the unhappiness of children torn between their father and their mother. Although divorce is legitimate when a couple is sterile, it solves no problem at all when they have children. Instead, then, one must go to the root of the evil; marriage without love—marriage which, too often, is nothing but an alliance "between pride and cupidity." This "moralization" of marriage and this defense of the family come from Pierre Leroux, who was also the mentor of George Sand. Indeed, André Léo (Léonide Béra), born in 1832 at Champagné-Saint-Hilaire in the Vienne, the daughter of a naval officer, had married a follower of Pierre Leroux, Grégoire Champseix. After the December 2nd coup d'état, they lived in Switzerland (most of André Léo's novels take place in that country). Their marriage was happy. They had two children, André and Léo, whose names made up their mother's *nom de plume*. Back in France after the amnesty, Grégoire Champseix died in 1863. His wife had to support herself and her children by writing. But she also entered into political activity; more precisely, into the struggle for women's rights. It was at her house that the platform of the *Société des Droits des Femmes* was discussed.[6]

In her study *Les Femmes et les Moeurs*, she took her turn at refuting the various arguments of the antifeminists. Physical inferiority? Woman was, as a matter of fact, the "first beast of burden," and even today one can see the chores women tackle in the country. Were the toils of pregnancy and labor, and the care devoted to children, also to count for nothing? The fact that woman's physical resistance was different from man's did not imply that she was inferior to him. As for the false ideal of the pale, vaporish woman, André Léo reduced it to what it was: a passing fashion. "When nerves are no longer in style, they will be put to much less use," she remarked sensibly. History has proved her right. The vapors, the swoons, the flacons of smelling salts—which, moreover, were reserved for women of "quality" during the eighteenth and nineteenth centuries—have disappeared completely. Intellectual inferiority? Women had never been given the possibility of training their intelligence. Let education be as complete for woman as for man, and it would be seen what happened to that pretext of inferiority. Motherhood was the only role that she was allowed to play. But woman would be more capable of raising her children if she were less ignorant, less denigrated as a moral and intellectual being. Besides, she was occupied with the duties of motherhood for no more than about fifteen years. And what about those who had no children? Actually, they were denied the right to knowledge and to work because society wanted to deny them independence, because society wanted to keep them in a state of subordination. Revolutionaries became conservatives on this question. Socialists were divided. Proudhonians were hostile. For them the family was to be "an absolute monarchy" in which the father was to reign uncontested. Well, "a woman in slavery can raise nothing but slaves." Democracy proclaimed that freedom was necessary to "the dignity and the morality of the human being." But when it came to women, freedom was "an object of suspicion and of terror." Democracy proclaimed humanity's redemption through knowledge, but knowledge for women would be a poison. Democracy believed in the virtues of fellowship, but marriage was supposed to be based upon obedience. And, returning to the arguments of Jenny d'Héricourt, André Léo recalled that even if woman's inferiority were admitted (and it was still to be proven), the social contract was not to be based upon the law of the strongest. Even if woman's inferiority were admitted, was the ballot "a doctoral diploma"? Either the principles of democracy were false, or else one had to grant women the same rights as men or risk repudiating those very principles.

It must be agreed that these were strong arguments. But the working-class public at the Vaux-Hall remained unmoved, stated Gustave Lefrançais. A friend of Pauline Roland, Gustave Lefrançais was to be a member of the Commune. He was not a Proudhonian, and acknowledged the justice of these criticisms. But, he claimed, they were relevant only to conditions in the bourgeoisie:

> What does it matter to working-women who ply the
> needle or the burnisher, or who bloody their fingers
> in fashioning the stems of paper flowers, whose health

is being ruined by twelve or thirteen hours' work
that does not earn them as much bread as they need—
what does it matter that they are not voters, that they
may not administer the property they do not possess,
and that they cannot deceive their husbands on an
equal basis?[7]

A wave of the hand and the problem is conjured away
again. This passage admirably illuminates a certain
"socialist" mentality, which denies all importance to the
problem of women in society. This mentality, confused
by the plight of the working class to begin with, is hence
not interested in other forms of social injustice. Unfortunately this was a rather common attitude among certain
leaders of the workers' parties, for whom the Revolution
was nothing but an almost ritualistic custom, void of all
its content of truth and justice. We know where this leads.
   An orator began his speech with *"Citoyennes et
Citoyens."* This appeal to the *citoyennes* produced an
"extraordinary effect" on the audience. But be assured that
he immediately added that the political rights claimed by
women were entirely "secondary." If women had the right
to vote and to be elected, would they "be considered less
as exploitable material in all forms by the capitalist exploiters, because of that"?[8] This was a sophism current in
that day. Universal suffrage appeared, even under a capitalist regime, as a weapon that the working class laid
claim to. Why, then, not claim it also for women? Furthermore, the subordination of women existed long before the
capitalist system. The disappearance of the latter did not
necessarily imply the disappearance of an age-old situation.
In reality, the old latent antifeminism, almost biological, is
behind all this. The schism cuts not only through classes,
but also through sexes. And it was with scorn that the

revolutionary Gustave Lefrançais spoke of the "rhetoric" of these ladies. Yet the Vaux-Hall discussions ended in a vote on principle that recognized the right of women to work, and as a result, to social equality.[9]

In the hall at Pré-aux-Clercs, the debates on marriage, divorce, and *union libre** went on between Catholics and socialists, in the presence of government agents. Olympe Audouard was called to order by a police commissioner for having declared that divorce would guarantee "family morals." She replied that this opinion was taken from *Idées napoléoniennes* by Louis-Napoléon Bonaparte, when he was at the fortress of Ham. Olympe Audouard had run *Le Papillon* and then *La Revue Cosmopolite,* but the board of directors had not let her change that publication into a political newspaper, for this authorization could be granted only to a French *man.*[10] She was a vigorous opponent, who did not hesitate to attack. In *Le luxe effréné des hommes* (1865), she neatly parried the criticism generally addressed to women. In *Guerre aux hommes* (1866), she showed how relentlessly a woman was quashed once she had shown some promise in the arts, science, or literature. "For woman to succeed in any career whatever, she must have ten times as much talent as a man, for he finds a spirit of cooperation ready to aid and sustain him, while she has to struggle against a stubborn attitude of ill will." What she asked for was simply that the law and the world treat her like an intelligent being, not like a child.

This whole movement culminated in the *Société de la Revendication du Droit des Femmes*—which brought together André Léo, Maria Deraismes, Louise Michel, Noémie Reclus, Mme. Jules Simon, and others—and in the newspaper *Le Droit des Femmes.*

* An *union libre* is the approximate equivalent of "common-law" marriage in Anglo-Saxon law.—*Trans.*

But politics does not consist solely of written or verbal manifestoes. It is a driving force. The movement which impelled women to demand their rights as adult, equal, free human beings, is inseparable from the total political situation. Thus we find women participating in the struggle of the republicans and the socialists. On November 1, 1868, there was a demonstration at the grave of the deputy Baudin. Victorine Brochon, who, as we have seen, had joined the International and participated in the organization of cooperatives, was there, and succeeded in eluding the police.[11] Pierre Bonaparte's assassination of the reporter Victor Noir threw the people of Paris into a turmoil. A huge meeting took place in Belleville. "We must put a stop to this," they said, and agreed to meet again the next day. "Women everywhere," Jules Vallès noted. "A good omen. When women get embroiled, when the housewife gives her man a push, when she rips her black flag of revolution down from the kitchen to raise it in the streets, it means that the sun will rise over a town in revolt."[12] The next day, January 12, 1870, two hundred thousand Parisians, men and women, swarmed over the Champs-Élysées. André Léo, and the schoolteacher Louise Michel—dressed like a man, "so as not to bother or be bothered by anyone," and dreaming of Harmodius— mingled among the crowd. Louise Michel had a dagger hidden in her clothes. "Almost everyone who turned up at the funeral expected to go home again as members of a republic, or not to go home at all."[13] The police were at every corner, ready to intervene. But old Delescluze and Rochefort won out over Flourens and the Blanquists: Victor Noir's body was carried directly to the cemetery to avoid an ill-prepared demonstration, which would have given the police a pretext for a bloody repression.

But the decaying Empire needed military adventure. War was declared against Prussia, under the worst imaginable conditions. A part of the people, deceived by official propaganda, raised the cry: "To Berlin!" But the workers of the Corderie* demonstrated in favor of peace; that war of dynasties did not concern the people.[14] Louise Michel, who certainly had moments of poetry, but was a bad poet when writing in verse, expressed this state of mind:

> Since they want war, since fighting must be done,
> People—your heads bowed down, and sad of
>   heart—
> Against the tyrants you must fight as one,
> And crush them both, William and Bonaparte.[15]

The disasters of this war became known immediately. The French Army withdrew. On August 14, the Blanquists Eudes, Granger, Brideau, and Flotte tried to seize weapons from the barracks in La Villette: the Empire had to be overthrown. They were arrested and condemned to death on August 29. Louise Michel, André Léo, and Adèle Esquiros—the wife of Alphonse Esquiros, and herself the author of several rather bad novels—circulated a letter from Michelet in the prisoners' favor. Thousands of signatures were soon appended to this letter. As often happens in this sort of appeal, a few nervous people wanted to withdraw their names: "I admit that I did not want to scratch out those two or three timid signatures," records Louise Michel. But this petition had to be got through to General Trochu. It was not easy to reach the Governor of Paris, but the three women did not let themselves be intimidated. They entered the general's antechamber; orderlies requested that they retire. They declared that, "coming on behalf of the people," they would not leave without an

---

* In other words, the members of the Federation of Syndicated Workers Chambers, which was located at 6, Place de la Corderie; this soon became the Paris headquarters of the International.— *Trans.*

answer, and settled down on the benches. In view of their stubbornness, a secretary went to get someone who claimed to represent Trochu. The petition's bulk seemed to impress him, and, to get rid of the intruders, he stated that their canvassing would be taken into consideration. Louise Michel was under no illusions: "That promise would have weighed little in the balance, had the Empire not been crumbling."[16] No matter. Some virtually unknown women had taken it upon themselves to carry the petition of thousands of Parisians to the Governor of Paris: this was an extraordinary act, bordering on scandal.

These intercessions on behalf of Eudes and his friends had at least one result: they were granted a stay of execution on September 2. On September 4, the Empire fell and the Republic was proclaimed. "The proclamation of the Republic, that dream dear to my childhood, was going to come true. I was so happy," wrote Victorine Brochon in her memoirs.[17] But Louise Michel, much more of an extremist, would not be taken in; the Empire had desecrated *La Marseillaise* that the crowd was singing. The song of the workers was that of Jacques Bonhomme:

> Bonhomme, bonhomme,
> Get an edge on your scythe,
> Ours is the revolt, and we need it.[18]

From that day on, an almost unbridgeable gulf existed between the bourgeois and the socialist Republics.

CHAPTER THREE

THE SIEGE OF PARIS

BY A TWIST OF FATE (of which we have seen other examples), those who had rejected war found themselves, when the country was invaded, fighting in the front ranks. When the Prussians were at the gates of Paris, the people, who in 1870 had hardly shown enthusiasm for a dynastic war, decided to fight. By contrast, caught between two problems—the Prussians on the one hand and the people on the other—the men of September 4th*preferred, for the most part, to negotiate with the former as soon as possible. Thus they would have been free to

---

*Those who proclaimed a Republic and set up a provisional government, called the Government of National Defense, with reactionaries as its most powerful members.—*Trans.*

re-establish order—their own order. The newly-proclaimed Republic was of the bourgeoisie, and it was understood that it would remain so. As in 1830 and 1848, the bourgeoisie had triumphed over the working class.

When Paris was besieged on September 19, there emerged a strange antagonism between a people which believed in the possibility of defense and victory, and a government which did not, and which organized a few absurd, bloody sorties as red herrings. That Siege of Paris became part of the folklore of Parisian families. When I was a child, my grandmother showed me a piece of "bread from the Siege" that had been kept as a symbol. Since then, the French have certainly known other suffering, but never has Paris been cut off, as it was then, from all its surrounding land, without which it was nothing but a desert of stone and asphalt, and reduced to asphyxiation and slow death. Cold, hunger, lines in front of stores—my generation lived through all that. But in 1871 our grandmothers experienced much more. An egg cost a franc then. Butter rose from 6, to 20, to 28 francs a pound. In the Faubourg Saint-Germain, a rabbit cost 45 francs, a cat 20, a dog's leg 6 francs a pound. No milk for children. Animals from the Jardin des Plantes appeared in the butcher-shops under the name of "fancy meats." The trees of Paris were cut down, but the green wood smoked and would not heat.[1]

From January 19 on, the bakers distributed bread only to people carrying cards: 300 grams for adults, 150 for children.[2] Even so it was an unidentifiable mixture, in which straw and paper were to be encountered.

Women suffered more than men: it was they who had to stand in line for hours, in mud, snow, and cold, trying to feed their families. "All food became so repugnant that to think of eating brought one almost to despair."[3] And one did indeed despair seeing children die of hunger and cold, despite the women's efforts. To the tune of the ballad of Fualdès,* they sang:

> Not a single store
> Has anything on display.
> Except in the baker's kitchen,
> Look wherever you may,
> It won't do any good.
> There's not even any wood.
>
> One day a poor mother
> Stands in line for a dole,
> Out of wood and coal,
> One day—one whole day.
> She holds against her breast
> Her baby, frozen to death. . . .[4]

Nathalie Lemel and her *La Marmite* carried out the difficult job of feeding hundreds of starving people. Louise Michel organized a soup kitchen for her students.[5] They were dining well at Brébant.

There was no work. At the ramparts of the town, the National Guard earned 1.50 francs a day, plus 75 centimes for their wives. This did not go very far when an egg cost a franc. Work, then, had to be given to women. But what work, except making soldiers' equipment? Victorine Brochon wrote:

> I signed up at the municipal building in the 7th arrondissement, since I was from that district. They gave me a soldier's jacket to make; they were satisfied with it. That way, I got 4 francs, but they only gave out three jackets a week to each of us, which was fair, in that more people were kept in work. This gave

* Fualdès was a magistrate assassinated in 1817; the subsequent trial created a great stir, and formed the basis of a popular ballad. —*Trans.*

me 12 francs a week, for four people. We could just
make out. Thousands of people did not have that
much.[6]

Mme. Poirier (Sophie Doctrinal), whose husband was
president of the 18th arrondissement Vigilance Committee, ran a workshop where clothing was made, and employed seventy or eighty women. She had the mayor of
Montmartre, Georges Clemenceau,* requisition her a
building at 64 Boulevard Ornano. This attempt was socialistic in inspiration, for the women did not earn a salary,
but instead shared in the profits. After the 10th of March,
Sophie Poirier, having no more work to give out, changed
her workshop into a medical center.[7] From this it can be
seen how difficult it is to clear a logical path (work for
women, medical centers, etc.) amid a ceaselessly shifting
reality, in which all activities are commingled and one
encounters the same people under various aspects. It is a
characteristic of revolutionary periods that the vitality of
life breaks down social functions and categories.

Workshops of this sort were organized in all municipal
halls. Work for women was one of the goals of the *Comité
des Femmes* on the Rue d'Arras, founded by Jules Allix.
He was a peculiar chap, slightly mad, although the organization and goals of this committee do not seem to be so:
work, education, social welfare, and rights for women.
Jules Allix advocated the establishment of communal
workrooms, in which women might find some work and
be fed during the length of the Siege. The Education
Committee organized meetings to propagandize in behalf
of the social Commune. One could sign up for work, for
nursing, for first aid, or even for the women's brigade
"being formed on the ramparts." Moved from 3 Rue
d'Arras to 14 Rue Notre-Dame, where the treasurer,

* The same Clemenceau who was to lead France during the last
years of World War I.—*Trans.*

Geneviève Vivien, lived, the Committee seems to have been greatly expanded during the Siege, since it comprised one undersecretariat per arrondissement, 160 district committees, and more than 1800 members. Except for André Léo and Elizabeth Dmitrieff, a member of the organizing committee, scarcely any of the women who were in it participated in the Commune. I noticed, in passing, the name of Juliette Drouet in the 9th arrondissement, without having been able to ascertain whether it was she who was Victor Hugo's sweetheart.[8]

But more frequently, the women of the bourgeoisie were in the *Société de Secours Pour les Victimes de la Guerre*. On an equal social basis, they became much more openly involved than the men of their class; perhaps because they were more naïve, and in any case less vulnerable to political wheeling and dealing. "Those members of the National Defense, who did so little defending, had heroic wives," acknowledged Louise Michel.[9] The still quite new International Convention of Geneva hastily organized the formation of hospital attendants; but General Trochu preferred nuns to these suspect laywomen. Victorine Brochon was accepted into the 7th Company of the 17th Battalion of the National Guard. She wrote, "I was happy, not because of the sorrows that burdened France, but because I believed in the accord of a national feeling of humanity. I thought that the problems and differences of opinion would dissolve in the face of imminent danger."[10] This illusion quickly disappeared before the absurdity of marches and counter-marches, the incoherence of the defense, and those ill-arranged sorties in which, despite dedication of the ambulance nurses, many dead men remained upon the battlefield. "It takes twenty-five years to make a man, and then he is killed. What a stupid role they have God play."[11]

The snow fell. The artillery shells fell. In that war in which civilians mingled with fighters, in which there was neither front nor rear, and in which everyone found himself equally involved since the enemy was at the gates and was bombarding the very houses, it was normal for women to follow their men up to the ramparts, carrying their rifles, accompanying them, with their children, as far as possible. They encouraged them, but they also heaped sarcasms on them when they lost ground, as did those housewives of the Boulevard Ornano who jeered at the deserters from the 32nd Battalion.[12]

The women worked as ambulance nurses and carried food. Constance Boidard, a buttonmaker who had no children to take care of, brought provisions to the 160th Battalion, whose sergeant-major was her husband.[13] The day-worker Palmyre Thierry (widow of Delcambre), brought food to the *Volontaires de Montrouge,* to which her lover belonged.[14] All these women, thus, served a common apprenticeship in the fight, shoulder to shoulder with their men. But some of them went further, demanding that a women's battalion be formed. André Léo dissuaded them from this: Paris did not lack defenders, and there was no need for a women's battalion.[15]

But the idea was in the air. On October 3, in *La Liberté,* one Félix Belly had suggested that ten battalions of "Amazons" be armed. Green posters had been pasted up to help spread the idea.

> In answer to the desire that numerous letters have expressed to us, and to the generous dispositions of a great part of the feminine population of Paris, there will be formed successively, in proportion to the resources given us for their organization and equipment, ten battalions of women, without distinction as to social class, who will be called the Amazons of the Seine.

They would, along with the garrison National Guard, be given the task of guarding the ramparts and the barricades, "bringing the soldiers all the domestic and fraternal services that are compatible with moral order and military discipline," and giving first aid to the wounded. They would be given small arms, and, like the men, would receive wages of 1.50 francs per day. And—since at that time people loved colorful uniforms—it was provided that their uniform consist of black trousers with orange bands, a black wool cowled blouse, a black peaked cap trimmed in orange, and a crossbelted ammunition pouch. An enlistment office was opened at 36 Rue Turbigo, where the applicants were to appear accompanied by a member of the National Guard, who would answer for their "morality." The battalion was to comprise eight companies of one hundred and fifty Amazons each, who would immediately be trained in how to handle a rifle.

To meet the expenses of this organization the "originator and provisional head of the first battalion" appealed to the generosity of "ladies of the wealthy classes." They would not hesitate to offer their bracelets, necklaces, and other jewels—of which, in any case, they would be divested if the Prussians entered the city. Thus they would attest to their civic feeling (and their awareness of their own best interest), and would contribute to overturning the barriers that had for too long separated them from the working classes (Félix Belly thought of everything). A ladies' committee would, moreover, function as a "family council." A doctor, preferably female, would be attached to each battalion. The arms and weapon manufacturers were invited to submit models of weapons which would be examined by artillery officers. In short, everything was arranged. And, concluded the poster:

> Every moment counts. The women, too, feel that their country and their civilization need all their strength to resist the savage violence of Prussia. They want to share our perils, sustain our spirit, give us the ex-

ample of fearlessness in the face of death, and thus be worthy of their emancipation and their civic equality. And may all of Europe learn with admiration that it was not only thousands of citizens, but also thousands of women, who, in Paris, defended the freedom of the world against a new Barbarian invasion.[16]

Women came to the Rue Turbigo to sign up—fifteen hundred of them, Belly claims—but General Trochu put an end to this project: Jeanne Hachettes and Jeanne d'Arcs are acceptable only as past history.[17]

During the Siege, then, women served in the fighting only individually, as ambulance nurses or canteen workers; but at the same time they were serving their apprenticeship in political life. Vigilance committees were organized in various quarters; there were two in Montmartre, one for men, the other for women. Louise Michel participated in both at once: "No one was very much bothered by the sex of those who were doing their duty. That silly problem was done with."[18] The Women's Vigilance Committee of the 18th arrondissement had been set up by Louise Michel, Mme. Collet, and Mme. Poirier, who, as we know, ran a sewing workshop. "This committee had the job of allocating work, receiving and distributing contributions, visiting the sick and the poor and caring for them in their homes," explained Mme. Poirier before the Council of War. "I was given the title of president. Besides," she added, "I was better known than the two working-class ladies, and I was known by all those with whom we had to do for the apportioning and use of relief funds to the sick."[19] Mme. Collet left for England on March 16; Louise Michel, on the other hand, became twice as active. She wrote articles: "When the country is in peril, we must point out danger wherever it is, and cowardice wherever it lurks. Let us be on our guard. . . . Here, in Paris, we breathe an odor of death. Treason is rampant. If Trochu follows Bazaine's footsteps, we must not let the people sleep. Let us be on our guard. . . ."[20] Often she presided over meetings, keeping discipline by brandishing an old hammerless gun at the "men of order," who, armed with bayonets, invaded, the room. At other times, accompanied by a member of the National Guard, she combed the churches. "I spent the finest hours of the Siege with the Montmartre Vigilance Committee and with the *Club de la Patrie en Danger*. One was a little more fully alive there, with the joy of feeling oneself in one's element, in the midst of the intense struggle for liberty." The members of the Vigilance Committees were to inflame the Clubs: "We took off every night around Paris, sometimes demolishing a club of slackers, sometimes fanning the Revolution."[21]

After September 4, when the theaters were closed, even more people were attracted to the Clubs. These Clubs, in which all opinions met and clashed, were of various leanings. Women brought their children along; there, at least, they were out of the cold, but they also attended because of political conviction, and did not hesitate to intervene in the proceedings. Nathalie Lemel spoke out at the *Club de l'École de Médecine*[22]; Louise Michel, at the *Club de la Patrie en Danger* and elsewhere. Both the defense of Paris and the sending of delegations to the Hôtel de Ville were discussed. Faced with the government's inertia, they demanded mass sorties; faced with the disparity of food provisioning, that measures be taken against the merchants. In a hall in the Faubourg Poissonnière, they raised the question of *unions libres,* so prevalent among the working classes. The "companion" of a National Guardsman should be accorded the same rights as a legitimate wife.[23] They discussed socialism: if men hesitated to form the Commune, it was the women who would show them the way to the Hôtel de Ville.[24] An orator voiced doubts about the fighting spirit of the workers of Belleville: "You could not find five hundred men determined to fight for the Commune," he said. Women rose up: "We will go first; we will ask them for bread."[25] Asking for bread is the primordial demand of women. On October 5 and 6, 1789, it was the women who went to Versailles looking for "the baker and the baker's wife and the baker's little boy."* And once more, it was the theme of hunger around which women organized against the Germans and the Vichy government, during the brutal winters of the 1940's. The politics of women moves first through the distribution of essential goods, the just administration of things.

Women also participated in street demonstrations. On September 18 they took the initiative in demonstrating in sympathy with Strasbourg, which had been besieged for more than a month. "The idea came to some among us— or rather, some women among us, for we women were in the majority—to get weapons and set forth to help Strasbourg defend herself, and to die with her."[26] Louise Michel and André Léo led a little group that set out for the Hôtel de Ville crying "To Strasbourg!" Women— many schoolteachers, young people, and especially students—joined them along the way. They stopped before the statue of Strasbourg to attest to their involvement, then set off again for the Hôtel de Ville to demand weapons. To their great surprise, Louise Michel and André Léo were allowed to enter, but it was only to be locked up with two other "prisoners," a student and an old woman coming from the grocer's. She had no idea of what had happened to her, and she "was trembling so much that the oil she had just bought spilled all over her dress." They let the old woman go, but an officer interrogated André Léo and

* This alludes to what was something of a hunger march on Versailles by a mob of irate women to demand bread on October 5, 1789. On their return to Paris they sang this song; their demands had been met and the royal family had agreed to live in Paris. —*Trans.*

Louise Michel at great length: "What can it matter to you if Strasbourg falls, if you are not there?" he concluded.[27] Such was the tone of the Republic's defenders. The two women were released, thanks to the intervention of a member of the Government who was arriving at the Hôtel de Ville.

At the end of November, some women wanted to go to the Hôtel de Ville to propose various means of defense, and to demand that they be recruited. They appealed to Louise Michel and the Montmartre Vigilance Committee to back their mission. Louise Michel went with them, although she was not in agreement with this venture, which she considered "more courageous than clear-sighted." "We went with them as women, in order to share their dangers, not as *citoyennes*," she explained. Naturally, Louise Michel, who was beginning to be recognized and dreaded, was the one arrested as the instigator. With insolent arguments, she denied any responsibility. She could not organize a demonstration that appealed to a government she no longer recognized; when she came to the Hôtel de Ville on her own behalf, it would be "with the people in arms." Finally, Mme. Meurice (speaking for the *Société des Femmes Pour les Victimes de la Guerre*), Ferré (in the name of the Clubs), and Victor Hugo intervened for her release.[28]

That day Louise Michel màde a date with the people of Paris. On January 22, in the square of the Hôtel de Ville, that date was indeed kept. The capitulation that was gradually sensed in the provisional government's ambiguous acts, in the endless hesitations of General Trochu, in those ill-prepared sorties which, despite the men's courage, all ended in failure—this capitulation (the word was pronounced on January 20, after the Buzenval sortie) was not desired by the people of Paris. They had suffered four months from hunger and cold and bombardment and misery; they had buried their dead without useless mourning. These people, called so fickle and inconstant, had borne everything with a patience, abnegation, and courage that had won them the admiration of all Europe. They wanted, at least, that all these sacrifices should not have been in vain. Moreover, these intelligent people did not understand that their forces had not been concentrated in battle all at once; that they had let themselves be nibbled away in little fragments, exhausted in ludicrous sorties. These intelligent people did understand that they had been deceived; that the famous Trochu "plan," with which they had been mollified for so long, had never existed; that the Government of National Defense had never been anything but a lure; and that the strong who rule the earth had, perhaps, settled down again on the people's back. The replacement of General Trochu by General Vinoy would not restore their lost confidence. During the night of January 21, the delegates from the National Guard, the Vigilance Committees, and the Clubs agreed to gather on the 22nd at the Place de l'Hôtel de Ville to oppose surrender. Those from the National Guard were urged to arrive armed; women, to go along to protest against the latest bread ration: people were willing still to put up with rationing, but only if it were for victory.

An enormous crowd filled the square. A great number of women were present, among them André Léo, Sophie Poirier, Béatrix Excoffon, and Louise Michel (who was dressed in a National Guard uniform). Deputations were received by the assistant to the mayor, Chaudey, who was in a rage. Outside, people were shouting "Death to the traitors!" From the windows of the Hôtel de Ville, Breton Mobile Guards fired into the crowd.* "The bullets made

* The French Army consisted of conscripted recruits, serving seven years. The annual "class" of eligible men was actually chosen by a lottery. Those receiving "bad numbers" served, unless they were rich enough to buy substitutes. The Mobile Guard had been instituted late in the 1860's by Napoleon III's Minister of War, Marshall Niel, to reform and strengthen the National Guard by giving special

the noise of a summer hailstorm."[29] The National Guard returned the fire, but some of them said later that they had aimed only at the walls. "I was not among those," wrote Louise Michel. "To act that way would mean eternal defeat, with its piling up of the dead, its long misery— it would even be treason." But she felt no hatred toward those men who were merely the helpless instruments of the powerful:

> Standing before those accursed windows, I could not take my eyes off those pale, savage figures who were emotionlessly and mechanically firing upon us, as they would have fired upon packs of wolves. And I thought: "We will have you one day, you scoundrels, for you kill, but you believe. They haven't bought you, they've tricked you. We need people who aren't for sale." And the stories of my old grandfather passed through my mind, stories of those times when hero against hero, the peasants of Charette, Cathelineau, and La Rochejacquelin fought implacably against the Army of the Republic.[30]

This feeling of respect, of fraternity for the enemy, is rare and noble enough to note in passing. Yet at the same time, Louise Michel was giving herself wholly to battle: "The first time you defend your cause with weapons, you live the battle so intensely that you are no longer yourself so much as a projectile." This division into actor and spectator ranks very high on the scale of human values.

Some people held the women responsible for the failure of the demonstration. At the *Club de Belleville*, remarks were made that set the room laughing: "How do you

---

training to its unmarried members. Although these goals were never fully achieved, the Mobile Guard was separate from, and elected the officers of, the National Guard. In the eyes of the Parisian National Guard, whose men were drawn mostly from working-class districts, the Mobile Guard consisted of the appointees of a deposed tyrant. —*Trans.*

expect to make virile resolutions in the midst of a bunch of women, children, and good-for-nothings who come here to digest their dinner? It is the Clubs that are ruining us. The enemy is immediately informed of our intentions."[31]

But that was not the Government's opinion. On the contrary: they feared the Clubs' activity and ordered that they be closed. They outlawed newspapers and sent out warrants for the arrest of the demonstrators, who were called "foreign partisans." Having done that, the Government had its hands free to sign the armistice. On January 28, four hundred thousand armed men surrendered to two hundred thousand. It was easier to reach an understanding with the Prussians—men of order—than with the workers in Belleville. On January 29 the German flag was flying over the strongholds.

Now it was a question of electing an assembly. The provinces sent to Bordeaux all the ghosts from the former regime, the heirs of the Restoration, the opportunistic politicians of the Second Empire, those petty squires exhumed from their country seats—everyone who was as narrow, as out of date, as clerical, as rancid as could possibly be found; everyone who was ready to unite against that city, Paris, whose very paving stones were always ready to rise up in the name of heaven only knew what sort of justice, liberty, or right. This *introuvable* assembly* found its leader, its symbol, and its style in Monsieur Thiers.

On February 26 the peace preliminaries were signed. France had to pay 5 billion francs and hand over all of Alsace, save Belfort, and a part of Lorraine, to the Germans. Paris felt, not vanquished, but betrayed. On the Place de la Bastille, where in former days the people had not left a single stone underfoot, the battalions of the

---

* An allusion to the *Chambre Introuvable*, elected in 1815; Louis XVIII gave it this nickname because of his gratified amazement that such a pro-Royalist group could have been gathered.—*Trans.*

Mobile Guard filed past. From time to time, a man would harangue the crowd, and women dressed in black would hang a tricolored flag from the column: "To the martyrs, the women of the Republic."[32]

The Assembly "of Notables," for its part, took the most reactionary measures possible: the bills that had fallen due between August 13 and November 13, 1870, were immediately payable, the moratorium on rent payments and the National Guard's pay were cancelled. In Paris, where commerce and industry had been paralyzed by the Siege, where famine was rampant, this meant that many people were rendered destitute.

But rumor had it that the German army was going to enter Paris. One thing, at least, that the Prussians did not have was the cannons. The Parisians considered these their property; they had paid for them by the subscriptions— from 10 centimes up—of the common people. Women and children went up the Faubourg Saint-Honoré toward the Parc Monceau. The guards opened the gates and "those people whom a flick of the finger had knocked over"[33] took down the cannons. On February 26 a singing crowd, an entire population—National Guardsmen, women, children, all together—triumphantly brought the cannons from the good neighborhoods toward Montmartre, Belleville, La Villette, and Les Buttes-Chaumont.[34]

On the first of March, the Germans entered a Paris that was deserted, gloomy, and darkened; they left again on the second, to camp in the outlying districts.

CHAPTER FOUR

THE 18TH OF MARCH

IT WOULD WITHOUT A DOUBT be an exaggeration to say that this day of revolution was the work of women. But they contributed a great deal, at least to the first part: the neutralization of the troops.

An end had to be made to it. At the order of Thiers, the army had entered Paris during the night. It had occupied the strategic points, and had effortlessly laid hold of the cannons at Les Batignolles. On Montmartre, a post of the National Guard's 61st Battalion stood watch in the Rue des Rosiers. Louise Michel had come there to deliver a message, when the National Guardsman Turpin was wounded by a bullet, in rather uncertain circumstances. Louise Michel and a canteen worker gave him first aid.[1]

The army had encountered no resistance, and it seemed that the whole business would quickly be taken care of. But General Vinoy had forgotten that, in order to move cannons, one has to have horses. He had forgotten the horses: a minor detail. The cannons from La Butte would have to be brought down by manpower.

During this time Montmartre had awakened. The housewives, who were going out to get their bread and milk, began to flock together and spread the news. Inquisitive groups formed about the soldiers. Around seven o'clock, the mayor of Montmartre, Clemenceau, climbed to the top of La Butte and asked to have the wounded man taken to the hospital. General Lecomte would not permit this. He formally opposed "the promenade of this corpse." A military doctor attended to Turpin.[2]

But the alarm had been sounded. The tocsin rang out in the churches of Paris. "I went down, my rifle under my coat, crying 'Treason,' " wrote Louise Michel. "A column was formed. The whole Vigilance Committee was there: Ferré, old Moreau, and all of them. Montmartre arose. The call to arms was sounded. I came back, indeed, but with others, to the attack on the fortified heights of Montmartre; we went up with the speed of a charge, knowing that at the top there was an army in battle formation. We expected to die for liberty. It was as if we were lifted from the earth. . . ."[3] And, since Louise Michel was gifted with a poetic sensibility for which sky, sun, and night were in constant attendance upon the actions of men, she added: "La Butte was enveloped in white light, a splendid dawn of deliverance." Suddenly, she saw her mother beside her—her mother, the old servant Marianne Michel whom she had never ceased, nor would cease, to love with utter tenderness: "I felt an appalling anguish.

She had been worried, and had come. All the women were there, going up at the same time as we were, I don't know how."[4]

The groups of housewives with their children—merely curious or bantering at first—had swelled and become threatening. Now, among the soldiers of the 88th Battalion and the National Guard, they formed a "veritable human barricade."[5] General Lecomte gave the order to fire. Then the women spoke to the soldiers: "Will you fire upon us? On your brothers? Our husbands? Our children?"[6] The statement of General d'Aurelles de Paladine on this subject is very significant:

> The women and children came and mixed with the troops. We were greatly mistaken in permitting these people to approach our soldiers, for they mingled among them, and the women and children told them: "You will not fire upon the people." This is how the soldiers of the 88th, as far as I can see, and of another line regiment found themselves surrounded and did not have the power to resist these ovations that were given them. People were shouting, "Long live the line!"[7]

Faced with this unexpected intervention, the soldiers hesitated. A warrant officer stood in front of his company and shouted: "Surrender!"[8] Then the 88th Battalion fraternized with the crowd. The soldiers arrested their general.

The women had assembled in the Rue Houdon. General Susbielle gave the order to charge. But, intimidated by the women's cries, the cavalry "backed up their horses," which made the people laugh.[9] Everywhere—in the Place Blanche, Place Pigalle, in Belleville, at the Bastille, at Le Château-d'Eau, and in the Luxembourg Gardens—the crowd, mostly composed of women, surrounded the soldiers, stopped the horses, cut the harnesses, forced the "bewildered" soldiers to fraternize with their "brothers" in the National Guard.

Disconcerted by this strange, this scandalous, victory of the people, General Vinoy ordered his troops to withdraw to the Champ-de-Mars. The field was left to the women. They had nothing to do but to go back home and fix dinner—which, for the most part, they did.

At the moment when, in the Rue des Rosiers, they were shooting both General Lecomte, who that morning had given the order to fire into the crowd, and General Clément Thomas, who remained in the eyes of the Parisian people the slaughterer of the June 1848 insurgents, the housewives of that morning had disappeared from the scene. But other women had swarmed over, mingling with the crowd, which was escorting and insulting the prisoners.

> Prostitutes, registered or not, came from the quarter of Les Martyrs, or out of hotels, cafés, and the brothels that were then so numerous along the old boulevards at the outer edges of Paris. On the arms of line soldiers, accompanied by a legion of pimps, they had surged out, the pathetic spume of prostitution upon the revolutionary wave. There they were: getting drunk at all the bars, howling their beggarly joy over this defeat of an authority that, for them, was characterized by the prefecture of police and its spies. It was they, plus a few poor women demoralized by the deleterious attacks of poverty, who, at the corner of Rue Joudon, cut up the flesh of the horse of an officer killed a few moments earlier. It was they who dragged the infantrymen along, hurling themselves upon the prisoners, uttering threats of death.[10]

This document is by neither Maxime du Camp, nor Jules Claretie, nor Dumas *fils*, but by a supporter of the

Commune, Gaston da Costa, who was an assistant to the Public Prosecutor of the Commune and was condemned to death by the Council of War. This account does not deny the violence or the excesses inherent in every revolution, but it does give an explanation for them. For da Costa, the women who that morning had placed themselves and their children between the troops and the National Guard were not the same ones whose insults, that evening, escorted the two arrested generals. But "this is not to say that the former cannot also suddenly become desperate Furies," he adds.[11]

The harpies, with their screaming, yells and violence, had attracted the attention of the Commune's enemies, who had indeed seen only these women; meanwhile, the supporters of the Commune noticed only "honest women of the people, and heroic *citoyennes*." Often the two were the same. Both, in any case, fought side by side, and knew how to die with equal courage upon the barricades.

It is necessary, then, to introduce shades of grey into a subject little suited for such nuances (Manichaeism is appropriate to revolutionary periods), and to try to relate the behavior of the masses to the only true reality: the almost biological truth about the individuals who made up the masses, at least to the extent that they can be understood and explained.

It was, again, women and children who, on the 19th of March, tried to wrest General Chanzy away from the escort that had taken him prisoner. In their eyes, every general was a traitor deserving immediate execution.[12]

Ten days later, when the Commune, elected on March 26, moved into the Hôtel de Ville, a crowd that included many women joyously welcomed the new power—the power of the people, and of hope.[13]

Suddenly, this hope became concrete in phrases that were very simple, but went to the heart of the poor people whom war and siege had made even poorer: the remission of the terms of October 1870 and of January and April, 1871; the suspension of the sale of articles that were deposited at the Mont-de-Piété.

But the government that had taken refuge in Versailles could not tolerate that other power which was holding its own in Paris. On April 2, Versailles attacked Courbevoie. Hearing the cannons anew, Paris awakened from its dream. Ever since the Commune had been established, they had been living in an atmosphere of fervor, confidence, and hope. Was a new siege beginning? The barricades went up again. The cannons were dragged up onto the ramparts.[14] The women on the boulevards formed the chorus of a Greek tragedy; their cheers inspired the National Guard, who were going to the outposts; their invective was heaped upon the idlers who stood around and watched them go by.[15]

And the women decided to carry out their own special activity. A call to women was launched in several newspapers:

Let's go to Versailles. Let's tell Versailles what the Revolution of Paris is. Let's tell Versailles that Paris has formed the Commune because we want to stay free. Let's tell Versailles that Paris has made ready to defend herself, because she has been slandered, because she has been betrayed, because they wanted to take her by surprise and disarm her. Let's tell Versailles that the Assembly is not the law: Paris is. Let's tell Versailles that the government has to answer for our brothers' blood, and that we hold them responsible, before all of France, for our bereavement. *Citoyennes*, women, let's go to Versailles, so that Paris can have made the last attempt at reconciliation. There can be no delay at all. Let us meet this very day at noon on the Place de la Concorde, and make this important resolution before the statue of Strasbourg.

The signer—*"Une Véritable Citoyenne"*—was anonymous.[16]

But let us listen to Béatrix Excoffon, whom we have already encountered at the Place de l'Hôtel de Ville, and whom we shall meet again. Béatrix Excoffon was born in Cherbourg on July 10, 1849. She was the daughter of a watchmaker, Ange Euvrie, who had been arrested for having opposed the December 2nd coup d'état. Although he was released, young recruits were forbidden to enter his store for a nine-year period.[17] (The ruling powers bear these grudges.) Béatrix was a nice young girl who had been living for more than four years with a printer's compositor, François Excoffon, by whom she had had two children. She bore his name, although they were not married. We have seen that *unions libres*—whether because of negligence, or distrust of bourgeois law, or anticlericalism—were very frequent among the working class.

On April 1 [Béatrix Excoffon was mistaken here about the date: it was the 3rd that she was speaking of] a woman neighbor, surprised to see me, asked me whether I had read the newspaper announcement of a women's meeting on the Place de la Concorde. They wanted to go to Versailles to stop the bloodshed. I told my mother that I was leaving, I kissed my children, and off I went. At the Place de la Concorde, at 1:30, I got into the procession. There were between seven hundred and eight hundred women. Some talked about explaining to Versailles what Paris wanted; others talked about how things were a hundred years ago, when the women of Paris had once before gone to Versailles to carry off the baker and the baker's wife and the baker's little boy, as they said then.

These reminiscences of the Revolution of 1789 reappeared everywhere during the ephemeral rule of the 1871 Commune, even to the use of the Republican calendar—just as the revolutionaries of 1789 had often draped themselves in the trappings of the Roman Republic.

At the gates of Versailles, the women ran into freemason parliamentarians, who, for their part, had tried to mediate. Tired to death, the *citoyenne* who led Béatrix Excoffon's group suggested that they regather at the Salle Ragache. Béatrix Excoffon was designated as her substitute. "They made me get up on a billiard-table and I said what I thought: that although there were not enough of us to go to Versailles, there were enough to go tend the injured in the Commune's marching companies."[18] But like Fabrizio on the battlefield at Waterloo, Béatrix Excoffon saw only one aspect of these demonstrations. Even today, with newspapers and memoirs, it is hard enough to reconstruct their chronology. Other groups of women were stopped at the fortifications by the National Guard, who dissuaded them from going farther for fear that they would be gunned down.[19]

On April 4, the demonstrations continued. A delegation of women dressed in mourning announced at the Hôtel de Ville that 10,000 (*sic*) Parisian women were preparing to march upon Versailles. Around three o'clock, some twenty women in the Boulevard Richard-Lenoir railed against the men "who would rather hide out than go fight against Versailles." They said further that 700 *citoyennes* had just left the Place de la Concorde, with red flag unfurled, "to march in the lead before the men."[20]

Around 3:30, a column of women carrying the red flag did, in fact, leave from the Place de la Concorde, and headed for Le Point-du-Jour. These were women of the people, "very neatly dressed"; some of them even wore black silk dresses and hats. Their bodices were adorned with red rosettes (the Council of War was to consider red among one's clothing a proof of allegiance to the Commune). About fifty street-urchins, singing *Le Chant du Départ,** went ahead of them. They declared that "they were going to Versailles to call upon the Government to stop sending bombs down on Paris," and they unsuccessfully invited the women along the way to join them. But again that day, the National Guard blocked their passage.[21] Around seven o'clock that evening, a woman was haranguing the crowd in the Place de la Bastille: "The bloodshed has to be stopped." She made a date with the women for the 6th of April.[22]

On the 5th, the watchwords—if watchwords there were, the initiatives, in any case—became entirely contradictory. At the Bastille, at Le Château-d'Eau, and at the Place de la Concorde, the women declared that they had given up the project of going to make the Versailles government listen to reason. It was decided that all the women, no matter what their class, would mingle among the National Guardsmen, thus avoiding bloodshed.[23] A utopian plan, some thought, for the presence of women had certainly not hindered the shooting on the 2nd of December.

In front of the Hôtel de Ville, a girl suggested to the Fédérés† that the wives of policemen living in Paris

* A famous patriotic song dating from the French Revolution, written by André Chenier's brother, Marie-Joseph.—*Trans.*

† The Fédérés—or the Federals, as they will subsequently be designated—were the members of the 215 battalions, out of some 270, who formed the Republican Federation of the National Guard on March 3, 1871. In the main, the members were from the working class or lower-middle class; in opposing the Versailles government they were interested in preserving the Republic, and the autonomy both of Paris and of the National Guard. Even today there is an annual May Day procession by labor organizations to the "Wall of the Federals" in the Père-Lachaise cemetery, where the last remnants of the Commune died fighting.—*Trans.*

march in front of them, so that the Versailles soldiers would hold their fire. "Bareheaded, with beautiful blonde hair, and an intelligent and dedicated face, she made a great impression on everyone around her," said a bourgeois woman, Mme. Blanchecotte, who was passing by and whose sympathies were surely not directed toward the Commune.[24] Another woman, "also blonde, decently dressed, serious and distinguished," called, in her turn, for resistance.[25]

From all these initiatives, one may conclude that on the 3rd, 4th, and 5th of April, the women were making an effort "to do something" to avoid the bloody clash between Versailles and Paris. But these outbursts seemed neither organized nor coherent. They were divided among various currents, from conciliation to resistance.

On April 6, in Jules Vallès' newspaper, a *citoyenne* (who may have been a *citoyen*) appealed for calm. "We were going to Versailles. We wanted to avoid bloodshed. In the name of the women of Paris, we were bringing our recent mourning for our fathers, husbands, and children to Versailles. We were not able to carry out our task of reconciliation and humanity. The government has attacked Paris. Blood has been spilled."[26] What should women do from now on? Disband their ranks, and stay "calm and earnest." "We have no politicking to do, we are human and that is all. Since we cannot prevent bloodshed, our primary mission is ended." Thus, women were to go back to the hearth, or, if absolutely necessary, keep themselves occupied at medical stations. Any other initiative would hinder the military movements and the execution of the Commune's orders. And finally—an odd argument, and that which makes me think the passage was drafted by a man, or upon his advice—"Any inopportune step on our part would cast a slur on the men's dignity." The women's attempt would live on, surely, as a protest against the Versailles government, which they held responsible for the blood that had flowed, and as an act of faith in the Commune, that "honest, simple government," made for all, which through liberty and work would bring "a little comfort into every sort of poverty." Let the women, then, disperse, crying "Long live the Republic! Long live the Commune!" and let them leave the men to take care of their own business. This document, worthy of the good Chrysale,* is signed *"Une Vraie Citoyenne."*

But the women hardly seemed inclined to go back to their houses. Moreover, to be popular the government needed the participation and mobilization of the masses. The Commune had decided to hold national obsequies for the first men who died fighting in the defense of the Revolution. And Courbet probably did not become involved in making the arrangements, as David had done earlier for the ceremonies of the other Revolution; nonetheless, the burials could not have been conducted with more ceremony. On April 6, at two in the afternoon, a crowd gathered at the Beaujon hospital, where the victims' bodies were displayed. The wives and mothers, "like Spartan women," Lissagaray tells us, uttered "cries of fury and vows of vengeance." Then the three biers, draped in black cloth and red flags, and borne by eight horses, moved slowly toward Père-Lachaise. In front were buglers, muffled drums, the *Vengeurs de Paris,* and then the members of the Commune. Behind them, the dead men's wives and the ambulance workers wore Geneva armbands and the red scarf of the Commune. All along the boulevards, "the Sacred Way of the Revolution," were thousands of sobbing women. There were two hundred thousand people at the Bastille. "The men of Versailles can no longer say that we are a handful of malcontents." And when they parted beside the graves, it was to the cries of "Long live the Republic! Long live the Commune!"[27]

* See note on p. 17.

On April 9, the guillotine at the foot of the statue of Voltaire—the "defender of Sirven and Calas"—was burned. The Commune wanted thereby to show that a new world had begun, one from which the death penalty was to be excluded, and in which justice would reign. Women were also represented at this symbolic ceremony.[28]

Any political system which demands the consensus of the masses and at the same time serves as the expression of the masses, must appeal to popular sentiment and organize a following. Religions, like political movements, need collective demonstrations. Women, who are more emotional than men, are doubtless even more susceptible to this communal appeal.

But the women also had good reasons for backing the new power. To be sure, the goals of the Commune, set forth in a Declaration to the French People, took no account of women's existence.[29] The men of the Commune did not foresee for a single instant that women might have civic rights, any more than did their "great forebears" of 1789 and 1793, or the 1848 revolutionaries. But certain measures, like the remission of rent payments or the discontinuation of the sale of articles deposited at the Mont-de-Piété, affected women directly.* A 600-franc pension was to be granted the wife, legal or not, of any member of the National Guard who had been killed defending the people's rights, after an inquiry that would establish her rights and needs. Each of her children, legitimate or not, could collect a 365-franc pension until he was eighteen. At the expense of the Commune, orphans would receive

* The Commune decreed that any rent payments made during the Siege of Paris were to be deducted from future payments, that any tenant could cancel his lease during the next six months, and that he could not be evicted for the next three months. They also decreed that pledges left at pawnshops could not be sold until further decrees established regulations for dealing with these articles, especially tools—the loss of which would hinder a worker in finding new work.—*Trans.*

the education necessary "to make their own way in society."[30]

This was an implicit recognition of the structure of the working-class family, as it really existed, outside the context of religious and bourgeois laws: the recognition of *unions libres*; of the right of children, legitimate or natural, to subsistence, and the disappearance of the old *macula bastardiae* of Roman Law, Church, and Civil Code. In this, the Commune, which was handling the Banque de France with kid gloves and did not venture to make any inroads into private property, undoubtedly took one of the most revolutionary steps of its ephemeral reign. That this measure outraged the bourgeoisie, that it was received with jubilation by the members of the Commune—both of these are indications of its significance. Arthur Arnould, a member of the Commune writes:

> This decree, which raises woman to the level of man, by putting her, in the eyes of morals and the law, on a footing of civic equality with man, placed itself upon the plane of living morality, and delivered a mortal blow to the religio-monarchical institution of marriage as we see it functioning in modern society. It was an act of justice as well, for it is time to have done with that iniquitous prejudice, that legal barbarism, which—in what today is called concubinage, as opposed to legal marriage—strikes only at the weak: the seduced woman and the innocent child.

And, detailing the moral nature of *union libre*, he adds, "The union of man and woman ought to be a fundamentally free act performed by two responsible people. In this union, moral rights, like duties, ought to be reciprocal and equal. When a man becomes a woman's lover and gives her a child, that woman is his wife, those children are his children." The society that did not condemn the man had no right to condemn the woman, still less the children. But this decree included a qualifying statement: in every arrondissement, a jury headed by a member of the Commune was to ascertain that the illegitimate wife was not a "sometime prostitute."[31] Another decree provided that a food pension be granted any married woman who asked for separation from her husband.

But the Commune could not hope to legislate for the future if it did not first defend its own existence. After the attempts at conciliation, the illusions were shattered. The Commune had to fight. On April 11, some *citoyennes* flung out a violent call to battle, in pure 1792 style.[32] "Paris is being blockaded. Paris is being bombarded. *Citoyennes*, where are our children and our brothers and our husbands? . . . Do you hear the roaring cannon, the tocsin ringing out the sacred call? To arms! The Nation is in danger!" Was it foreigners who were coming to attack Paris, threatening those triumphs known as "liberty, equality, and fraternity"? "No, these enemies, these murderers of the people and of liberty, are Frenchmen." And the women explained the meaning of the struggle: "This is the final act in the eternal antagonism between right and force, between work and exploitation, between the people and the people's torturers." For what the Commune wanted was the end of man's exploitation of man. "No more exploiters, no more masters; work and well-being for all; government of the people by the people." And they recalled the noble watchword of the proletarian struggles: "To live free, working, or to die fighting." The Versailles government felt no fear of having to account for itself one day before the court of the people; it did not shrink before the greatest crime of all: civil war.

Citoyennes of Paris, descendants of the women of the Great Revolution, the women who, in the name of the people and justice, marched upon Versailles and carried Louis XVI off as a captive—we, the mothers, wives, and sisters of the French people, will we go on allowing poverty and ignorance to make enemies out of our children? Allowing them to kill each other—father against son, brother against brother—under our very eyes, for the whim of our oppressors, who want Paris handed over to foreigners and annihilated?"

The cause of Paris was the cause of all Europe, and the Commune's revolution had a universal importance. Germany was trembling in the wind of revolution; Russia was watching the defenders of liberty perish, but another generation was arising in its turn, "ready to fight and die for the Republic and for social change." Ireland and Poland, Spain and Italy, were recovering their strength to join in the international struggle of the people. England was feeling the effects of a revolutionary movement; Austria was obliged to crush the revolts of the Slavic population that she held in bondage. "*Citoyennes,* the chips are down. We must win, or die." Those who said, "What do I care about the triumph of our cause, if I must lose my loved ones?" had to realize that the only means of saving those they loved was to fight, for this fight could finish only in the victory of the people. Besides, as far as their husbands and brothers were concerned, their lives were already at stake; it was the children who would pay for their defeat; for "neither we nor our enemies want mercy." Let the women prepare, then, to defend and avenge their brothers: "And if we have neither rifles nor bayonets, there will still be paving stones to crush the traitors with."

This passage, clearly expressing the ideas of the International about the class struggle, was signed by "a group of *citoyennes*." It was the first official act of the *Union des Femmes Pour la Défense de Paris et les Soins aux Blessés.*

An announcement followed: the women had met on April 11, at 8:00 P.M., at Larched Hall, 74 Rue du Temple, and at the Grand Café des Nations, there to make up arrondissement committees. Summing up the appeal, the announcement addressed itself to *citoyennes* "who know that the present social order bears within itself the seeds of poverty and of the death of all liberty and justice . . . who welcome the rule of work and equality, and who are ready to die for the triumph of the Revolution."

Following the April 11th meeting, the Central Committee of the *Union des Femmes* was provisionally appointed. With no time wasted, Elizabeth Dmitrieff and seven women workers—Adélaïde Valentin, Noémie Colleville, Marquant, Sophie Graix, Joséphine Prat, Céline and Aimée Delvainquier—told the Executive Commission of the Commune: "At this hour, when danger is imminent and the enemy is at the gates of Paris, the entire population must unite to defend the Commune," which stood for "the annihilation of all privilege and all inequality," and which was to take account of all just demands, without distinction as to sex. This distinction had been maintained by the "necessities of the antagonism upon which the governing classes' privilege had rested." Social reform, which was to ensure "the rule of work and of justice," thus possessed an equal importance for all citizens, male and female. Consequently, a great number of women had resolved that "in the event that the enemy should come through the gates of Paris," they "would fight, and win, or else die for the defense of our common rights." But this organization could succeed only if the Commune backed its action. It demanded, then, that the Commune give it a hall in every municipal building in which its committees could have permanent quarters, and that it take on the printing costs of the circulars and posters that were needed for publicity. There had to be collaboration between the *Union des Femmes* and all the official organisms of the Commune: "The government commissions would need only to turn to the Central Committee of *citoyennes,* in order to have the necessary number of women ready to serve in the medical centers or, if need be, at the barricades."[33]

But the revolutionary current that the *Union* stood for was far from expressing all the leanings of the women of Paris, even among those who had rallied around the Commune. Actually, the women were as much divided by their social origin as were the men. On May 3, a poster pasted up on the walls demanded peace in the name of "a group of *citoyennes.*" "The women of Paris, in the name of the Nation, in the name of honor, in the name of humanity itself, ask for an armistice." They believed that the courage and resignation they had displayed that winter during the Siege gave them the right to be listened to by the various parties, and they hoped that "their capacity as wives and mothers will soften hearts in Paris, as well as in Versailles." This vocabulary is obviously vastly different from that of the militant women of the International. Tired of suffering, terrified by the unheroic misfortunes that threatened them, they appealed to the generosity of Versailles and Paris, begging both sides to lay down their arms and to try to find a peaceful solution. All women, they said—those who feared for their children's lives, those whose husbands were fighting because of conviction, or else to "earn their daily bread at the ramparts," the calmest women and the most "exalted"— all demanded peace.[34]

This was by no means the opinion of the *Union des Femmes* which, on the 6th of May, replied with an indignant manifesto:

In the name of the Social Revolution that we hail, in the name of the demand for working rights, for equality, and for justice, the *Union des Femmes Pour*

la Défense de Paris et les Soins aux Blessés protests
with all its might against the shameful proclamation
of *citoyennes* which appeared and was posted the day
before yesterday, and which issued from an anonymous group of reactionaries. . . .

How could anyone appeal to the generosity of Versailles,
the generosity of the "villainous murderers"? There was
no possible conciliation "between liberty and despotism,
between the People and it torturers." Conciliation would
be treason, the negation of all the hopes of the working
class—hopes for total social reform, abolition of all
privilege, the substitution of the rule of work for the rule
of capital, the worker's liberation by the worker. This
struggle could end only in the victory of the people, and
Paris ought not to flinch from it, for

> it bears the banner of the future. . . . United and
> resolute, ennobled and enlightened by the suffering
> that social crisis always draws in its wake, profoundly
> convinced that the Commune, representing the inter-
> national and revolutionary principles of the people,
> carries in itself the seeds of social revolution, the
> Women of Paris will prove to France and to the
> world that they too, at the moment of supreme
> danger—at the barricades and at the ramparts of
> Paris, if the reactionary powers should force her
> gates—they too know how, like their brothers, to give
> their blood and their life for the defense and the
> triumph of the Commune, that is, the People. And
> then victorious, at one in uniting and agreeing upon
> their common interests, working men and working
> women, in full solidarity, with an ultimate effort, will
> annihilate forever every vestige of exploitation and
> exploiters. Long live the social and universal Repub-
> lic! Long live work! Long live the Commune![35]

CHAPTER FIVE

THE UNION DES FEMMES

WHAT, THEN, WAS THIS *Union des Femmes Pour la Défense de Paris et les Soins aux Blessés,* whose call we have read? It was actually the women's section of the French International. Its contemporaries[1] were not unaware of its affiliation and its importance, both of which became more significant in the parliamentary inquiry into the March 18th insurrection. Barral de Montaud did not hesitate to attribute to the *Union* every initiative taken by women during the Commune[2]—no doubt an exaggeration.

The *Union des Femmes* was organized—we do not know when—by a friend of Karl Marx, Elizabeth Dmitrieff, who was already helping to administer the *Comité des*

Femmes created by Jules Allix. She was a strange person, whose importance would never have been suspected from the almost empty dossier the Council of War kept on her[3] —indicating the extent of the negligence with which these military men conducted the inquiry. "It has not been possible to ascertain what the Dmitrieff woman was doing before March 18," we read there. Well, you would have only to refer to one document—also preserved in the War Archives[4]—to see that she had already participated in the *Comité des Femmes*. No testimony was sought out. As far as the officers of the Council of War were concerned, Elizabeth Dmitrieff, born somewhere in Russia, came out of the blue on March 18. They recall only her elegance, comparable to that of Théroigne de Méricourt:* she always wore a riding habit, a felt hat trimmed with red feathers, and a silk scarf of the same color fringed with gold, which "crossed her bodice from right to left," as the insignia of her rank. For the rest, there are a few copies of articles under her name, and a certificate of citizenship taken out in the name of the *citoyen* Henri Colleville. Slim pickings.

Today, however, we are much better informed. The young woman known in Paris during the Commune as Elizabeth Dmitrieff was born in 1851, in the province of Pskov. She was the daughter of a former hussar officer, Louka Kouchelev, and a young nurse, Nathalie Troskevitch. In her father's will, he acknowledged her only as his "ward." Like Louise Michel, Elizabeth Dmitrieff was of irregular birth. This common origin may have predisposed them to a keener resentment of social injustices. But the harshness with which the former officer treated his serfs was, perhaps, also not without influence on his daughter's revolt. However that may be, Elizabeth re-

---

* A heroine of the French Revolution who ran a *salon* and later helped to storm the Bastille; she was nicknamed "the Amazon of Liberty."—*Trans.*

ceived an excellent education and, as was customary in Russian high society, learned several languages. In her father's library at Saint Petersburg, she found works in French, German, English, and Italian, and read them avidly, as she did the newest Russian periodicals to which her mother subscribed. These were the years of the sixties, when the young Russian intelligentsia was "going to the people" and passionately discussing "new ideas": the emancipation of the serfs and of women, the reform of education and of justice, the theories of art for art and art for society, materialism and spiritualism, the value of science, and many other questions—we find them echoed in the works of Dostoyevsky. Besides Tolstoy, Turgenev, and Dostoyevsky, who were at the height of their talents, a new, more "radical" type of writer was appearing: the poet Nekrasov, the dramatist Ostrovsky, the critic Dobroliubov, and especially the philosopher Chernyshevsky, who was then in Siberia paying for the boldness of his social ideas. In Saint Petersburg, Elizabeth participated in all these discussions. But in Russia, as in France, women were forbidden to study in the universities. Thus Elizabeth decided to leave Russia and, like many girls of the Russian intelligentsia, to study in Switzerland. To that end, she agreed to a *mariage blanc* with Colonel Tomanovsky; he was much older than she, and tubercular, but he was in favor of women's emancipation. This model husband thus gave her a social position, a rank among the nobility, and freedom. In Geneva, Elizabeth met a group of young Russian revolutionaries, who gave their allegiance to the First International. She was the person whom they selected to go to London to contact Karl Marx. "Dear citizen," they wrote to him, "allow us to present to you our best friend, Elizabeth Tomanovskaya, who is sincerely and profoundly devoted to the revolutionary cause of Russia. We should be happy if, through her, we might know you better, and if, at the same time, we could acquaint you in more detail with the circumstances of our activity, of which she will be able to speak to you extensively. . . ." Elizabeth arrived in London during the summer of 1870. She rapidly formed a friendship with Karl Marx and his daughters. In a letter (January 7, 1871) to Karl Marx, she wrote: "I thank you for your kindness and for the interest you show in my health. Naturally, I do not want to take up your time, but if you had a few free hours on Sunday night, I am convinced that your daughters would be as happy as I to see you at our house." At the same time, she informed him about the agrarian situation in Russia:

> As far as concerns the alternative that you foresee in the problem of how communal property will fare in Russia, unfortunately it is very probable that it will be transformed into small individual properties. I venture to send you a copy of the *Narodnoye Dielo* (*The Cause of the People*), in which this problem is examined. Certainly you know the study by Hoksthausen, which appeared in 1847, describing the communal system in Russia. If perhaps you do not have it, let me know; I own a copy and could send it to you immediately. In the articles on landed property which you are reading at present, you will see that Chernyshevsky mentions it often, and quotes passages from it. . . .

This is a valuable letter, indicating not only the friendly nature of the relations between Elizabeth and Marx, but also their intellectual affinities. This very young woman— twenty years old—showed herself to be quite well aware of Russian social problems, and gave relevant information to the man who was already considered, along with Mikhail Bakunin, the leader of the international revolutionary movement. Karl Marx was deeply impressed by the personality of Elizabeth Tomanovskaya: it was she whom in 1871 he entrusted with a mission to Paris, doubt-less a mission of inquiry, but also one of organization; for we meet her again leading the *Union des Femmes Pour la Défense de Paris et les Soins aux Blessés.*[5]

Under her stimulus, the *Union des Femmes* was formed on April 11. From then on meetings were held regularly in different neighborhoods of Paris. On April 13, the second meeting took place in the municipal building of the 3rd arrondissement, in the Rue du Temple; the third, in the municipal building of the 4th arrondissement;[6] and so forth. In the *Union,* there were several women who had belonged to Jules Allix's group. But it is impossible to compare the social origin of the supporters of these two associations, for only in the second case, and then incompletely, do we know their professions. André Léo, who belonged to a committee of the former, did not figure in the second group. Nathalie Lemel's case was the opposite. In the 11th arrondissement, ten members of the committee of Jules Allix went over to Elizabeth Dmitrieff's union; six went over in the 8th arrondisse-ment, five in the 17th, four in the 5th, six in the 7th. But these were exceptions. Elizabeth Dmitrieff was recruiting militant women who were new and who came from a distinctly proletarian background. In the 13th arrondisse-ment, for example, we find one maker of men's clothing, one linen-draper, three seamstresses, two bootstitchers, and one woman whose profession is not indicated. In the 16th arrondissement, there are one garment maker, four seam-stresses, one linen-draper, and one bookstitcher. Out of 128 members, we know the professions of 60. All women's trades are represented there: fifteen seamstresses, nine waistcoat-makers, six sewing-machine operators, five dress-makers, five linen-drapers, three makers of men's clothing, two bootstitchers, two hat-makers, two laundresses, two cardboard-makers, one embroiderer of military decora-tions, one braid-maker, one necktie-maker, one schoolteacher, one perfume-maker, one maker of jewelry, one gold-polisher, one bookstitcher, and one bookbinder. The Central Committee, which in principle was made up of twenty members representing the twenty arrondissements of Paris, accurately reflected this social composition. The list that has come into our hands does not indicate who had the responsibility in the 2nd and the 15th arrondissements. But for the rest, we come across the seamstress Anna Mallet (1st arrondissement); the sewing-machine operator Marquant (3rd); the hat-maker Angelina Sabatier (4th); the embroiderer of military decorations Victorine Piesvaux (5th); the bookbinder Nathalie Lemel (6th); the linen-draper Octavie Vataire (7th); Marie Picot (8th), whose profession, if any, is unknown; the seamstress Bessaiche (9th); the dressmaker Blanche Lefebvre (10th); the seam-stress Marie Leloup (11th); the seamstress Forêt (12th); Mme. Chantraile (13th), who had no profession; the waistcoat-maker Rivière (14th); the bookstitcher Aline Jacquier (16th); Aglaé Jarry, without profession (17th); the gold-polisher Blondeau (18th); the seamstress Jeanne Musset (19th); and the cardboard-maker Gauvain (20th). And finally, Elizabeth Dmitrieff.

The general staff of the *Union des Femmes,* its Execu-tive Committee, was composed of four workers—Nathalie Lemel, Aline Jacquier, Blanche Lefebvre, and Marie Leloup—and three members who had no occupation— Aglaé Jarry, Elizabeth Dmitrieff, and a Mme. Collin, whose arrondissement is unknown (unless it be the 2nd or the 15th, which had no representatives).[7]

The *Union's* organization is detailed in statutes that were picked up by the press:[8] "A responsible organization among the *citoyennes* of Paris who are resolved to support and defend the cause of the people, the Revolution, and the Commune, has just been founded to give assistance in the work of the government's commissions, and to serve at ambulance stations, at canteens, and at the barricades."

In each arrondissement there were created committees responsible for recruiting women who wanted to participate in these services, for the administration of funds coming from voluntary subscriptions, for summoning the women of the *Union* "at any hour of the day or night" and giving them chores at the order of its Central Committee and upon the request of the Commune commissions. The arrondissement committees, then, were charged with the mobilization of women: every day they had to send the Central Committee a report of their activity.

These arrondissement committees were composed of eleven members. They had to be open day and night, and hold a plenary meeting at least daily. The president was designated by rotation. She was aided by a board, subject to dismissal, consisting of a general secretary, two assistant secretaries, and a treasurer. Every other day, a financial report had to be sent to the Central Committee, as did whatever funds exceeded that which was essential to the functioning of the arrondissement committee. Every member of the *Union* had to give a contribution of 10 centimes (the same dues as those of the International) and to acknowledge the authority of the Central Committee.

As we have seen, the Central Committee was made up of delegates from each arrondissement. It, too, had to be open twenty-four hours a day. The plenary sittings took place twice a day. The board was composed of a general secretary, three assistant secretaries, and a treasurer. A seven-member executive committee was entrusted with maintaining liaison with governmental commissions. The members of the executive committee wielded a card stamped with a seal and signed by the members of the Central Committee. They wore a red rosette in their buttonholes as an insignia.

The money that remained in the coffers, after the administration costs had been met, was to be used in the following manner: for supporting impoverished or ill members of the *Union,* for paying the committee members who had not the means to devote their full time to the *Union,* and finally for "buying kerosene and weapons for the *citoyennes* who will fight; should the occasion arise, weapons will be distributed according to the drawing of lots." This Article 14 has hardly been given due attention; yet it seems very important. It would be absurd to think that this kerosene was bought to light lamps; the kerosene and the weapons appear to belong in the same category. They are means of combat. The *Union des Femmes,* then, foresaw the eventuality of incendiarism as a defensive measure. There is no way of escaping this conclusion: any other interpretation would be erroneous. But it would be equally erroneous to become more indignant about the incendiary kerosene of the Commune than about the incendiary shells of Thiers.

At the Ministry of War, I discovered the archives of the 7th arrondissement committee; these allow us some slight grasp of the committee's everyday life.[9] It was not, perhaps, too significant a committee. Of its ten members, who do not correspond entirely to the general report drawn up by Elizabeth Dmitrieff, we find a linen-draper, Octavie Vataire, and nine other women whose professions we do not know. Six came from Jules Allix's committee—a very high ratio, which we do not find elsewhere. As the *Union*'s statutes prescribed for them, these women worked out a set of rules for procedure. Every step had to be taken by two members, and people had to be present at the "office" from eight in the morning to seven at night. The office was open until nine o'clock. Each member was to receive 3.50 francs per day, which seems considerable (in the 9th and 12th arrondissements, the municipality paid 2 francs).[10] If one confines oneself to the account book's entries from April 24 to May 17, the revenues of the *Union* in the 7th arrondissement were radically reduced. On April 25 there were 2.20 francs in the till, and in the evening the Central Committee was sent what remained after the day's expenses: 1.20 francs. On April 27, a *citoyen* gave them a 50-centime gift, but on May 3, 30 centimes had to be given to the delegate to the Central Committee, so that she could take the bus. As for asking the members for the 10 centimes' membership fee, this seems to have been entirely omitted. As one member of the municipality observed, how can one ask 10 centimes from women "who have not even the wherewithal to buy bread"? Since the Central Committee did not reply, the 7th arrondissement committee gave up collecting this membership fee. On May 15, the treasurer concluded that she had no more funds to keep. Indeed, there remained, on May 17, 5 centimes in the till.

But this penury did not hamper the committee's activity. It sent to the Central Committee an ambulance nurse from the 106th Battalion, who had no more medicine and wanted to know if she could obtain any. It summoned women to the twentieth meeting of the *Union,* which was to be held in the municipal building on May 8. It made a list of the working women in the neighborhood, and asked for the concession for sandbags that women could sew for the barricades, in order to distribute work throughout the arrondissement. On May 17, the Gros-Caillou gunpowder factory exploded, and the *Union* attended to giving clothing to the victims, and finding them new lodgings.[11]

In the other arrondissements we find similar activities. The members of the 2nd, 10th, and 11th arrondissements went to look among the debris for the inhabitants of Neuilly who had been bombarded by the Versailles army.[12] In the 5th arrondissement, they reminded a colonel of the elementary rules of military discipline: "It is urgent that you refuse passes to all the Guards' wives." These visits provoked disorder, and hindered defense; and "this causes much unpleasantness to the service of our nurses who are devoting themselves to tending our wounded."[13]

But if the defense of Paris and first aid for the wounded appeared as the primary objectives of the *Union des Femmes,* the organization of work seemed to be even more important, for this carries within itself the seeds of that social reform which gave the Commune its historical significance. As a consequence of the war, the Siege, and then the events of March 18, a great number of shops had closed their doors. Their owners had preferred to leave Paris for safer places, Versailles or the provinces. Although most of the men were mobilized in the National Guard, unemployment was rampant. In the besieged city, the manufacture of cartridges, sandbags for the barricades, and military equipment provided the women with some means of sustenance. Women came to the military supply office and the Ministry of Labor, asking to be given work. Three thousand women seem to have been employed making cartridges.[14] Vuillaume, in *Mes Cahiers Rouges,* tells us that he supervised a workroom of five hundred to six hundred pretty girls who were assembling fulminate cartridge caps.[15] And Lissagaray describes the workroom in the Corps Législatif building where fifteen hundred women were sewing sandbags for the barricades: "A tall and beautiful girl, Martha, distributed the work; she wore a red, silver-fringed scarf that her friends had given her. Happy songs shortened their tasks. Every evening, the wages were paid out, and the workers received full payment for their work, 8 centimes per bag. The middleman of former days would have left them 2 centimes at the most."[16] Saint-Pierre-de-Montmartre had been changed into a workroom which employed fifty women in making military uniforms.[17] But these were only stopgap measures.

Since the 18th of March the contractors who remained in Paris had lowered wages. Perhaps this was an attempt thus to create a current of hostility against the new government, by aggravating the economic situation. A report on contracts for military clothing negotiated with the firm of Monteux-Bernard makes it clear that at a payment of 3.75 francs for a jacket and 2.50 for trousers, it was impossible for the women to live. The working-women's associations gave 6 francs for the same thing. If the Commune accepted this competition between capitalist work and cooperative work it "would lose its dignity," and the women would again see their piece-rates decrease. Nor should the Commune have recourse to buying from intermediaries: "This would mean that the enslavement of the workers would continue, through centralization in the hands of the exploiters. . . ." Léo Frankel concluded that the Commission for Labor and Exchange should demand that the purchases that could be made directly from the cooperatives be entrusted to them.[18]

Indeed, numerous demands were addressed to the Commission for Labor and Exchange. On May 3, Octavie Tardif, one of the directors of the *Union des Femmes,* who was at the same time responsible for the International in her arrondissement, presented the Commission with a petition bearing eighty-five signatures: "We have to have work, for our brothers, our husbands, and our sons cannot provide for the needs of our families." But this work had to be distributed in each arrondissement to avoid traveling, waste of time, and "the much greater inconvenience of neglecting our children." The outfitting of the National Guard could provide immediate work.[19]

During the course of a discussion by the Commune about the articles deposited at the Mont-de-Piété, Frankel adopted Octavie Tardif's suggestion. The women of Paris had no work; the National Guardsmen had only 30 sous a day to live on. Poverty was widespread among the workers of Paris. Workshops had to be organized, but not "National Workshops," like those of 1848. "These would be workshops that would hand out work; the women would be given work to do at home. For, while we are obtaining work, we think that it is important, at the same time, to bring about reforms in work for women."[20] These reforms went in the direction of the Proudhonian current, even though Frankel belonged to the Marxist group of the First International: if women must work, they should at least be able to remain at their own fireside.

We see a plan for the organization of women's work which reflects the ideas put forth by Frankel before the Commune. This plan is neither signed nor dated, but the printing order is signed by Benoît Malon.[21] This is one of the most important documents for understanding the Commune's deeper meaning, beyond its mistakes and shortcomings.

> The March 18th Revolution, spontaneously achieved by the people amid circumstances that were unique in history, is a great victory for the Law of the People, in the implacable struggle that they carry on against all tyrannies—a struggle begun by the slaves, continued by the serfs; a struggle that the proletariat will have the glory of ending in the achievement of social equality. The movement that has just been born was so unexpected, so decisive, that professional politicians have understood nothing of it and have seen in this great movement only an insignificant and aimless revolt. Others have insisted on limiting the very idea of this Revolution by reducing it to the simple demand for what they call municipal franchise.

But the people were not tricked by that. What they saw in the Commune was indeed communal autonomy, but also "the creation of the new order, that of equality, solidarity, and liberty, which shall be the crowning of the communal revolution that Paris has the honor of having initiated." Paris, then, was not only to think of defending itself, but also was to enter vigorously upon the path of social reform. The Commune had an imperative duty toward the workers from whom it had sprung: to take decisive measures in their behalf. While the men were fighting, the Commune should concern itself with their wives and children, should give them support and work. But charity workshops were not to be trusted. "The crisis we are passing through is a terrible one. We must act, and act quickly, all the time refraining from resorting to expedients, to attempts which sometimes may fulfill the exigencies of an unusual situation, but create for the future dreadful difficulties like those that followed upon the closing of the National Workshops in 1848." Therefore, the stopgap of charity had to be rejected. "Assistance, in the strict sense, presents dangers of another order. It tends to encourage laziness, and to debase character. The Commune, then, should abandon the old mistaken procedures, be inspired by the very difficulties of the situation, and put into practice those means which will outlive the circumstances that gave them birth."

How to attain this goal? There would be special workshops for women's work, and sales outlets for the finished products. Each arrondissement would provide receiving centers for raw materials, which would be allocated to the women individually or in groups, and places to store and sell the products. To put this plan into effect, there would be an appeal in every arrondissement to a committee of women. The delegate to the Financial Commission of the Commune would open a credit account with the municipal councils for the plan's realization.

This organization of work would be taken in hand by the *Union des Femmes*. Elizabeth Dmitrieff, representing the *Union,* sent a very detailed report to the Commission for Labor and Exchange. She emphasized the significance of the socialistic, not charitable, nature of this plan.

The reorganization of work, which tends to assure
the product to the producer, can be effectuated only
by means of free productive associations, which make
advantageous use of the various industries for their
collective profit. In taking work away from the bondage of capitalistic exploitation, the formation of these
organizations would eventually allow the workers to
run their own business.

It would modify not only the social relations of production, but also the forms of work, which were inhuman.
It was absolutely necessary that there be variety, for "the
continual repetition of the same manual movement has a
deadly influence upon the organism and the brain." The
shortening of the working day should also be taken into
consideration, for "the exhaustion of physical strength
inevitably brings about the extinction of moral strength."
Finally, it would be a good idea to abolish "any competition between workers of both sexes," since, in the struggle
they were waging against capitalism, their interests were
identical. Wages ought to be equal for equal work.

If these associations were to develop, each of their
members had to belong to the International, and the
State had to grant them a social loan, at 5 per cent
interest, repayable by annuities.

Elizabeth Dmitrieff had few illusions about the pro-
fundity and duration of the women's enthusiasm for the
Commune. The organization of work was urgent, for
"it is to be feared that the feminine element of the
Parisian population, revolutionary for the moment, would
return because of continual privation to the passive and
more or less reactionary state to which it belonged in the
past."

Therefore, the Central Committee of the *Union des
Femmes* asked that the Commission for Labor and Exchange give it the task of outfitting the military, and that

it put at the disposal of the *Associations Productives
Fédérées* the money necessary to take advantage of factories and workshops which had employed women, and
which were abandoned by their owners. Next came an
enumeration of feminine professions, ranging from typog-
raphers to glassblowers and illustrators, and naturally
including all the clothing trades.[22]

Statutes explain that all the working women's productive associations were to be federated, and to be responsible to the arrondissement committees of the *Union des
Femmes.* The Central Committee was to maintain liaison
with similar foreign organizations, to facilitate exportation
and exchange of products. The cadres of the *Union des
Femmes*—the Central Committee, Executive Committee,
and the arrondissement committees set up to participate
in the defense of Paris—could also serve to organize work
upon a socialist basis. The arrondissement committees
would keep registers in which women of various occupations would come to enroll, in order to form federated
productive associations, and also keep a record of women
working in their homes.[23] Each arrondissement committee
was to nominate five members, forming the Federation of
Women's Associations. Aided by the Central Committee
of the *Union des Femmes,* a committee would draw up
final statutes, which would be submitted to the arrondissement committees and approved by the general assembly.
A purchasing committee, in agreement with the Commune's Commission for Labor and Exchange, would de-
cide what expenses to incur. A member of the Central
Committee would have a permanent seat on the former
Ministry of Public Works (a woman in a ministry: what
a bold innovation!). A committee would choose which
samples to manufacture; another, composed of cashiers
and accountants, would establish the cost price. Yet another would keep a record of the buildings abandoned
by their owners.

Military outfitting would furnish the women with immediate work, but the future had to be provided for. Linens were of prime importance for Parisian commerce. "If convents and prison enterprises were done away with, it would be possible to raise wages." Feathers and artificial flowers were luxury items, true, but "it is important to prepare a new future for this industry." Besides, seasonal unemployment was considerable in this type of work, and the women of this group had to be brought together to do other tasks. The ideal was still for women to do their work in their houses. "Sewing-machine operators would be able to work at home, if society helped them to own the instruments of their work."[24] Thus, in these revolutionary plans it was not a question of collectivizing the means of production, but of furnishing the producers with their working implements.

But the state of a society is not altered in a few weeks. Despite the willingness of the Commune and the *Union des Femmes* to make a radical change in working conditions, the situation of working women remained precarious, and worsened from day to day. There were too few cooperative workshops to prevent factory managers from bringing wages even lower, or to force them to set more equitable prices. Promises were not kept. "They said that military trousers would be paid for at 2 francs, and jackets at 4 francs." But "just as in the good old days," the prices had gone down to 1.40 for trousers and 2.50 for jackets. "This shameful exploitation must cease. We must have the women with us at any cost."[25] The women who sewed National Guard uniforms wrote in *Le Vengeur*, May 14: "The intelligent, hard-working woman must cease being the victim, slave, and dupe of the owners, who enrich themselves by her suffering and at her expense." They asked that the previous prices be re-established, or else that they be given full power to make use, for their own profit, of the enterprise in which they were working.[26]

In any event, the men and women of the Commune, in an isolated city in the heart of a hostile country, entered into a merciless struggle against a government that had both army and money on its side. As if they had the future before them, these men and women were getting ready for a basic transformation of production, and seeking to blaze a path of social justice. It was because of this faith that the Commune and its supporters are admirable, and, to a certain extent, exemplary; the efforts of the Paris Commune in 1871 inspired the social reorganization of Communist Yugoslavia.

Moreover, the *Union des Femmes* did not limit itself to these projects. On May 10, it invited working women "with substantial practical and theoretical knowledge" to meet in the municipal building of the 10th arrondissement in order to reach an understanding with the Central Committee about the measures to be taken for the reorganization of work. And on May 15, the *Union* informed these women that this reorganization had been approved, and advised them to register in the municipal buildings.[27]

Without delay, poor women who did not even have the 10 centimes to pay for their membership in the *Union des Femmes* responded to this registration that the arrondissement committees were undertaking. We have, for the 5th, 7th, 10th, and 11th arrondissements, lists of women ready to participate in these new workshops.[28] These lists accurately reflect the division of feminine occupations. Out of 71 women signed up in the 10th arrondissement, we note 26 seamstresses, 9 laundresses, 3 burnishers, one worker in gold; all the others are connected with the clothing trades. In the 11th arrondissement, 140 out of 238 women list themselves as seamstresses; then there are one sewing-machine operator, one bootstitcher, one gold-hammerer, and one gold-polisher. Among the non-proletarian professions, there are three schoolteachers, one trained nurse, one accountant, one salesgirl, one pianist, one cellist, and one chorus-singer. The others—linen-drapers, dressmakers, corset-makers—all have to do with sewing. In all of this there are few industrial workers.

In accordance with the Commission for Labor and Exchange, Elizabeth Dmitrieff, Nathalie Lemel, Aline Jacquier, Blanche Lefebvre, and the other members of the Executive Committee of the *Union des Femmes* called a meeting of all working women on May 18, at the Bourse; there they named each corporation's delegates and thus made up the syndical chambers. Each of the latter would elect two delegates, who would make up the Federal Chamber of Working Women.[29] On Sunday, May 21, the working women were again brought together at the Hôtel de Ville for the final drafting of the syndical and federal chambers.[30]

But on that same Sunday the Versailles troops entered Paris. It was no longer a time to build the future, but to fight in order to preserve the present.

CHAPTER SIX

THE CLUBS

HOWEVER GREAT THE IMPORTANCE of the *Union des Femmes,* it would be wrong to attribute to it all women's demonstrations and activities during the Commune. Just as the International was not the sole power behind the Commune, the *Union des Femmes* accounted for only a part of feminine action. The women who spoke in the Clubs, cared for the wounded, brought provisions—and the soldier-women who elicited the sympathy and enthusiasm of some, and the criticism and sarcasm of others—were not, for the most part, affiliated with the *Union.* Louise Michel did not take part in it, although she was a member of the International. André Léo's membership is open to conjecture. The Montmartre

Women's Vigilance Committee, which was already in existence during the Siege, carried on its independent activity. Sophie Poirier, Béatrix Excoffon, and Anna Jaclard were active in the Vigilance Committee, and none of them belonged to the *Union*.

Anna Jaclard had been a member of Jules Allix's committee. Like Elizabeth Dmitrieff, she was born in Russia, the elder daughter of an artillery general, Vassily Korvine Krukovsky, who believed that he was descended from the kings of Hungary. On her mother's side, she was the granddaughter of General Schubert, a member of the Academy of Sciences. This doubly aristocratic origin did not prevent the secretary of the Russian Embassy in Paris, in 1871, from styling her a "harpy" and a "*pétroleuse*." From the estate at Palibino, where she spent her youth in luxury, Anna Vassilievna Korvina Krukovskaya had traveled a long road to the streets of Paris.

Sophie and Anna, General Korvine Krukovsky's two daughters, had been brought up with the greatest care. But like Elizabeth Dmitrieff, they were infected by the great wind of revolution which, during the sixties, was blowing over the young generation of intelligentsia. Sophie, who became a very distinguished mathematician and held a chair at the University of Stockholm, has left us some memorabilia of this revolution. "It can be said that at this time, between 1860 and 1870, one single problem preoccupied the educated classes of Russian society: the conflict between the young and the old. A sort of epidemic spread among children, and especially among young girls, the desire to flee from the paternal house. . . ." It was learned that a girl from the neighborhood had escaped abroad, and that another had left for Saint Petersburg to join the "nihilists." At Palibino, a student, the son of the local Orthodox pope, was the one who spread this news. Under his influence, Anna began to read philosophy and sociology, and to write. *A Dream,* signed (again!) with the masculine pseudonym of Yuri Orbelov, was published by Dostoyevsky in the magazine *Epoch,* which he ran, in 1864. A correspondence ensued between the writer and the general's daughter. They met each other at Saint Petersburg, and excitedly discussed literature and politics, about which they did not agree. Consequently, with his own brand of logic, Dostoyevsky asked for Anna's hand in marriage. She refused. "Sometimes I am astonished myself," she explained to her sister, "that I am unable to love him. He is so good, so intelligent, so kind. But he needs a woman who would devote herself to him fully. I cannot do that." However, the two sisters had to find a way of escaping the general, the estate, and the family. Like Elizabeth Dmitrieff, Sophie entered into a *mariage blanc* with a young scholar, Vladimir Kovalevsky, and, thanks to this chaperon, crossed the frontier, taking her sister Anna with her. The trio parted immediately. Vladimir remained at Vienna to study geology and paleontology, Sophie went to Heidelberg to take courses in physics, and Anna went to Paris to devote herself to social problems. The separation angered the general, who refused to send Anna money. To earn a living, she started work as a bookbinder in a printing shop. This lofty aristocrat discovered poverty, the necessity for work, and the workers' revolution all at once. "When I left for France," she wrote in 1869, "I did not suspect that the dream of throwing over the bourgeois regime was so close to being realized." It was during a Blanquist meeting that she met Victor Jaclard, a medical student, whom she married. But pursued by the police of the Empire, Victor Jaclard sought refuge with his wife in Switzerland. They followed political events closely. She wrote her sister:

Jaclard is impatiently awaiting information about the state of mind in Paris. The news of the French defeats and the disturbances in Paris keep us on the alert. We have decided to go there despite the danger—a danger which, for Jaclard, is even greater, since he has been sentenced to deporation. But in the face of the present circumstances, one cannot remain idle. The lack of resolute men, men who have heads on their shoulders, is too self-evident for thoughts of saving one's own skin.[1]

The Empire fell; Victor Jaclard and his wife went back to France. Jaclard took part in the battle of October 31, and then was named an assistant to the mayor of the 13th arrondissement, a colonel of the 17th Legion, and a member of the Central Committee of the National Guards. As for Anna, she took part in Jules Allix's *Comité des Femmes* in the 18th arrondissement[2] and, with André Léo, in the Montmartre Vigilance Committee. Since she seems to have met Elizabeth Dmitrieff in Switzerland, in the Russian section of the International, it is odd that Anna did not join the *Union des Femmes*.

The relations between the Montmartre Vigilance Committee and the *Union des Femmes* do not seem always to have been of the best. On April 22, Anna Jaclard, André Léo, and Sophie Poirier issued an appeal to the women of Montmartre to form ambulance stations.[3] The *Union des Femmes* took umbrage at seeing André Léo's name at the bottom of the poster, and published a protest in the newspapers.

The Central Committee of the *Union des Femmes pour la Défense de Paris et les Soins aux Blessés* deems it necessary to inform all members of the *Union* that the *citoyenne* André Léo, in giving an explanation of the motives that were involved when she put her name to a committee alien to our union, declared

that she had no official connection with the afore-
mentioned Vigilance Committee, and attested to her
desire to remain a member of the 10th arrondissement
committee of the *Union des Femmes pour la Défense
de Paris et les Soins aux Blessés.*[4]

Thus, the *Union des Femmes,* scarcely on its feet, assumed
all the characteristics of a "monolithic" party which intended to rule all activities of its members and to retain
a monopoly over their initiatives. Moreover, we do not
know how André Léo followed up this affair. The only
certain fact is that her name does not figure in the list of
members of the *Union des Femmes* which is preserved in
the War Archives.

The Montmartre Vigilance Committee, like the *Union
des Femmes,* ran workshops, recruited ambulance nurses,
aided the impoverished wives of the Federals, sent women
speakers to the Clubs, and went hunting for draft dodgers.[5]
Its activity, therefore, exactly duplicated that of the *Union
des Femmes,* but it had eluded the *Union*'s control—
whence, no doubt, the latter's annoyance. The certainty
of being in the right, and the resulting intolerance, are
characteristic of every revolutionary party. But the 18th
of March was not a day for any one party. The Commune
was the outgrowth of various tendencies—Jacobin, Blanquist, Internationalist—whose vague outlines we discern
among the women. But the women who spoke out in the
Clubs, with more eloquence or less, most often did not
represent anyone but themselves, or a spontaneous expression of popular opinion: that of the chorus in Greek
tragedy.

The Clubs, which had already exerted great influence
during the Siege, regained all their importance during the
Commune. Many women participated in them; some
Clubs were even exclusively for women. "We want to give

them a major share of our space," we read in the newspaper *La Révolution politique et sociale.*

Yet the greatest space will be reserved for the abstracts
concerning the *citoyennes'* clubs. It is time for us to
halt the injustices and prejudices of which women are
victims. When we shall have placed every *citoyenne*
in a position where she can earn a living, when strong
men no longer steal from them the work that is theirs
by right, our daughters will no longer sell their honor
to the vilest shopclerk. . . . I shall never cease to protest against the ill fate that the egoism of modern
society has imposed upon them.[6]

Once again, the opinions of contemporaries were dia-
metrically opposed, and are worth quoting next. Maxime
du Camp: "On May 3, out of curiosity, I went to the open-
ing of the *Club de la Révolution Sociale,* in the church
of Saint-Michel des Batignolles. I have hardly ever seen a
sillier spectacle. Many women; a few men affectedly keeping their hats on their heads; babies squealing; Commune
members girt with their red scarves, acting self-important
in the churchwarden's pews." The organ intoned *La
Marseillaise.* "Screeching women's voices, men's bassi-
profundi, yapping voices of children. . . . The organ played
Le Chant du Départ, and the assembly began to bray
even more impressively." Naturally the statements could
have been nothing but stupid: " 'It has been long enough
that our oppressors have kept the people, without which
they would be nothing, in darkness. . . .' Tomorrow they
will expound upon a weighty question calling for the
meditation of all patriots: 'Woman in the Church and
Woman in the Revolution.' " To Maxime du Camp's eyes,
this question is utterly ridiculous.[7] The Commune's
Journal Officiel depicts the same meeting in these terms:
"The church was overflowing; women were in the major-

ity. One had the feeling that the husbands going off to fight for the Commune had left a hardy seed of revolutionary ideas behind them at home. . . ." No longer were the men and women braying: "The organ opened the meeting with *La Marseillaise,* sung all the way through by the club's *citoyens* and *citoyennes* with admirable enthusiasm. This patriotic song, reverberating in the vaulted ceiling, produced a majestic effect. . . ." After several "very interesting" revolutionary speeches, people left to *Le Chant du Départ,* having settled the order of the day on the subject "Woman in the Church and Woman in the Revolution."[8] It would be impossible to find two passages that were at once more in agreement, and more contradictory. The whole difference is in the tone, in the mind of the narrator. Benoît Malon and Lissagaray also emphasized the importance of the Clubs. In them the "holy revolt of the poor, the exploited, the oppressed, against the exploiters, against the tyrants"[9] was preached. If few precise ideas could be extracted from these discussions, at least they were "stockpiles of fire and courage."[10]

Let us walk, then, through Paris, touring the Clubs of the Commune; but let us be wary of the eyewitnesses who guide us. Fontoulieu, the Abbé Amodru, the Abbé Delmas, and the Abbé Ravailhe are somewhat horrified by this occupation of the churches by henchmen of the antichrist. One might well imagine. A correspondent of *The* [London] *Times,* in his turn, escorts us into a women's meeting in which that bourgeois feels himself to be in very evil surroundings.

Several "Red" newspapers had alerted him that meetings would soon be organized at which *citoyennes* "might congregate" and give vent to their enthusiasm. He is dubious whether a man can attend without personal danger, but he hearkens only to his courage and his professional conscience; thanks to the protection of "a female newsvendor who occupies one of the kiosks on the Boulevards," he and a friend slipped into one of these assemblies of ill repute. It was held on the Boulevard d'Italie, in a dilapidated outbuilding over which a red flag was flying. The room was glutted with women and children, women of "the lowest order of society," naturally, wearing "loose untidy jackets" and "white frilled caps upon their heads." At the end of the room, there was a table "littered" with papers and books, behind which stood *citoyennes* wearing red scarves. One of these, young and pretty (curious that this reporter did not *see* her as old and ugly—we have here a proof of "objectivity"), spoke—held forth, I should say—upon the rights of women. She spoke in a foreign accent that shocked our Anglo-Saxon (this may have been Elizabeth Dmitrieff); what she was saying, moreover, seemed to him utterly idiotic. It was a diatribe against the stupidity and cowardice of men, and an appeal to the women of Paris to defend the barricades. The words of the lady orator were, essentially, of little importance to the reporter. What struck him more was her beauty. "She seemed very handsome, and might have sat for the portrait of one of the heroines of the first Revolution." However, this man was put off by something about her appearance. He would "not like to have been her husband." The second orator, however, "seemed tolerably respectable," with her black dress and her bonnet. But her speech, still according to this reporter, was as "rambling and inconsistent" as the preceding one. Perhaps it would not be necessary to defend the barricades, but there remained for the women the imperative duty of gathering the wounded up from the battlefield, and thus of saving countless lives. It was also necessary to take care of the field kitchens. The woman speaker recalled the example of Jeanne Hachette and the women in the Revolution of 1789, and hurled a few harsh words at the clergy. As for the third speaker, she attacked society's exploitation of the poor and defended the Republic. "A vague and unnecessarily repetitious speech." Thereupon, professional duty done, our reporter and his friend prudently ducked out, for, he said, their presence had been noticed and God only knew what might have happened to them. As they left, a lady "held out a bag and solicited a trifle on behalf of the new society."[11] Such was a Women's Club during the Commune, as seen by an English bourgeois.

Let us continue our stroll. At Saint-Jacques du Haut-Pas and at Saint-Séverin there were Clubs for both men and women. Fornarina de Fonseca often spoke at Saint-Séverin.[12] She was an Italian, whose family had a strong revolutionary tradition. Her grandmother, Eléonora de Fonseca, who was a lady-in-waiting to Marie Caroline, Queen of Naples, had espoused the ideas of the French Revolution and had founded a newspaper, *Il Monitore Repubblicano*. Arrested by order of the king, she had been freed by the French in 1799. But upon the restoration of Ferdinand IV she was condemned to death and executed.[13] Her granddaughter proudly revived this heritage, and never failed to invoke her grandmother's memory whenever she spoke in a Commune Club.

The church of Saint-Sulpice was defended by its parishioners, and the Club did not move in there until May 14.[14] Women were in the majority, and made up the Club's clerical staff. Paule Minck and Lodoyska Kawecka often gave speeches there. The latter, too, was of Polish origin. Her husband, the doctor Constantin Kawecki, had studied at Strasbourg and had been appointed Commandant of the 202nd Battalion of the Federals, then Lieutenant Colonel of the Turcos of the Commune. Lodoyska contributed to *Le Journal des Citoyennes de la Commune*, and was soon to fight for the defense of the Gare Montparnasse. Both of them would ultimately seek refuge in London.[15] In the 15th arrondissement, the *citoyens* and *citoyennes* of the *Cercle des Jacobins* met in the basement of the church of Saint-Lambert de

Vaugirard.[16] The *Union des Femmes* held a meeting there
on April 26, presided over by an Austrian, Mme. Reiden-
reth, who, it was said, exerted a great influence on the
women living in Vaugirard. "She was a woman in her
forties, tall, strong, of very high color, and wearing a
Zouave uniform. Her hair fell over her shoulders in long
coils wound around with red ribbons. At her belt hung
two very richly worked American revolvers." Two women
attended her: Julie Bourroit, a seamstress, and Anna Lavigne, a canteen worker. At this meeting, only women
were admitted. They discussed the influence of religion.[17]

At Sainte-Élizabeth-du-Temple, the offices of Mary's
month went on being celebrated in the Virgin's Chapel,
while to the right the Women's Club of that quarter was
holding a meeting.[18]

On April 27, the church of Saint-Nicolas-des-Champs
was occupied by the Club which had formerly held its
meetings in the Salle Molière.[19] In that first meeting they
considered prostitution and the means of wiping it out.
The parish priests were outraged to hear "the most
scabrous subjects treated without circumspection before
an audience composed for the most part of women and
children," and would not permit any religious exercises to
be held in a church that had been thus desecrated.[20] The
Club took little heed of these protestations. The red flag
was raised over the church and the president, Landeck,
declared in the name of the Commune that these monuments belonged to the nation: "let the priests say Mass
there when they wish to but we shall also carry out our
tasks there."[21] Not many women were there at the outset.
An identity card, countersigned by the Club's secretaries,
had to be shown at the entrance. But this measure was not
enforced, and the "lost women" of the quarter flowed in.[22]
And certainly, in the 3rd arrondissement, there must have
been many prostitutes in the audience. It was all the more
understandable that the prostitutes—despised by every-

one, even though people showed only amused indulgence for the men who used and exploited them—often viewed the revolutionary government of the Commune as a possibility of bettering their class in the new society. Prostitution considered as an economic consequence of low wages and of poverty was part of the order of the day, and people were looking for the means of making it disappear.

Alongside of Landeck, a jewelry maker, Marie-Jeanne Bouquet, *femme* Lucas, sat on the platform. She was a friend of Félix Pyat and of several officers in the Federals.[23] In the audience, one saw a bootstitcher, Clotilde Vallet, the widow of a certain Legros, and "companion" of a delegate to the Central Committee, Gandon, by whom she had two children, in keeping with that habit of the Parisians of not getting married either at the church or the municipal building, but of practicing faithful *unions libres*.[24] There was also the wife of a savings-bank employee, Jeanne-Marie Jobst.[25] A woman, Pauline Mengue (Paule Minck?), arriving from the provinces came to declare that the communal movement was making great progress there, and that sympathy and admiration for Paris were increasing[26]—words of hope that warmed people's hearts.

On May 4, the curé of Saint-Eustache received orders to put the church at the disposition of the Club. On the 5th, the crowd moved in. "It really must be said," notes Abbé Coullié in horror, "that women form the bulk of this terrifying mob." But, in compensation, it was the ladies of La Halle who brought a threatening petition before the Commune, demanding that "their venerable curé be set free."[27] Besides, even though "under those holy vaults, evil doctrines and more than one impiety" had been heard, the curé acknowledged that the church had not been subjected to any looting, and that the sanctuary had never been occupied.[28] Seen from the other side, the "impieties" became "an admirable sermon." One witness noted a speech worthy of the Gospel According to St. John, to which liberty and equality had been added. "The people were gathered as if at Divine Worship. What more religious, indeed, than the Revolution? The numerous women were assembled. . . ."[29] In this Club, they were listening to a canteen worker of the 84th Battalion, Mme. Brossut, as well as Joséphine Dulimbert (who in 1870 had edited *Le Moniteur des Citoyennes*), Élizabeth Deguy, and Marie Menans, whom we shall meet later upon the barricades.[30]

The *Club des Libres Penseurs* met at Saint-Germain-l'Auxerrois. There too, the Club was of mixed sexes, and we re-encounter Lodoyska Kawecka, dressed in Turco trousers and a crimson velvet hussar's vest adorned with embroidery. She had gold-tasseled boots and a hat with a red cockade. From her blue sash hung two revolvers. When she was not with the Federals, she came to the Club for target practice.[31] Nathalie Lemel, too, was there.[32]

Before an audience of men and of women "who smoked"—which was particularly horrible—were put forth the "impious" doctrines of the liberation of women. A resolution favoring divorce was voted for by acclamation. "We must admit," remarked an editor of *Le Cri du Peuple*, "that the supporting arguments, developed with a veritable eloquence, seemed to us irrefutable."[33]

The *Club des Prolétaires* met at Saint-Ambroise. There, too, many women were present. Mme. André, a laundress, was its secretary. We have fairly complete information on this Club, thanks to the minutes of its meetings preserved in the Archives of War.[34] *Citoyenne* Thiourt (or Thyou), who spoke many times, displayed great violence and zeal. In the Place de la Bourse, she had asked directions of a *citoyen*; he had answered that, in that quarter, there lived no citizens, but ladies and gentlemen. Consequently, on May 13, she demanded that cannons be placed on that square to silence all the reactionaries. On May 16, she called for the arrest of all priests until the end of the war. On the 18th, she announced the presence of twelve chassepot rifles hidden in the Rue Neuve-des-Boulets, and plunged into the search for draft dodgers. *Citoyenne* Madré, on the other hand, thought that women should not take weapons to look for hidden traitors, but should form groups to work on the barricades (May 18). On May 20, *citoyenne* Valentin urged women to "guard the gates of Paris, while the men go to battle." Then she demanded that the clothing left in the religious communities be sold or distributed "to dress poor children," and that "the flowers upon the altars, in the chapels, and all around the madonnas, be given to schoolchildren as prizes, to decorate the garrets of the poor." The proposition was unanimously adopted. Perhaps I am wrong in lingering over this detail, unworthy of a "serious" historian. But I find it admirable that in the midst of fighting, in the midst of poverty, in the feverish atmosphere of the Clubs, a woman should think of giving flowers to children. This seems to me quite indicative of a deep sensibility which rarely appears in revolutionary movements, which, because they must confront the most urgent situations, have to be schematic.

At the church of Saint-Eloi, we see *citoyenne* Valentin again,[35] as well as a seamstress, Marie-Catherine Rogissart, who belonged to the 12th arrondissement women's group responsible for seeking out draft dodgers.[36]

On May 12, about thirty women led by Lodoyska Kawecka, who seems definitely to have played an important part in the Clubs, went to ask the beadle of the church of the Trinité to turn over the keys of "that communal edifice" to the *Club de la Délivrance*. They were accompanied by several unarmed Federals. That evening, the meeting opened at eight o'clock, before an audience composed mostly of women. The president seems to have been twenty-five years old. Lodoyska Kawecka preferred the role of adviser, so that she might take part in the discussion. Women gave speeches about means of regenerating society. André Léo reasonably set forth the tenets of socialism; an old woman, called La Mère Duchêne in that quarter, was particularly violent. A hundred draft dodgers ought to be executed as an example: "What are the lives of a few bad citizens, when we are concerned with founding liberty?" Nathalie Lemel urged women to take up arms for the defense of the Commune: "We have come to the supreme moment, when we must be able to die for our Nation. No more weakness. No more uncertainty. All women to arms. All women to duty. Versailles must be wiped out. . . ."[37]

Let us go on to Notre-Dame de la Croix, in Ménilmontant. Paule Minck went there to ask the curé for permission to hold meetings. The ambulance worker Lachaise was among its most diligent members.[38]

At Saint-Christophe de la Villette, an old woman urged those present to sing *La Marseillaise* instead of hymns, for "there is no more God."[39] And Sidonie Herbelin summoned women to meet "in the Black Crows' barn."[40]

Louise Michel often presided over the *Club de la Révolution,* which met at the church of Saint-Bernard de la Chapelle. On May 13, they voted to do away with the magistracy and the statutes then in force, and to substitute a "legal committee entrusted with working out a legal plan which would have some relevance to the new institutions and to the people's aspirations." They voted, as well, for the abolition of religious worship, the arrest of priests complying with "monarchist dogs," and the execution of one hostage every twenty-four hours until Blanqui, who was imprisoned by the Versailles government, was returned to Paris. Then there were social measures: the articles deposited at the Mont-de-Piété were to be remitted without charge to the defenders of the city and to citizens in need, the licensed houses of prostitution were to be abolished, and the Commune was to consign the projects it undertook to "working women's corporations."[41]

On May 3, the *Club de la Révolution Sociale* was opened in the church of Saint-Michel des Batignolles.[42]

There, too, women were in the majority. The dressmaker Blanche Lefebvre, of the *Union des Femmes,* played an important role. Wearing a red scarf and a revolver at her waist, she gave speeches almost every night. Tall, thin, and sunburnt, she loved the Commune "as others love a man"; she was to die for it on the barricades. She reported young men who were obtaining from the Commune passes which enabled them to leave Paris. "If these abuses continue, we, *citoyennes*—we shall be obliged to climb up on the ramparts to avenge our brothers who have been abandoned by cowards." She asked that women's leavetakings, as well, be watched: "Let one woman be placed at every gate with a secret word, so as to know if the *citoyenne* may or may not pass." She also demanded that counter-revolutionary newspapers be banned.[43] A laundress, Victorine Gorget, demanded "a strong organization that would allow us to use all the vital energy of the population for resistance; without this we shall have to open the gates to the army of Versailles."[44] The seamstress Marie Ségaud, *femme* Orlowsky, "who also goes in for literature," haunted the *Club Saint-Michel.*[45] The rumor went around that the Bishop of Paris and the Abbé Deguerry had been freed. The Club delegated *citoyennes* Lescluze and Efligier, and *citoyen* Franklin, to make sure that these men were still in prison; they felt that it was important to keep these hostages, since Blanqui had not yet been freed.[46] But the invasion of the church by these infidels aroused the indignation of the damsels of the parish. These pious young ladies, whom we know only by their first names—Maria, Cécile, Félicité, Angèle—decided to blow up the Club, and the church along with it. Fortunately, the curate cooled their worthy ardor.[47]

Let us end our promenade with the *Club de la Boule Noire,* where we recognize our old friends of the 18th arrondissement Vigilance Committee. Sophie Poirier was its president, Béatrix Excoffon its vice-president. The latter seems to have exerted a moderating influence on the members of this club; this, at least, is what she told the Council of War. She intervened, once to defend nuns against a woman who demanded their execution, and at other times concerning the abolition of prostitution and the organization of work. "At the next-to-last meeting of the *Boule Noire*," stated Béatrix Excoffon before the Council of War,

> a *citoyen* named Barois made a motion whose objective was to demand the exchange of Blanqui for the Archbishop of Paris, and the execution of that prelate if the proposition was not accepted. In my role as vice-president, since Mme. Poirier had blocked the motion, I submitted the proposition to the assembly, which accepted it unanimously; it was decided that the report of the meeting be sent immediately to the Commune. At the last meeting, on May 20, the same *citoyen* asked if the assembly wanted the Archbishop to be shot. Everyone's reply was negative.[48]

The question of pulling down the Vendôme column was also brought up: "I said once that the Vendôme column had cost four million men, and it would have been better to fight against the Prussians with the soldiers who could have been fathered by the victims of the First Empire, than to own a pile of bronze."[49]

CHAPTER SEVEN

OPINION AND ACTION

THAT TRIP THROUGH the Clubs enables us to make out what subjects were being passionately and violently discussed there.

There is no doubt that the women in the Clubs had only very vague ideas concerning socialism. But what they did know, what they did feel in a confused and visceral fashion, was that they had worked all their lives for ridiculous wages, and that, if nothing were to change, their children would be like them: poverty-stricken and exploited. To a young man who was expounding the goals of the Commune, an old working woman in a blue apron, with a square kerchief on her head, got up and answered:

He tells us that the Commune is going to do something so that the people aren't dying of hunger as they work. Well, that's fine; it's not a bit too soon! Because here I've been a washerwoman for forty years, I've been working every blessed day of the week, without ever having anything to put in my mouth or to pay the rent. Food is so expensive! And so why is it that some can rest from one New Year's Day to the next, while we are always at work? Is that fair? It seems to me that if I were the government, I'd manage things so that working people could be given their turn to rest. If the people had vacations like the rich do, *citoyens*, they wouldn't complain so much.[1]

Women like André Léo, Louise Michel, and Nathalie Lemel came to speak and to set forth ways of transforming society: the abolition of capitalistic exploitation and the handing over of tools and workshops to the workers.

To this claim for justice to the working class was added that of women, who were doubly exploited. At the *Club de la Révolution Sociale,* they discussed woman's situation "according to the Church and according to the Revolution."[2] A motion in favor of divorce was approved at the *Club des Libres Penseurs.*[3] At Sainte-Élizabeth-du-Temple, they demanded that women having a specified number of children receive a pension. This proposition seemed grotesque to the reactionary onlooker who reported it; but is it not the origin of family allowances?[4] The Clubs, depicted by the adversaries of the Commune as lairs of bandits, drunkards, and prostitutes, were demanding measures whose morality was entirely puritanical. The Vigilance Committee of the republican *citoyennes* of the 18th arrondissement voted for a motion which would tend to make the prostitution that had been increasing for some time disappear from the streets. The motion was signed by the president, Sophie Poirier, the secretary, Anna

Jaclard, and two assistants, Mmes. Barois and Tesson. Four hundred signatures followed.[5] The *Club de l'École de Médecine* demanded "that all women of suspect morality plying their shameful trade on the public thoroughfares" be immediately arrested, and likewise "the drunkards who have forgotten their self-respect"; that the cafés be closed at 11 o'clock at night; that "stag parties" be forbidden. This document was unanimously approved.[6] The residents of the 1st and 2nd arrondissements congratulated the municipal council of the 11th for having taken measures concerning prostitutes and drunkards, and asked that a decree of the same sort be applied to their neighborhoods. Nobody could take a step without being scandalously accosted by women of ill repute, especially in the Rue du Petit-Carreau, Rue de Montorgueil, Rue Saint-Honoré, etc. It does not appear that this expansion of prostitution, which a century later exists in the same streets, can be attributed to the circumstances created by the Commune.[7] In response to this appeal, the municipal council of the 2nd arrondissement had the licensed houses of prostitution closed.[8] The members of the Commune in the 15th arrondissement had prostitutes and drunkards arrested: "Any intoxicated member of the National Guards will be deprived of his pay for four days; his pay will be distributed to the neediest children in his company."[9] Staff officers who had been banqueting with tarts at Peters' restaurant were sent to Bicêtre, with pick and shovel, to dig trenches; the girls were sent to Saint-Lazare to make sandbags.[10] Édouard Moreau, Civil Commissioner to the Delegate for War, proposed that every drinking establishment from which a drunken man was seen to leave be closed, and that no woman not possessing a regular pass be permitted to enter forts or entrenchments.[11] The ideal Commune would have been Savonarola's Florence.

What was to become of these prostitutes who could no longer ply their trade? Some of them turned up at the

Hôtel de Ville asking to be allowed to care for the injured. They were refused this honor, for, Louise Michel noted, the men of the Commune wanted pure hands tending the Federals. But for Louise Michel, these women, the victims of poverty and of society, had a right to their place in the new world which was being born, and which ought to reject any moral condemnation. "Who, then, would have more of a right than they, the saddest victims of the old world, to give their life for the new one?" Therefore she directed them to a committee of women (the 18th arrondissement Vigilance Committee? the *Union des Femmes?*) "whose spirits were generous enough to let these women be welcomed." "We shall never bring shame down upon the Commune," these prostitutes said. Many, indeed, died courageously on the barricades during the Bloody Week in May, as did that "Henriette-Tout-le-Monde" whose story has been told by Maurice Dommanget.[12]

The Clubs were also interested in everyday life, organizing soup kitchens,[13] and helping the poor. At the *Club des Prolétaires, citoyenne* Mayer was outraged that assistance had been refused a mother of nine, ostensibly because she had been employed by a convent.[14]

In that newly-besieged Paris, they lived in terror of informers and of policemen. It was the gendarmes who were accused of bombarding Paris, when the commandant of Mont-Valérien would have refused to carry out this task.[15] The agents of Versailles were suspected of having blown up the cartridge factory on Avenue Rapp. Thus all Thiers' toadies, their families, all those whose sympathies were with the Versailles government, were distrusted. People demanded the enrollment of able-bodied men into the Federals. Louise Leroy, Octavie Tardif, Antoinette Decroix, and others whose husbands were fighting for the Commune, protested against "the cowards who . . . not content with merely hiding while their brothers are avenging desecrated Paris, still dare to scoff at good citizens doing their duty at the risk of their lives." If they refused to sign up, the women demanded that they be put under house arrest and publicly called to shame.[16] *Citoyenne* Gérard, of 159 Rue Amelot, wrote: "The primary duty of a government is that of enforcing its decrees. If it does not possess that firmness, its enemies will not fail to exploit its weakness, and even its most ardent supporters will be demoralized." While the republicans were fighting and dying for the Commune, able-bodied men were calmly going about their business and making fun of the fighters. This situation could not go on.

> My husband is part of the 7th Marching Company of the 141st Battalion. He has been at the Issy fort since Sunday, April 30. There he is fighting to defend our rights. I am not sorry for that, for I myself encouraged him to do it; it is his duty. But also, my heart bleeds when I see that absolutely no men but those who feel like it are fighting. The cowardice of the draft dodgers remains unpunished.

There were Federals who had abandoned their posts, and yet were continuing to draw their pay. She did not want to make any denunciations, but she feared that the Commune's weakness would frustrate all its plans for the future. "The feeling of the fighting men is that the Commune should, as quickly as possible, proceed to a general census of the population, and the immediate induction of all able-bodied male citizens."[17]

Under the pressure of public opinion and of the Clubs, General Cluseret decided that every man from nineteen to forty years of age be obliged to serve in the National Guard: a useless measure, since it provided only a very weak contingent of men who were really eager to fight (the partisans of the Commune had long ago been at the ramparts and the forts). A clumsy measure, too, since it gave the Commune the appearance of being dictatorial (which it scarcely was), inquisitorial, and intolerable—and all the while ineffective.[18]

However that may have been, the women were given the responsibility for this policing of the people. In the 12th arrondissement a "battalion of women" was formed, in which the seamstress Marie-Catherine Rogissart, whom we already encountered at the *Club Eloi,* played an important part. According to an eyewitness whom she accused of being a Versailles spy, she had said; "I'll make you all go fight, you're nothing but a bunch of chair-warmers. Me, I'm a woman, and I have more courage than any of you. Like it or not, you're going to fight the Versailles murderers."[19] Joséphine Taveau, *femme* Semblat, led the search for sailors for the Commune.[20] A housewife, Marie Audrain, *femme* Vincent, appears to have been a sort of recruiting agent. She tried to enlist all the men in her neighborhood, and even talked about giving the women weapons "to go avenge their murdered husbands and brothers."[21] The textile-carder Françoise André, *femme* Humbert, sought out two draft dodgers.[22]

Lacking policemen, most of whom had left for Versailles, the Commune women attacked their wives and families who had remained in Paris. The cook Mélanie Jacques, *femme* Gauthier, denounced a policeman's wife: "Assuming that the government of the Commune was a legal one, she believed that she was doing a patriotic deed by denouncing this woman."[23] At the head of twenty Federals, Claudine Lemaître, *femme* Garde, had a policeman's widow arrested and had all his uniforms, symbols of a loathed domination, thrown out the window.[24] Louise Arzelier, *femme* Jumelle, called "The General of the Commune" in the neighborhood, denounced a policeman's niece as a Versailles agent.[25] The laundress Suzanne Peru, *femme* Dutour, denounced a wine merchant for his remarks. He was said to have declared that "the Versailles government really ought to send all the *Communards* to Cayenne."[26]

One could give example after example, taken from the dossiers of reprieve or the archives of the Councils of War. Most of these women were acting out of political conviction. The writs accusing them noted the "fanaticism" of their opinions, that is, their conviction in favor of the Commune, and stated with astonishment that they "had no previous criminal record." Out of all these denunciations, however, one may assume that a few sprang from private vengeance.

Moreover, the Clubs found that the women entrusted with hunting out draft dodgers and Versailles agents did not put into their task all the zeal that could be desired. The *Club Saint-Ambroise* complained that the women did not put posters up on the draft dodgers' doors, as they had been told to.[27]

The women, then, sounded the call to armed struggle, to the preparation of the barricades, not only in the 18th arrondissement Vigilance Committee and the *Union des Femmes,* but individually and at random, during conversations in the Clubs and in the streets. At the *Club Révolutionnaire, citoyenne* Frenozi demanded that "if the Versailles government has not returned *citoyen* Blanqui to us within two days, the hostages we have in our hands be shot. It's been almost a month now that we have been negotiating," she added, "let him be returned to us! This is the simplest means of forcing them to hurry up and return him."[28] The softness of the Commune was criticized, but its activity was passionately supported. At the National Circus, in the Boulevard des Filles-du-Calvaire, before six or seven thousand people, a woman, *citoyenne* Baule, back from the provinces, demanded that the Commune establish a program that would combine the claims of Paris with the aspirations of "our friends beyond the

Seine." This was, she asserted, the only way of getting the provinces' support. "The provinces love us, love the Commune. But they do not understand us yet. They do not exactly know where we are going, and what they would involve themselves in by following us." Millière, who presided at the meeting, congratulated the speaker. They decided to designate sections by *départements*; in these, men and women would group themselves according to the province they had come from, and study the possibilities of Commune activity in the *départements*.[29]

This picture of public opinion would be incomplete if one passed silently over the deeply anticlerical nature of the Clubs. This anticlericalism had strong and far-reaching roots: in the novels of George Sand, Eugène Sue, and Victor Hugo, who had been the intellectual leaders of the people throughout the nineteenth century. For Victor Hugo, the abbey, and the convent in particular, was "one of the dankest secretions of the Middle Ages." It was "a congregation of owls trying to face daylight."[30] For George Sand, it was a place "of lies and imposters."[31] Tales circulated about the corpses in the Église Saint-Laurent, or about the instruments of torture in the Picpus convent—tales which seemed to issue from the novels of Eugène Sue, and which found a naïve credence in the audience of the Clubs. People were outraged. They demanded that the nuns in hospitals and schools be replaced by *citoyennes*[32] and that priests and nuns be arrested until the end of the fighting. All of this did not take place without excess and violence, usually verbal; the critics of the Commune have compiled anthologies of these. In the eyes of the people of Paris, the Church was closely allied to bourgeois interests: the one was rejected along with the other.

CHAPTER EIGHT

EDUCATION

TO ESTABLISH the future society of which it dreamed, the Commune had to mold men and women who were free of the stamp of clericalism. It was necessary to organize a secular system of education, and to make provisions for new schools for girls, whose schooling had always been so badly neglected—especially technical schools, which would prepare them to earn a living.

As early as March 26, the Society for New Education named delegates who were to present a project for educational reform to the Commune. This committee consisted of three men—Menier, Rama, and Rheims—and three women, Henriette Garoste, Louise Laffitte and Maria Verdure (daughter of the schoolteacher Augustin Verdure, a member of the Commune). Without wasting any time, on the first of April the delegates brought the Commune an educational plan reminiscent of the one drafted in 1849 by the *Association des Instituteurs, Institutrices et Professeurs Socialistes,* under the direction of Pauline Roland.

It was necessary for a republic to "make young people ready for self-government through a republican education." This problem took precedence over all others; without its solution, serious and lasting social reforms could never be envisaged. Therefore, all the educational establishments maintained by the Commune, the *départements,* and the State had to be opened to all children, regardless of their faith. In the name of freedom of conscience and of justice, religious or dogmatic instruction had to be abolished in State establishments: "Let neither prayers, nor dogmas, nor anything that is reserved for the individual conscience be either taught or practiced there." Questions that were within the domain of religion, therefore, had to be removed from examinations. Teaching methods should always be "experimental and scientific," based upon "the observation of facts"; therefore, teaching organizations could exist only as private or non-State establishments. In short, schooling had to be considered as a public service; it had to be free, complete (with the exception of competition for professional specialties), and obligatory, whatever the social position of the parent. In response to the delegates of the Society for New Education, the Commune answered that it was in complete agreement with their plan, and that it considered this first step "an incentive to set out on the path that it had decided to take."[1]

The Society of Women, Jules Allix's *La Commune Sociale de Paris,* and the Society for New Education joined forces to organize a meeting upon the theme "Social Planning and Education."[2] Twice a week, on Thursdays and Sundays, the Society for New Education brought teachers and parents together to discuss the reforms to be effected in the programs and methods of instruction.[3] In a hall on the Rue d'Arras, Edmond Dumay gave lectures every night about the new education, the family, and the rights and duties of children and parents. "The husband and wife should be equal before the law and before morality; there can be only physical or intellectual inequalities, and different functions, in their association." This association could be lasting only if it were based on "a community of national elementary education." On the other hand, families based on passion, self-interest, convenience, or the domination of "the head of the house" were unstable. The dowry was an immoral custom: "The true dowry is the worth of the fiancée."[4] For her part, Louise Michel sent the Commune a summary of an educational method that she had been thinking about for a long time. It was necessary to teach as many elementary ideas as possible with "the fewest, simplest, and most comprehensible words possible." She attached great importance to the moral training of her pupils. Their conscience ought to be developed to the point that "no reward or punishment can exist apart from the feeling of having done one's duty, or having acted badly." As for the religious problem, that should be left to the will of the parents.[5] With her friends in the Montmartre Vigilance Committee—Sophie Poirier, Marie Cartier (née Lemonnier), and Mme. Dauguet—Louise Michel demanded secular professional schools and orphanages to replace "the schools and orphanages for ignoramuses."[6]

Maria Verdure, and Félix and Élie Ducoudray, representing the *Société des Amis de l'Enseignement,* proposed a plan for the reorganization of day nurseries. The problem of very young children was difficult for working women to solve. The ideal would be to excuse mothers from all work during the nursing period "by means of the social reforms we are planning." But, in the meantime, the day nurseries could do considerable service. They should not merely be considered places to keep children of the poor; they should give them a start in education in pleasant surroundings. First of all, boredom, "the greatest malady" of little children, ought to be avoided. Therefore the nurseries would include gardens, aviaries full of birds, and painted or carved toys representing animals, trees, and real objects. Bright colors everywhere. There should be ten women for the care of a hundred children—gay young women. Medical supervision would be provided for.[7] This dream of the *Communards,* which then seemed a demagogic utopia, is what people today are trying to attain within any of a variety of social structures.

But they were not content with vows and plans. As if the political part were already won, they put themselves courageously to work. At 40 Boulevard Victor-Hugo, they established a National Guard orphanage for the children of Federals and of working women who made military clothing or were ambulance nurses and thus were unable to take care of their children. "The Republic will open its arms to them, offer them a bed, clothing, and food. It will teach them to be decent, hard-working, and brave."[8] In the 8th arrondissement, the mayor, Jules Allix, took a census of the children. Out of 6,251, only 2,730 attended schools. The others were simply not enrolled, although some of them received instruction at home. The private schools did little. Two Congregation schools had shut down. They had to be reopened. "All children between the ages of five and twelve should be placed in school immediately, or, at least, it should be proven that someone is teaching them or having them taught."[9] The girls' school on the Rue de la Bienfaisance was turned into a pilot school, as we would say today, under the guidance of Geneviève Vivien. Children as young as three were admitted to it. Between five and seven, they were to get some conception of reading, writing, arithmetic, and spelling.[10]

Paule Minck opened a school at Saint-Pierre de Mont-martre.[11]

But they were also struggling against the religious communities, whose teaching went against the social goals of the Commune. In the 4th arrondissement, the priests and nuns were thrown out of the public schools. "The Commune has no intention of offending any religious faith, but it has a strict duty to be on the watch lest the child, in his turn, be done violence by assertions which his ignorance does not allow him to judge or to accept freely." Schoolteachers from that time on had to inculcate the children with a secular ethic: "Teach the child to love and respect his fellows, inspire him with love and justice, and also teach him that he must learn for the good of the common interest."[12]

This battle for secularization needed volunteers. The Commune urged citizens of both sexes who hoped to obtain jobs in elementary schools to bring their supporting papers and offer themselves as candidates at the Commission for Education at the Hôtel de Ville. For having accepted a teaching post in a nuns' school, a young bookseller from the Rue Monge, Anne Denis, would be summoned to appear before a Council of War.[13]

This was indeed a direct participation in the Commune struggle, for the priests and nuns did not allow themselves to be ousted without a fight. Marguerite Tinayre, appointed inspector of girls' schools in the 12th arrondissement, went to visit the religious school on the Passage Corbes, in Bercy, and informed the Mother Superior that from then on the latter would have to address all her requests to her. Two weeks later, the mayor of the arrondissement, accompanied by a dozen women, expelled the nuns, who took refuge at Charenton.[14] The women who ran the school on the Rue Saint-Dominique complained that before the nuns closed their establishment, they had allowed a certain number of children to leave. People came to demand the return of two of them. "I count upon your good will," she wrote in a rage to Raoul Rigault, the delegate to the Prefecture of Police, "to have them brought back home."[15] At the school on the Rue des Bernardins, "harpies"—a Commune supporter is speaking: to each his own harpies—harpies, then, flogged the new schoolteachers; whereas at the school of the Marché aux Carmes, tradeswomen threw a newly-appointed principal down the stairs.[16] Faced with this resistance, the delegate to the Commune's Commission for Education, Édouard Vaillant, decided to have diehards arrested.[17]

But the problem was not only that of secularizing elementary education. Édouard Vaillant asked the municipalities to establish professional schools. People were particularly concerned with women's technical instruction, which would eventually enable girls to earn a living. Mme. Manière, a schoolteacher, organized a temporary workshop-school in the Rue de Turenne. She submitted to the Hôtel de Ville an organizational plan for professional schools which would supplant the convent workrooms. From their twelfth year on, girls would receive a responsible general and professional education, under the guidance of teachers or specialized craftswomen. "The various disciplines would provide a favorable environment for a progressive education." When the pupils were skillful enough, they would be paid for their work.[18] In the 8th arrondissement, Jules Allix organized a workshop which was to be both a school and a shelter for young girls without either family or occupation.[19] The drawing academy on the Rue Dupuytren was reopened; under the direction of Mme. Parpalet, it became a professional school of industrial art for young girls, giving instruction in drawing, sculpture, and wood- and ivory-carving—all the fields in which the art of design can be applied to industry. Also, literary and scientific instruction was to be carried on at the same time as the practical courses.[20]

The evening before the troops of the Versailles government entered Paris, the Commune's Commission for Education had decided to raise teachers' salaries: 1,500 francs for teaching assistants; 2,000 francs for principals. For the first time the equality of men's and women's salaries was declared, "seeing that the necessities of life are as numerous and imperative for women as for men, and, as far as education is concerned, women's work is equal to that of men."[21] This revolutionary, anti-Proudhonian decision is far from being universally applied even today. At the same time, a committee composed of André Léo, Anna Jaclard, and Mmes. Périer, Reclus, and Sapia was given the responsibility of organizing and superintending girls' schools.[22]

It is quite certain that in two months, petitioned on all sides by claims as urgent as they were various, the Commune could not successfully have carried through its educational reform. But guidelines had been drawn which the bourgeois Republic was to follow in its efforts to secularize and organize the education of girls. Women took an important part in formulating and partially implementing these plans—which were much less utopian than they were said to be.

CHAPTER NINE

A GREAT JOURNALIST

T HE GOALS OF THE COMMUNE, the coherent thought which quickened the best of the *Communards*, are both expressed by André Léo's excellent articles. And one might wonder through what injustice of History a woman whose novels are above average, and who played an important role in the Commune, has nowhere found her rightful place. Benoît Malon—who, one must admit, became her husband—paid her this tribute: "This woman, whose name is among those of the greatest writers of our time, and whom Rossel, who knew what he was talking about, called *citoyen* André Léo, was equally devoted to the cause of the people and to serving it with her writings, her speeches, and her total support."[1] Yet literary historians who set third-rate writers up in the eyes of posterity never even mention her name, and the historians of the Commune scarcely notice her. No doubt there are several reasons for this. The first is that André Léo was a woman, and women need much more talent than do men in order to be recognized. Second, André Léo was implicated in the Commune, and literary historians generally tend to be very traditionalistic. Third, however devoted André Léo may have been to the Commune—a devotion that she retained all her life—she did not figure among its extremists, and did not hesitate to criticize the mistakes and violence of the Commune's supporters. Tending toward Bakunin rather than Marx, she thus cannot be ranked among the prophets and saints of the First International. In the eyes of orthodox Marxists, André Léo is an "individual," someone smacking of anarchism, and vaguely disturbing. In the eyes of anarchistic revolutionaries, she is much too reasonable. In the eyes of the bourgeoisie, she is a revolutionary. In short, there is no category for her; she is among those people who could not be annexed by any single cause.

In the newspaper *La Sociale*, André Léo thus became the zealous but lucid promoter of the Commune. As early as the 9th of April, she recorded the isolation of Paris, the mutual lack of understanding between the capital and the provinces. "Both are in the wrong, and for Paris, the more intelligent, the fault is perhaps greater." Thus it was necessary for Paris to enlighten the countryside and the provinces, and explain that they all had the same oppressors. It was right for Paris not to imitate the violence its enemies had done to thought and liberty, not to transgress the principles that were the very bases of its demands. In this, André Léo implicitly poses the eternal question of means and ends. How can just policies be enacted by unjust means, when the end is always contained in the means put forth to achieve it, the means which determine it? "We must support our faith in a worthy manner; we must show in all its brilliance the idea we have the honor of representing; we must not let it be obscured by error or vituperation, must not disturb the conscience of those who see ideas only through men." Therefore, one should not proclaim a Commune and then act as if it were the Constituent Assembly. As a Commune, Paris should accept the assembly elected by the provinces. Fighting against this assembly, Paris was no longer the Commune, but the Revolution. Thus it was right to make a frank avowal of the social idea, the revolutionary idea, that one represented. "Now it no longer has anything to contrive. If it does not yield to the lesser, it will not yield to the greater." It was, then, a fight to the death between Revolution and Monarchy, between poor and privileged, between worker and parasite, between people and exploiters. The peasant, too, was among the exploited; but his condition was hidden from him by his antiquated ideas. Thus he had to be shown where his interest lay. Granted, it would be preferable to appeal to his intelligence. But whose fault was it? Who had abolished freedom of the press? Who had refused the people education, "without which universal suffrage is nothing but a trap in which democracy is caught, and perishes"? The responsibility devolved upon the men of lies and treason who had wanted merciless, bloody battle.[2] Next came a manifesto, drafted almost entirely by André Léo, addressed to the rural workers. It was necessary to end the antagonism between workers and peasants, between the city and the country (a problem against which all the twentieth-century revolutions would stumble). "Brother, you have been deceived. Our interests are the same. What I am asking for, you want too; the freedom that I demand is your own. . . ." What did it matter whether the oppressor was called landowner or industry? Everywhere, the producers of wealth lacked the necessities of life. Everywhere, they lacked "liberty, leisure, the life

of the mind, and the life of the heart." For centuries it had
been said that property was the fruit of labor. This was a
lie. That house, that land, on which the peasant worked
all his life, did not belong to him; or if they did belong
to him, they were burdened with debts, and he or his
children would have to sell them. "The rich are lazy; the
workers are poor and will remain poor." Against this
injustice Paris had risen and wanted to change its laws.
"Paris wants the peasant's son to be as well educated as
the son of the man who is rich, *and rich for no reason,* for
human knowledge is the common good of all men." Paris
no longer wanted a king or highly-paid offices. These econ-
omies would make it possible to establish homes for the
elderly. Paris wanted those responsible for the war to pay
the 5 billion francs owed to Prussia. Paris wanted justice
to be free, and to be done by judges chosen by the people.
Finally, Paris wanted "the peasant to have his land, the
worker to have his tool; work to be available for every-
body." It was said that the Parisians were socialists, "dividers." But who said that? The thieves who cried "Stop,
thief!" to put people on the wrong track. The real "dividers" were "those who do nothing but get fat from the
work of others." The cause that Paris was defending and
the cause of the worker were thus the same. The generals
who that day were attacking Paris were those who had
betrayed France: the deputies appointed by the provinces
wanted to restore Henri V. "If Paris falls, the yoke of
poverty will remain on your neck, and will pass on to your
children."[8]

Several times André Léo came back to the necessity for
making the countryside aware of the truth about Paris, for
purging the provinces of the poisonous calumnies spread
by the Versailles press. "Can we let this infamous old man
[Thiers] dishonor Paris? Do we want the provinces and
Paris to end up as mutual strangers, more enemies to one
another than are the rival nations?" France was being sold,

and nothing but Paris stood in the way of the transaction; therefore Paris had to be wiped out. Let Paris proclaim the truth. "The truth is the religion of every honest heart. The only atheist is he who does not possess it." Therefore it was a question, not of supporting or fighting the Commune, but of proclaiming truth: "The men of the revolutionary government have their faults and errors; so be it. But it is nonetheless true that by means of their risks and perils they support the great, the true, the only genuine revolution of this century, the breaking of the monarchical sac in which the embryo revolution has been choked for more than seventy years."

But since, as a rule, women are practical, André Léo did not stop at generalities, nor at vows. She proposed the founding of a newsletter which Paris, through the *Union Républicaine,* would send twice a week to all the papers in the *départements,* to give them accurate information on how things stood.[4]

If channels of information in Paris were free to operate, André Léo said again on May 16, the urban and the rural population would understand that they had to unite against their exploiters. For both of them hated the war. That was why the peasants had voted "for peace." What people in the provinces condoned most in the Parisian Revolution was that it had killed some generals. "A great cry must be raised, powerful and unanimous enough to reverberate in the very heart of the villages—the cry that never goes unheard: that of the martyr dying for his faith." This was the faith in communal liberty, in the Republic, in Equality.[5]

Paule Minck went back to the provinces to try to make them listen to the voice of the Paris Commune. But she was preaching in the desert.

In the midst of political passions, André Léo continued her efforts at clarification and truth; moreover, whatever its errors and faults, she was convinced that the Commune was on the side of historical truth and justice. Thiers had promised to apply "the common law" to Paris. But what, then, was "the common law"? "We live in an age when words have to be defined. The common law of Thiers and of the Assembly is the liberty of ignorance and the slavery of thought." While villages had the right to choose their mayor, cities of more than six thousand inhabitants had the right to nothing but a mayor appointed by the government. Why this difference of rule? Either

the countryfolk, farmhands, masons, shepherds, and so on are all philosophers, who in solitude balance the strong and the weak of things human, from Seneca to Montaigne, in the shadow of the oaks of Saint Louis and the beech trees of Vergil; while on the other hand, the towns are populated by loathsome, faithless, lawless bandits, all, as is well known, habitual criminals, who in this topsy-turvy century have come out of their traditional caves into the daylight of Belleville, Montmartre, and Les Batignolles

—or else the villages were illiterate, "reduced to the sermon and the almanac," while the towns knew more or less how to read, write, make judgments, form opinions, as Thiers himself had done, through study and discussion. Intelligence was precisely what Thiers and his "men of order"—those legitimist notables, Orléanist bourgeois, financiers, landowners, big businessmen—did not trust. It was all too clear why.[6]

The municipal law of Paris, just voted in by the Versailles Assembly, furnished yet another proof of the notables' great fear. Passy, an aristocratic district with 42,000 residents, was to have the same number of deputies as Popincourt, inhabited by 183,000 workers. And one had to have lived at least three years in the same place in order to vote. "For that assembly of stick-in-the-muds, immobility is a sign of virtue. The oyster is the symbol of sagacity." Furthermore, municipal offices would be unpaid. "Well-done! Workers, my friends, be advised that you will appoint one of yourselves to administer your interests. You may do it; nobody has forbidden you. Just one thing: the men you elect will have to have an independent income, or learn to live without food." You want "the common law": here it is. Equality? Take it. "The strongbox is God, and the Assembly is its prophet."[7]

But although André Léo ceaselessly attacked the Versailles government, she did not shrink from criticizing the actions of the Commune. She was outraged at the suppression of reactionary newspapers, and dissented with the editors of *La Sociale,* who had approved of this measure. "On this point I must disclaim any responsibility, out of respect for the principles which constitute all the power and the reason of democracy. In my opinion, to deny these principles is to deny our mission. If we act as our enemies do, how will the world choose between them and us?" Always the question of means and ends, which sadly poses itself to every revolutionary conscience. Let lies and calumny, when necessary, be attacked with justice, but "let freedom of thought be inviolable."[8]

She was equally indignant when the Commune was silent, particularly in the serious cases like that of Rossel, delegate to the Ministry of War. We know the lofty and magnificent letter of resignation that Rossel threw in the face of the Commune, when he was exasperated by its anarchy and weakness: "Provisionally appointed by you to the Ministry of War, I find that I am no longer able to bear the responsibility for a command in which everyone deliberates and no one obeys. I cannot remove the obstacles, for the obstacle is you, and your weakness; I do not want to make an attempt on public sovereignty. I resign; I have the honor of requesting a cell in Mazas."[9] André Léo energetically took Rossel's part: his letter was "the cry of a conscience," she wrote. If he was wrong, let it be proven; if he was right, let justice be done, not to citizen Rossel, but to the abuses that were ruining the Commune, which he was not the only one to note. "Why these reticences? Why this winnowing of facts? Why these closed doors? Are there, then, some things that are good to tell the public, and others that are to be hidden from them? But by what right? Do we not know that this is the denial of popular sovereignty and of the rights of Truth?" This conflict that exploded among the leaders of the Commune jeopardized not the ideas it was defending, but the men who represented and temporarily personified them. Men were interchangeable; they could always be found. The real savior was Truth. What was there to hide? Why were the Commune meetings secret? Did not the Commune have to account to the people? "The people who are dying for this cause have a right to know who is serving them, and who betraying them. A true democracy is not distrustful of truth, for it is made of truth. It comes from truth, it moves toward truth; it dies only for want of light."[10] The next day, André Léo returned bravely to battle, defending Rossel against the Commune and the Central Committee that had accused him of conspiracy. It was an indictment against the Central Committee. She accused certain of its members of being at the bottom of a monarchical conspiracy; it was against their will that the 18th of March became a social revolution. This accusation compels the historian's belief no more than does the charge brought against Rossel, which it so neatly countered. But André Léo was right in declaring, along with Édouard Vaillant, Jourde, Delescluze and many others, that the Central Committee had augmented anarchy and indiscipline, undermined the Commune, and greatly contributed to its incapacitation and impotence.

What has the Central Committee done since the election of the Commune? It had announced in noble words that it was stepping down without ulterior motives, but its actions have contradicted its words. It has set itself up as a rival of the elected power. It has sown disorder and division in the ranks of the National Guard. It has stirred up the soldiers against the commanders, and the commanders against each other. . . . It wanted to take over the administration of the military, and this administration is in a deplorable condition. . . .

In short, the Central Committee was following only one principle of organization, "that of disorder." "When an heroic people are fighting for a great idea, they have the right to ask their representatives for a little clear-sightedness, courage, and common sense," she continued. But she was not content with defense and accusations. Ever practical and concrete, she asked the Commune to appoint immediately a commission of inquiry to seek out the truth. But let them make haste, for the provinces, which were coming closer to the Commune, were disgusted by all these disputes. The Versailles government was taking advantage of their internal discord to secure its position.[11]

Unlike most of the men of the Commune, who so often went astray into vain discussions, devoting themselves to details and neglecting what was essential, André Léo never lost sight of the two objectives that, if the Commune were to triumph, were the most urgent: the indispensable support of the provinces, and the armed struggle against Versailles. In a very fine article, she extolled the soldiers of the Commune, those sixty thousand men who, for more than three weeks, had held their own against a hardened army of old soldiers, policemen, and gendarmes. Who were they, then, these dead men whose names and professions were listed every day? A shoemaker, a stonecutter, a carpenter, a blacksmith.

The soldier of the present Revolution is of the people. Just yesterday, he was in his little shop, his chest bent down to his knees, plying his awl or his needle, or hammering iron. How many people passed by without knowing, without believing, that a *man* was there? Today, this stonecutter, this shoemaker, this carpenter, this smith suddenly straightens up and, putting aside his tool and his apron, heads for the battlefield. He does the greatest thing that a human being can do: he dedicates himself to his faith, he fights for an idea whose victory he may not be there to see. This poor man gives the most precious human good—his life—to humanity.

There was an abyss between the imposed discipline of the soldier and the "free resolve" of the revolutionary fighter—the man who took his rifle and renounced all his attachments, renounced his very life, for his idea. Where did this devotion, this heroism come from? Not from "advanced classical studies and from that worship of virtue which do such a good job of inspiring the young bourgeois." What these men of the people made one realize was that "humanity has not degenerated, France is not dissolute."[12] André Léo upbraided the neutrals and the cowards, the people who tended to their little chores while others were fighting. If they were against the Commune, let them go to Versailles, where people were plotting "against justice and liberty," where people were fighting to defend the exploitation of man." But if they were "for communal liberty, for the idea that is not written, but lived," for liberty in equality, let them join the ranks of the defenders of the Commune. Doubtless the men representing the Commune were not above criticism. But they were, for the most part, men of good faith; moreover, they could be changed by election. Others were marred by "certain intemperances." Certainly, one had to take measures, although fatigue and the lack of healthy food had much to do with these abuses. These were not, in any case, adequate reasons to excuse oneself from serving the Commune.[13]

Finally, she summoned the women to join the struggle. If democracy had been vanquished until that time, it was because the democrats had never taken women into account. At that moment, it was a question not only of national defense, but of the defense of the law and of liberty. At that time, Paris was far from having too many fighters. Women like Louise Michel and Mme. de Rochebrune had given an example "and were the pride and the admiration of their brothers-in-arms." Let women fight, therefore, alongside their sons, their husbands, their brothers; then the Versailles soldiers, who had been duped by slanderous lies, would understand that they were not facing a group of sedition-mongers, but the people united. All women could not fight, but all could care for the injured or organize the feeding of the troops. "Therefore let General Cluseret now open three registers, for armed activity, aid to the wounded, and mobile kitchens." The women would come in droves to sign up.

But when the women wanted to answer the appeal of the Commune, they came up against the incomprehension of battalion commanders and doctors. André Léo looked for the causes of this, and patiently resumed the discussion, as we shall see later.[14]

Thus, in all her articles, André Léo displayed lucidity and practicality. With clarity she distinguished urgent necessities from illusory reforms which could be really applied only after victory; in this she showed herself to be infinitely more realistic than most of the men of the Commune. First it was necessary to win, and this meant that Paris must obtain the support of the provinces; hence her explanations to the peasants. It was necessary to fight; hence her praise of those volunteers who had chosen to give their lives for the Commune, and her appeal to women. But André Léo never lost sight of the fact that the end did not justify the means, that the truth had to be the people's weapon against reaction, whose domination could rest only upon a network of lies. It is a pity that being a woman, André Léo was not able to sit among the members of the Commune. In the midst of all the chattering, she might have been able to make them listen to words of common sense, reason, and intellectual integrity.

Artists, too, put their talent at the service of the Commune. At the Tuileries, concerts and popular performances were organized for the benefit of widows and orphans of the Republic. The people took over those royal apartments where they had not set foot since 1848. They crowded in, peaceful and joyous. Many spectators were not able to enter, but they refused to take back the price of their seat, 1.50 or 3 francs. They were given, as a souvenir, a red cockade and a copper medal in the shape of a Phrygian cap.[15] Rosalie Bordas, who had become famous in Paris by singing *La Canaille* the day after the assassination of Victor Noir, and then *La Marseillaise* at La Scala after the declaration of war, appeared dressed in a short white skirt and a huge red sash, which trailed behind her. Once again she sang *La Canaille*, and the refrain was picked up and chorused by the crowd:

> In the old French city
> There's a race of iron men,
> The furnace of their fiery soul
> Has forged to bronze their skin.
> Their sons are born on straw,
> Their palace is a slum.
> That's *La Canaille*—
> Well, I'm one of 'em.[16]

At a sign from Rosalie Bordas, a Federal came out of the wings and handed her a red banner; she slowly unfurled it and wrapped it around herself. She went on singing. "It was a thrilling sight," Vuillaume tells us. "The red of the gold-fringed banner was like a bloodstain on the white skirt: her hair spreading out on her bare shoulders, her broad chest, her solid, muscular arms, her gaze fixed on high, as if in a brutal ecstasy—she symbolized the heroic *canaille* who were fighting on the ramparts."[17]

Agar (Mme. Charvin), of the Comédie Française, also contributed to the popular performances at the Tuileries. In each drawing room, she declaimed Auguste Barbier's *Lyre d'Airain,* and *L'Hiver,* by the destitute and consumptive poet Hégésippe Moreau.[18] This participation in the Commune festivities won her, from Versailles, the insults of *Le Figaro.* "Once upon a time there was a princess who prided herself on protecting the arts, since she was an artist herself. For some reason, she became infatuated with a mediocre tragedienne, with a bleating and doughy delivery," and forced her upon the Comédie Française as a full member. After the fall of the Empire, this ingrate began to recite Hugo's *Les Châtiments* against her benefactors. "At the present time, rolling upon this slope of cowardice, flattering the sovereign *canaille,* as she used to flatter the Empire and its entourage, the ex-protégée returns to the Tuileries, with red ribbons on her bodice, to gabble socialist verses and to slobber insults upon a society which found an undeservedly high place for her." And, the editor promised her, she would be deported to Cayenne, along with the *"citoyenne"* Duguerret, who had dared to give performances at the Vaudeville for the benefit of the Federals. To these threats Agar replied with dignity. Yes, she had recited *La Lyre d'Airain* and *L'Hiver* at the Tuileries, for the benefit of the wounded, the widows, and orphans. "I often recited these poems during the Empire, in front of the Emperor, and often in the drawing rooms of Princess Mathilde. I have never recited *Les Châtiments,* and the entire Théâtre Français will bear witness that I have refused to recite it." As for her gratitude and esteem, these belonged for all time to Princess Mathilde. This declaration of fidelity toward a member of the imperial family is not without elegance, after the fall of the Empire and in the full sway of the Commune. She added, moreover, "I am ready to go to Cayenne. For that, I await a new denunciation from you. I do not fear your attacks at Versailles any more than I fear the Commune in Paris." She would continue, therefore, to give assistance to those who were suffering, from whatever cause.[19] Agar was not to go to Cayenne: but, blacklisted after the Commune's fall, she left with a road company for Switzerland, and had to quit the Comédie Française in 1872.[20]

But let us leave these very Parisian anecdotes.

CHAPTER TEN

---◈---

AMBULANCE NURSES, CANTEEN WORKERS, SOLDIERS

WE SHALL SEPARATE these three domains for the purpose of logical exposition. But life is not logical, least of all during a period of revolution. During the Commune struggle, the boundaries among such manifestly diverse activities were not well established. On the battlefield, Louise Michel was tending the wounded and firing; she was part of the 61st Battalion, the army corps commanded by Eudes. After having taken Les Moulineaux, they entered the Issy fort.

Two or three days afterwards, red flag unfurled, about twenty women came to see us—Béatrix Excoffon, Malvina Poulain, Mariani Fernandez, and Mmes.

Gaullé, Dauguet, and Quartier. They were answering the appeal that had come out in the newspapers; they tended the wounded, but they also took up the rifles of the dead. . . . There were also several canteen workers there, Marie Schmitt, Mme. Lachaise, Victorine Rouchy . . . many others, whose names could fill a book.[1]

Those burning with revolutionary passion involved themselves to the fullest in the multiple tasks the Revolution demanded of them. We are dealing, not with functionaries, but with living people, people who freely chose the total fulfilment of their destiny. This is why, throughout this study, we re-encounter the same women—in the Clubs, the committees, the ambulance squads, and even, rifle in hand, at the last barricades. And behind every name, as well as all the anonymities that make up the "masses" and supply material for statistics, there is a living person, unique and irreplaceable in his own single being.

On the 13th of April, the Commune had decreed that ambulance companies be organized. Each was composed of twenty doctors and health officers, ten vehicles, and one hundred and twenty stretcher bearers. In each arrondissement, two, three, or four squads had to be ready day and night. To each squad were to be added two women attendants who would walk along with the stretcher bearers. They would be given the pay of 1.50 francs, and the rations allotted to non-commissioned officers and National Guardsmen.[2] Anna Jaclard, André Léo, and Sophie Poirier responded to the summons of the Commune by the following appeal.

The *citoyennes* of Montmartre, who held a meeting on April 22, have decided to put themselves at the disposal of the Commune to form ambulance companies which will follow the corps that are fighting the enemy, and carry our heroic defenders from the battlefield. The women of Montmartre, inspired by the revolutionary spirit, want their actions to attest to their devotion to the Revolution.[3]

In the name of the 18th arrondissement Vigilance Committee, Anna Jaclard, Sophie Poirier, and Béatrix Excoffon organized a meeting at the *Club de la Boule Noire,* "for all *citoyennes* who want to lend their active support to the demand for all our rights, to go and help the wounded on the battlefield, or to care for them in the hospitals."[4]

Indeed, changes in public welfare were added to the care of the wounded. The 18th arrondissement Vigilance Committee again, in a petition with two hundred signatures, protested against the presence of nuns in hospitals and prisons, and demanded that they be replaced "by devoted and courageous mothers of families, who would do their duty better than the nuns."[5] These measures for secularization were demanded by all the Clubs. In the arrondissements, the Catholic boards of charity gave way to communally sponsored relief: "Alms must be replaced by the spirit of solidarity which binds republicans together and imposes it upon them as a duty."[6] The relief offices on the Rues Thouin, Boutebrie, Saint-Jacques, and the Rue de l'Épée-de-bois were taken over by women loyal to the Commune.[7] In the Saint-Lazare prison, as in the Beaujon hospital, nuns were replaced by women of the people.[8]

Therefore, in the realm of public welfare, the Commune acted as a revolutionary power. It shattered the pre-existing apparatus, and attempted to substitute another system conforming more to its own viewpoint: in this case, secularity. Insofar as it was a revolutionary power, the Commune would have done better to take over the Banque de France than to carry out measures on a secondary level, which disorganized the hospital services and contributed to futile and inextricable disorder. But the men of the Commune did not discern the hierarchies of urgency. Their debates, like their decisions, were often marked by revolutionary childishness.

The ambulance women of the Commune, for their part, published a very urgent appeal. They declared that they

do not belong to any society whatever. They live only for the Revolution; their duty is to tend, on the very field of battle, the wounds made by the poisonous bullets of Versailles, and when the hour demands, to take up their rifles like everyone else. In the event that, as might happen, reaction is triumphant somewhere, they have the right to set fire to powder; for wherever it may be, the Revolution must not be vanquished. Long live the Commune! Long live the Universal Republic!

This document is signed by Louise Michel, who must have drafted it (her style is recognizable), and by her friends Mariani Fernandez, Malvina Poulain, and Mmes. Gaullé, Quartier, and Dauguet.[9]

The *Union des Femmes pour la Défense de Paris et les Soins aux Blessés* also recruited ambulance nurses, canteen workers, and soldiers. The 4th arrondissement Women's Committee urged all "devoted and patriotic" *citoyennes* to meet at the municipal building "to organize and come to the aid of the wounded."[10]

All these appeals did not remain theoretical. The women of the 18th arrondissement organized a permanent ambulance station at l'Élysée-Montmartre.[11] Louise Michel and her friends organized a mobile ambulance station at Neuilly; Béatrix Excoffon and eighteen other women formed another one at Issy.[12] The *Union des Femmes* ran a station for eight ambulance nurses at Petit-Vanves.[13] Béatrix Excoffon has preserved for us, in a vivid account, the impromptu character of these ambulance stations.

"We'd left for the Porte de Neuilly. Along the way, many people gave us linens and bandages; I bought what medicine we needed at a druggist's. And there we were, turning Neuilly upside down to see if there were any wounded left, not suspecting that we were right in the middle of the Versailles army." A lieutenant of the Federals asked them what they were going to do, with their red banner. "I replied that we were going to tend the wounded, and that we had wanted to cross the bridge because that brought us nearer to the place where we could hear cannons." Even though they did not have passes from the Commune, the lieutenant authorized them to continue on their way, since they were not armed. Having crossed the bridge, they heard the cannons toward Issy. A young woman advised them that if they wanted to go farther they should call the bargeman "on the island." But, she added, "you must say that you are women from the Commune. Otherwise he will not let you cross in his boat."[14] The bargeman let them into the cabin, cut off a long tree branch and fastened to it the red flag that Béatrix Excoffon portrayed herself as holding. From the bank, the gendarmes fired, without hitting them. Finally, they reached the Issy fort, where they met Louise Michel and the 61st Battalion. Béatrix Excoffon remained at Issy for about two weeks, as ambulance nurse to the Enfants Perdus.[15]

Others continued to tend the wounded of the Commune, as they had tended the wounded during the Siege. Such was that "distinguished" old lady of whom Vuillaume tells us, who is guilty of no other crime,[16] or Victorine Brochon, who was sought as a *pétroleuse,* and who left us valuable memoirs about the Siege and the Commune. We also find her at Issy in the heat of battle, tending, with ridiculously inadequate equipment, the wounded who had been fatally injured by the "nicked bullets" of Versailles.

Unfortunately, we lacked everything. We had no bandages for dressings. We had to make those wretched men drink from little cartridge boxes. In spite of everything, these disabled men did not voice a single complaint or regret. They suffered, but they seemed happy to have retaken the fort, happy to be giving their lives to establish a more just and fair society. For all of us, the Republic was a magic word.

The medications that were so sorely lacking were redis-covered too late in an abandoned military van. The wounded died during the night. "If I were to live a hundred years, I could not forget that terrible slaughter."[17] Another nurse, Alix Payen, gives us a concurring state-ment in a letter to her mother. She came from the Milliets, a family of Fouriérist republicans, and obtained a nurse's certificate that allowed her to follow her husband onto the battlefields of Issy, Vanves, Clamart, Levallois-Perret, and Neuilly. She observed the men's discontent, because of "bad administration, excessive fatigue, and especially because the trenches were badly defended; there were only a quarter of the men necessary." But she also observed the courage, the nobility, and the thoughtfulness of "those children of Paris."[18] A Federal, Alphonse Freye, asked the editors of *Le Cri du Peuple,* May 3, to be so kind as to give him "a corner in the paper" to thank an ambulance nurse of the 169th Battalion of the National Guard, who had been caring for the wounded on the battlefield and had saved his life.

But, in this struggle to the death, Versailles had no more mercy for nurses than it had for prisoners: both were shot. Lieutenant Butin, sent with truce flags to gather up the injured at the Vanves fort, was greeted with rifle fire by the Versailles soldiers despite his white flag and the flag of the Geneva Convention; he had to return in haste to the lines of Federals. An ambulance

nurse who was about to lift up a wounded man was raped
and killed by five Versailles men.[19] The Commune seized
upon the affair, and considered applying the decree concerning hostages which had been voted in on April 5,
after the massacre of Flourens, Duval, and prisoners taken
by Versailles. This decree aroused the indignation of all
right-minded people, but was merely a response to the
murders committed by order of Thiers. Moreover, the
debate revealed that the men of the Commune were much
more respectful of their enemies' lives than were their
adversaries. Urbain, under the influence of his mistress
Marie Leroy (herself influenced by a Versailles agent,
Barral de Montaud), asked that ten hostages be shot within
twenty-four hours, in reprisal for the murder of the ambulance nurse; but the Commune's Public Prosecutor,
Rigault, declared that as far as he was concerned, he would
rather let ten guilty men escape than strike down a
single man who was innocent. Consequently he asked that
a grand jury be formed.[20] The decree concerning hostages
was not actually applied in reprisal for the murder of the
ambulance nurse. It would take the mass murders of
Federals by the Versailles army, during the Bloody Week
in May, for the exasperated crowds to abandon themselves
to violence against the hostages.

Despite their good intentions, the volunteer nurses
were often not well regarded by the officers. In *La Sociale,*
André Léo recounted the mishaps of the nurses from the
17th arrondissement. Provided with an order from the
municipality and with a Red Cross armband, they appeared at the Porte de Clichy to offer their services. The
commandant of the 34th Battalion accepted four of them.
The others went on to Levallois; from there they were
sent to the staff headquarters of General Dombrowski,
who was at Neuilly. There they were the targets for the
officers' equivocal jokes. "Why all this red tape?" they
asked the officers. "Do Paris and the Revolution have an

excess of devotion at their service?" They encountered
Louise Michel who, with two friends, was cooling her
heels in a little room. She had left the Issy fort for Neuilly,
where the fighting was the most fierce. But they refused
to put her to work. "Ah," she said, "if only they would
let me tend our wounded! But you would never believe
how many obstacles, how much teasing and hostility, there
have been!"

Everywhere along the outposts, André Léo noticed a
dual attitude toward the ambulance nurses. The officers
and surgeons were clearly hostile to them; the troops
were in favor of them. Similarly, in 1849, Jeanne Deroin,
offering her (illegal) candidacy, had encountered only
sarcasm in the bourgeois districts, whereas those who
heard her in the Faubourg Saint-Antoine greeted her
sympathetically.

> Alongside of that bourgeois, authoritarian mentality,
> so narrow and so petty, which unfortunately exists
> in so many of our commanders, there blazes in our
> *citoyen* soldiers the keen, exalted, profound sentiment
> of the new life. It is they who believe in the great
> forces that save the world; they acclaim these, they
> do not outlaw them. They know that the right of all
> is contained in their right. Whereas most of the
> commanders are still only military men, the soldiers
> are real citizens. . . .[21]

Rossel—that student at the École Polytechnique who
became the Commune's Minister of War, and who was
without doubt one of the strangest and most attractive
figures of the Revolution—expressed his regrets at the
situation André Léo pointed out to him, and asked her
to tell him "through the public press" (a consistent revolutionary, Rossel was a foe of secrecy) how to set it right.[22]
"The noble and frank tone of your recent proclamations,"

answered André Léo, "made me sense a man who was incapable of common bias. You know better than I what you can do to make use of the devotion of republican women, for that is inherent in your power. . . ." Women were running up against masculine prejudices and the surgeons' *esprit de corps* at a time when, on the contrary, it was necessary to move toward "that responsible brotherhood of men and women, that unity of feelings and ideas, which alone can form, in honor, equality, and peace, the Commune of the future." The Republic could be established only upon such a recognition of equality. André Léo submitted to Rossel an idea of Dr. Jaclard, the head of the 17th Legion (as we have seen, his wife Anna played an important role in the organization of the ambulance stations). Doctors without antifeminine prejudices, and the three or four young women who had passed their examinations at the École de Médecine, were to be placed in charge of several ambulance stations. "These women had the courage to force the doors of science; they will certainly not fail to serve Humanity and the Revolution."[23] But, by contrast to Rossel, General Dombrowski displayed an eminently reactionary attitude toward women. André Léo sharply reminded him that without the participation of women, the 18th of March would have ended in failure: "You would never have been General of the Commune, *citoyen* Dombrowski." She asked the general to do a little reasoning. Could the Revolution have been accomplished without women? That had been the mistake of the First Revolution: women had been excluded from freedom and equality; then, returning to Catholicism, they had strengthened the forces of reaction. The republicans were full of inconsistencies: they did not want women to be under priestly thumbs, but they were upset when women were free-thinkers and wanted to act like free, equal human beings. The republicans had dethroned the Emperor and God, but only to put them-

selves in the place of both. The republicans needed subjects—or, at least, subjected women. They did not want
to admit, then as before, that woman was responsible to
herself. "She should remain neutral and passive, under
the guidance of man. She will have done nothing but
change her confessor." But God possessed one enormous
advantage over man: he remained unknown, which
enabled him to be ideal. Religion condemned reason and
knowledge. The Revolution, on the other hand, postu-
lated that reason and liberty be exercised in the search for
Truth and Justice. "The Revolution is the liberty and
the responsibility of every human being, limited only by
the rights of all, without privilege of race or of sex."
Therefore women could not but be concerned; yet people
talked about the freeing of man, but not of woman.
Women were rejected and discouraged when they wanted
to serve the Revolution. It is in this sense that their
rejection was a reactionary step. A history of the period
since 1789 could be written under the title "A History of
the Inconsistencies of the Revolutionary Party."[24] But this
attitude of many Commune officers toward women corre-
sponds to an age-old feeling that is too deep and too
widespread for it to be easily changed, despite various
interventions. Thus the *Club de la Révolution Sociale*
in its turn asked the 17th arrondissement municipal
authorities to intervene on behalf of ambulance nurses
with the surgeons and battalion commanders.[25]

Armed women, whether canteen workers or soldiers—
often they were canteen workers and soldiers simultaneously—drew the attention of the Commune's admirers, as
well as its critics. With their chassepot rifles, their revolvers, their cartridge cases, their red sashes, and their
fantastic Zouave, naval, or infantry uniforms, they were
the target of caricaturists; a woman wearing pants was a
scandal in itself. With astonishment, Mme. Blanchecotte
described "those Federal women's faces, sinister, fate-

ridden, almost all of them very young, and some very beautiful."[26]

We find them scattered in the midst of the troops. In principle, there were four canteen workers per battalion, but often there were many more—accompanying their husbands or lovers, fighting and firing beside them. Often there were groups of them, marching in line, with their red banner, before the astonished onlookers in the street. "A band of women armed with chassepots passed by the Place de la Concorde. They were going to join the Commune fighters," noted *La Sociale* on April 5. A women's company, under the command of Colonel Adélaïde Valentin and Captain Louise Neckebecker, was incorporated into the 12th Legion.[27] On May 14, a hundred or so women went to the Hôtel de Ville to ask for weapons. Gambon, a member of the Committee of Public Safety, had some distributed to them.[28] The reactionary newspaper *La Justice* adds, with an irony that is at once scornful and uneasy, "One would like to smile. Might we be returning to the Vésuviennes of 1848, and might the laurels of *citoyen* Bormes be disturbing *citoyen* Gambon's sleep?"*[29]

* The Vésuviennes was a women's political club formed during the Revolution of 1848. Through its connection with an ancient superstition that laurel protected people from lightning, this may refer to Gambon's reservations about the advisability of Bormes's carrying out his plans to give the Commune Greek fire, the precursor of the contemporary flame thrower. "Greek fire" designates any of several highly inflammable compositions (some say saltpeter, others naphtha, sulphur, and quicklime) mentioned in early works on the art of war, and during the Middle Ages. As the discomforts of the Siege of Paris worsened, many people began to hope for "miracle weapons"; this hope came to the fore again during the struggle against Versailles. Bormes, a chemical expert and a devoted Versailles partisan, was hired by the Scientific Delegation of the Commune to make a successful explosive compound. He was arrested on May 18, suspected of manipulating the compounds—which, indeed, he probably did—so that no explosives could be made. He was freed on May 24.—*Trans.*

These canteen workers and fighting women were involved in all military engagements. Insofar as they were women—those "females," as Dumas *fils* said—they were doubly insulted and maltreated by Versailles.

On April 3, at the time of a sortie when Flourens and General Duval were murdered by Versailles soldiers, the geographer Élisée Reclus, taken prisoner, gives us the following account of a canteen worker. "The poor woman was in the row in front of mine, alongside of her husband. She was not at all pretty, nor was she young: rather, a poor, middle-aged proletarian, small, marching with difficulty. Insults rained down upon her, all from officers prancing on horseback along the road." A very young hussar officer said. "You know what we're going to do with her? We're going to screw her with a red-hot iron." A vast, horrified silence fell among the soldiers.[30]

Often these women were heroic. Even the most ardent antifeminists have rarely denied that women have courage. At Neuilly, a canteen worker with a head wound had the wound dressed and then returned to combat. Another, chased by a gendarme, suddenly turned around and killed him point-blank. Her comrades and the crowd cheered her when she came back within the Paris walls.[31] On the Châtillon Plain, a canteen worker was the last to retreat, with a group of National Guards, and turned around every minute to fire her gun again.[32] In the 137th Battalion, a young canteen worker—almost a child—never stopped firing the cannon despite the shells, coming from Châtillon, which were falling all around her.[33] When the Federals had succeeded in evacuating the Vanves fort, by means of the catacombs and quarries under the region, the newspapers noted that "it was women who, in this situation, showed the most calmness, presence of mind, and courage. The ambulance nurses wanted to carry off the wounded. The canteen workers were distributing stimulants, and keeping watch over the torches."[34]

The canteen worker for the 68th Battalion was killed by an exploding shell.[35] Among the Federals killed in a battle at Neuilly, *The* [London] *Times* correspondent noticed three women's bodies. One of them was still holding the broken stub of a saber. "She was a beautiful girl, with black hair braided around her head."[36]

Most of these women remained anonymous. Others, killed in battle or dissolved into defeat, are not much more than a name: Mme. Oudot of the 208th Ménilmontant Battalion;[37] Honorine Siméon, cited at Clamart for having stayed constantly in the trenches, and having "done cartridge duty under enemy fire, when the National Guards themselves were hesitating to get cartridges."[38] *Citoyenne* Lens, of the 261st Battalion, mother of three, "an honorable woman, respected by all," was killed at the Issy fort.[39] Victorine Rouchy, of the Commune Turcos, was congratulated by her comrades for "the courage that she showed in following the battalion into fire, and the humanity she had for the wounded during the battles on April 29 and 30."[40]

Marguerite Guinder, *femme* Lachaise, was, like Victorine Rouchy and many others, simultaneously a canteen worker and an ambulance nurse. But we are a little better acquainted with her. Born in Salins in the Jura in 1832, she was a clothier by profession. She had been married to someone named Prévost, and had had a child by him; but she was separated from her husband, and for eleven years had been living with a bronze-setter, Lachaise, whose name she bore. This is another example of those unions which could not be legitimized because of the ban on divorce, but which were as faithful and durable as legitimate ones. The officers of the Councils of War always seemed to consider this "concubinage" as an indication of immorality, and one further charge against the women; yet at this time, adultery in polite society was regarded with the greatest indulgence. Never has "class" morality

been so flagrantly displayed. Both Lachaises went with
the 66th Battalion to Issy and Meudon.[41] The Federals
of the 66th requested that the Commune extend recognition to the heroism of their canteen worker:

> In the fighting of the third *inst.* [April], before
> Meudon, she displayed conduct beyond all praise,
> conduct of the greatest virility, remaining all day long
> upon the battlefield despite the harvest of shots falling
> around her, busy caring for and bandaging up the
> numerous wounded, in the absence of the services
> of any surgeon. In testimony of which, citizen mem-
> bers of the Commune, we are come to draw your
> attention to these acts, in order that the most perfect
> courage and unselfishness of this republican *citoyenne*
> be done justice to.[42]

Certainly the style of this citation leaves much to be
desired, but the defenders of the Commune were humble,
and often illiterate, people.

Rifle in hand, Mme. de Rochebrune avenged the death
of her husband.[43] Victorine Louvet, General Eudes' wife—
his "companion," as was the expression among the Blanquists to whom Eudes belonged during the Empire—is as
frequently cited for her courage. She was a life-long friend
of Louise Michel. In 1865, they spent their vacation together; Victorine was then preparing for her "exams."[44]
She was courageous and, furthermore, combined civil
courage with military courage (the two are not quite the
same thing); she displayed both when her husband was
arrested, after the raid on La Villette in August, 1870.
The examining magistrate knew that Eudes was hiding
Blanqui. He urged Victorine Louvet to disclose the revolutionary's hiding place. But no threat (true, they did not
talk in terms of torture, in those days) could make her
break her silence.[45] Naturally, Maxime du Camp and
others have heaped mud, abuse, and slander upon this

woman. In their eyes, a physical blemish was a sign of moral decadence: "With her wide eyes illuminating a delicately-colored face, framed by lavish, light-chestnut hair, Mme. Eudes could have passed for a perfect beauty, were it not for the nasty strawberry-mark which, spreading down between her eyebrows, made this madonna-like face horribly crude." Maxime du Camp considered her vulgar, pretentious, and coarse. He was outraged at seeing her fence with Raoul Rigault, the young Public Prosecutor of the Commune: "I imagine that she has given up on being a woman, or, at least, that she would have wanted to be a woman with a beard."[46] Such is their tone. Louise Michel points out that "Mme. Eudes did not fire badly, either," at the Issy fort.[47] And *The Times* correspondent saw her as another Jeanne Hachette, "carrying, not a hatchet, but a real rifle, which she used with remarkable coolness, always picking out her man and taking her own good time to aim accurately."[48]

But among all these women who soldiered for the Commune, a place apart must be given Louise Michel; her great figure dominated them all. She was everywhere at once: soldier, ambulance nurse, orator. She was to be found in the Clubs and on the battlefields, in the Mont-martre Vigilance Committee and in the ambulance stations she helped to organize. She also proposed to undertake a strange mission: that of going in person to Versailles to assassinate Thiers, whom she believed to be the most responsible for the situation. Ferré and Rigault, to whom she disclosed this plan, succeeded in dissuading her from it; the murders of Generals Clément Thomas and Lecomte had already aroused public opinion against the Commune. Besides, they added, "you won't be able to get as far as Versailles." Louise Michel wanted to prove to them that this plan, although perhaps absurd, was feasible. She got so dressed up that "I did not recognize myself," reached Versailles without interference, and made

her way into the park in which the army was camped;
there she propagandized for the March 18th Revolution,
and left as tranquilly as she had come. Then she bought
newspapers in a large bookstore. Since she did not lack a
sense of humor, she enjoyed reading the greatest ill of the
bloodthirsty Louise Michel. Finally she came back to
Paris, bearing the Versailles newspapers as trophies.[49] But
her courage and audacity were not satisfied with these
dangerous pranks. She was everywhere—at Neuilly, at
Les Moulineaux, at the Issy fort—with her rifle in her
hand. "Thus I had, as comrades-in-arms, the Enfants
Perdus in the Hautes-Bruyères, the artillerymen at Issy,
and at Neuilly, the scouts of Montmartre"[50]—and, especially, the Federals of the 61st Battalion, to which she
belonged. "An energetic woman fought in the ranks of the
61st Battalion; she has killed several policemen and gendarmes."[51] They gave her a Remington rifle instead of
her old one. "For the first time, I have a good weapon."
She has left us several vignettes of that war, at once work-
manlike and murderous: "Now we are fighting. This is
battle. There is a rise, where I run ahead crying 'To
Versailles! to Versailles!' Razoua throws me his saber, to
rally the men. We clasp hands on high, under a rain of
shells. The sky is on fire." She opposed the timorous and
shamed the hesitant. A panic-stricken Federal wanted to
surrender the Clamart station: "Go ahead if you want to,"
she said, "but I will stay here, and I'll blow up the station
if you surrender it." And she sat herself down with a
lighted candle, at the doorway of a room where ammunition was stored.[52]

She also gathered up the wounded and bandaged them
on the battlefield. As in the early days at Vroncourt, her
pity extended even to animals: she went under fire to
rescue a cat. But she was also an intellectual who was
introspective in the midst of action. One night, when she
was on guard duty at the Clamart station, with a former

pontifical Zouave who had joined the Commune, we overhear this strange dialogue. "What effect is the life you lead having upon you?" "Why, the effect of seeing before us a shore that we must reach," replied Louise Michel. Under fire, she read Baudelaire with a student and played the harmonium in a Protestant church at Neuilly, near a barricade. She jotted down, during a march, the impressions of a poet: "We are going to the Issy fort by way of a little rise among some hedges. The path is strewn with violets that are being crushed by the shells. . . ." Or again, on guard at the Montmartre cemetery: "Some shells came at regular intervals. One would have said a clock was striking, the clock of death. In this clear evening, balmy with the fragrance of flowers, the marble seemed to come alive. . . ."

CHAPTER ELEVEN

BLOODY WEEK

NEVER HAD THERE BEEN so many flowers as there were that Spring.[1] On Sunday, May 21, the weather was fine and people felt much more like going for a stroll than like fighting. Many Parisians attended the concert given at the Tuileries, for the benefit of the widows and orphans of the Commune. During its May 19th session, the Commune had concerned itself with theaters, and the Versailles bombardment of Paris had stripped the ramparts bare.

The Versailles troops entered the city that Sunday at three in the afternoon. The Commune was not informed of this until seven o'clock; the Parisians did not learn the news until Monday morning, the 22nd.

Paris, which had seemed enfolded in the sweet sleep of Maytime, awakened. But upon the walls there appeared clumsy posters which, in the long run, disorganized the defense: "Enough of militarism. No more staff officers with braid and gilt along every seam . . ."[2] This appeal was directed to no one but "bare-armed fighters," those who had revolutionary faith. Thus the last vestiges of discipline—indispensable to any armed combat, revolutionary or not—were destroyed. Paris would fight, then, district by district, street by street, house by house, barricade by barricade, without an over-all plan, but with savage, insane, desperate heroism.

The entire population was summoned to the barricades. "Let even the women join their brothers, their fathers, their husbands! Those who have no weapons can tend the wounded, and can haul paving-stones up into their rooms to crush the invader. Sound the tocsin; set the bells ringing; fire all the cannons."[3]

Everywhere the streets bristled with barricades, despite the admirable plans of Haussmann, who had taken all possible precautionary measures in order to prevent them. "What could I have been thinking of," wrote Jules Vallès; "I believed that the city was going to play dead before being killed. And here are all the women and children getting into the fight. A beautiful girl has just raised a brand new red banner, and above these grey stones it has the effect of a poppy on an old wall. Your paving-stone, citizen."[4] Women in rags and women in silk dresses,[5] young girls and old ladies, were sewing and filling sandbags, were working with pickaxes and mattocks, all day and, by gaslight, all night. The ladies of La Halle erected, in half a day, a sixty-five-foot-long barricade, at the intersection of the Place Saint-Jacques and the Boulevard Sébastopol.[6] In the Place du Panthéon, a barricade was built by women and children who were singing *Le Chant du Départ*. "Federal" women, wearing long red scarves

and red cockades on their black dresses, led the work.[7]
And a regiment of women, led by a white-bearded officer,
was seen crossing Paris. "While we admire the courage
of our modern heroines, we think wistfully of the time
when people engraved on the tombstones of Roman
matrons: 'She stayed at home and spun wool,' " observed
an editor of *La Vérité*, with a touch of nostalgic anti-
femininism.

Who were these women who were building barricades?
Some of them can be identified by means of the proceedings of the Councils of War which have come down to us,
and which condemn them "for having made, or helped to
make, barricades in order to oppose the action of the civil
police." There was the wine merchant Modeste Trochu,
femme Mallet, born in 1829 in Bourg-des-Comptes (Ille-
et-Vilaine): in order to construct a barricade in the Rue
Saint-Jacques, she distributed among the Federals some
pickaxes which men from the Highway Department had
stored with her; she gave them drink, planted a red flag
on the barricade, and cried "Long live the Commune";
and she reported her neighbor at 346 Rue Saint-Jacques,
because the latter had hidden her husband "so that he
would not march along with the others."[8] And Joséphine
Mimet, *femme* Bernard, stocking-mender, born in 1833
at Adilly (Deux-Sèvres): she brought coffee, night and
day, to the fighters at the barricades, and was seen, rifle
in hand, on the Rue Saint-Antoine.[9] And Virginie Lenor-
dez, *femme* Vathonne, who ran a small snack shop, and
was born in 1823, at Saint-Pierre-Église (Manche): she had
urged her son to fight for the Commune, had worked on
the barricades at the Rue des Charbonniers and the Rue
d'Aligre, and challenged passersby: "Your paving-stone,
citizen!"[10] And the braidworker Rosalie Gaillard, born
in 1836 in Saint-Gervais-les-Bains (Savoie): she had been
seen, all day long on the 23rd, and all the night of the
23rd–24th, sewing sandbags in the garden of the Tour-

Saint-Jacques.[11] And Élodie Duvert, *femme* Richoux, born in Toulouse in 1826, who kept a little restaurant on the Rue Saint-Honoré-Chevalier. Élodie Richoux came from a bourgeois family. Her husband, a civil engineer, had been killed during the Italian campaign; her brother was a painter in Meudon. "Courage, friends!" she cried to those who were building the barricade at the corner of her street and the Rue Bonaparte, "Courage, hurry up, we'll wipe out those Versailles swine!" And she went with the Federals to break down the door of the bookseller Repos, whose books were used for construction material. She brought food to the fighters, and a mattress on which they could rest.[12]

Then there was the feather-dealer, Eugénie Dupin, widow of Léger, born in 1836 in Bussy-Saint-Georges (Seine-et-Marne): she had urged her lover to serve the Commune, and had helped to build the barricade on the Rue Ténier.[13] And Alphonsine Blanchard, called "The Peasant," a dayworker, born in 1844 in Saint-Jean-de-la-Ruelle (Loiret): with a rifle slung across her back, she worked at building the barricade on the Rue de Lyon, and forced passersby to lay down their paving-stones upon it.[14] And Célina Chartrus, widow of Godefroy, born in 1832 in Agen, a professional nurse: armed with a revolver, she carried paving-stones for the barricade on the Rue de Meaux.[15] And Joséphine Courtois, widow of Delettra, a seamstress who was no longer young, being born in 1820 in Laroche (Haute-Savoie): she had already fought at Lyon in 1848, where she had been called "The Queen of the Barricades"; yet the years had taken away none of her revolutionary faith. She had been seen attending the *Club de la Boule Noire* and the *Club de l'Église Saint-Bernard;* now, armed with a rifle, a red scarf over her dress, she was requisitioning Gallier's empty casks to build a barricade at the corner of the Rue Doudeauville and the Rue Stephenson. She handed out cartridges, and even had her little girl carrying them to the fighters.[16] Around her there were other women, among them Marie Cartier, née Lemonnier, clothing maker, born in 1833 in Rainfreville (Seine-Inférieure): we saw her before as a member of the 18th arrondissement Vigilance Committee, signing, along with Louise Michel, a petition to obtain professional schools and secular orphanages. She, too, was rolling Gallier's casks along to build the barricade.[17] And also there was Jeanne-Marie Quérat, *femme* Jobst, born in Guignen (Ille-et-Vilaine) in 1824, married to a savings-bank employee: she used to attend the *Club Saint-Nicolas-des-Champs,* and had urged her son to fight in the ranks of the Commune.[18] And Madeleine Billault, widow of Brulé, born in 1820 in Châtellerault, shoe saleswoman: she handed out shovels and pickaxes to the Federals, got them to requisition a moving-man's wagons, and carried orders in the midst of the firing.[19] And Marguerite Fayon, dayworker, born in 1835 at Coren (Cantal), whose lover was a second lieutenant in the Federal Guard and a member of the Vigilance Committee: in the thickest of the fighting, she carried cartridges to the men defending the barricades.[20] And Marie-Augustine Gaboriaud, born in 1835 in Ardelay (Vendée), whom the neighborhood had named "La Capitaine": she was the "companion" of a stonecutter, Jules Chiffon, captain of the 121st Federal Battalion. Sashed in red, armed with a revolver, she led him to the barricades at the Pont d'Austerlitz and the Boulevard Mazas, organized an ambulance squad, and let the Federals into a house to defend the barricade at the Avenue Daumesnil.[21] And Eugénie Rousseau, *femme* Bruteau, a hairdresser born in Warcq (Ardennes) in 1826: she called her neighbors to the barricades, cleaned rifles, washed them to cool them off, recharged them, and brought them to the fighters; she went under fire to gather up the rifles of the dead. She had made a banner out of a red rag, and started a barricade at the corner of the Rue

Myrrha and the Rue Poissonnière and remained there until the end. When everyone else despaired, she was still crying out her hope: "See, Dombrowski has arrived! We're saved! Long live Dombrowski! Long live the Commune!"[22]

A remark is called for here. A large proportion of these women were born in the provinces. As for the men, the proportion was less, but still quite considerable: the Parisian insurrection of 1871 was carried out by provincials. There are doubtless several explanations for this paradox. These men and women who had broken ties with their villages and come to Paris, had given proof in their private lives of a will to renewal, a spirit of adventure, which also were what impelled them to join the ranks of the Social Revolution. Doubtless, too, they were less integrated into traditional urban life. Those who are settled always compose the bulk of conservatives; peasants are adequate proof of this. These hypotheses are certainly worthy of further research.

The Versailles troops advanced slowly and cautiously. They had learned at some cost, during the last two months, that these barefoot people fought bravely. They preferred to go around them rather than give frontal attack. Suddenly, Thiers' soldiers made it clear that the struggle would be ruthless: at the Babylone barracks, sixteen Federals who had been taken prisoner were immediately put to death, and the Versailles troops shelled the Finance Ministry. The firemen of the Commune extinguished this first act of incendiarism.[23]

The women fought shoulder to shoulder with their men: mostly unorganized, they had come there either because their husband or lover was involved in the battle, or because a barricade had been built at the end of their street. But a committee of the *Union des Femmes pour la Défense de Paris,* for its part, had met one final time on May 21, at the municipal building in the 4th arrondissement, presided over by Nathalie Lemel. On the orders of the Commune, they left, red flag in the lead, to defend Les Batignolles.[24] One hundred twenty women held the barricade at the Place Blanche, and halted the troops of General Clinchant for several hours. Not until 11 o'clock, exhausted and without ammunition, did they withdraw; those who had been taken were killed on the spot.[25] Among them fell the dressmaker Blanche Lefebvre, of the Organizing Committee of the *Union des Femmes*—she who had "loved the Revolution as one loves a man." The survivors doubled back onto the Place Pigalle, where they held out for three hours more; then the last of them retreated to the barricade at the Boulevard Magenta. "Not one survived. This is one of the many episodes of this legendary barricade," remarked Lissagaray.[26]

Nathalie Lemel doubled back from Les Batignolles to the Place Pigalle, where she had planted a red banner. She does not seem to have done any firing. She cared for the wounded, and urged the Federals to resist. "Her appearance impressed me," says an eyewitness, "for she was the only older woman amid a group of young girls, all armed with rifles and wearing ambulance nurses' armbands as well as red scarves." Elizabeth Dmitrieff, for her part, flung a last order to the 11th arrondissement committee: "Muster all the women, and the committee itself, and come here immediately to go to the barricades."[27] We find her at Montmartre with Louise Michel; at the Faubourg Saint-Antoine with Frankel. Louise Michel held the Montmartre cemetery with about fifty men from the 61st Battalion. Soon they were no more than twenty, then fifteen; they retreated to the barricade on the Chausée Clignancourt. Suddenly the National Guards arrived. "Come on, there are only three of us," cried Louise Michel—but they turned out to be from Versailles. They seized her, and threw her back into the barricade trench. When she got up, half-dazed, her comrades had disappeared. The Versailles men were ransacking the houses. "I saw only one means of stopping them, and I cried out to them, 'Fire! Fire! Fire!' "[28]

At this point we definitely must bring up the question of the fires for which eyewitnesses and bourgeois historians have ascribed full responsibility to the *Communards*. These fires actually had several causes: first, the incendiary shells and the kerosene bombs which the Army of Versailles had been using since the beginning of April. Many houses in Paris and the suburbs were burned thus, during the Second Siege of Paris, by the shells of the friends of order and property. These were, no doubt, "good" fires— regrettable, certainly, but normal facts of war. Some of the fires during the last week of May were also attributable to Bonapartist agents, who were trying thus to eliminate any traces that were compromising for the personnel of the Empire. In fact, it is strange to note that the *Communards*, those "dividers," did not attack the houses of the rich; that the *Communards*, those anticlericals, did not burn down churches; but that what disappeared in flames were buildings like the Court of Accounts, the Council of State, or the Ministry of Finance—buildings that contained the archives of the Empire's administration.[29] Perhaps, too, certain people hoped to receive large indemnities.

But, having made these reservations, it is certain that the Federals bore a great part of the responsibility for the Paris fires. "Fever of the besieged," "the madness of despair," "revolutionary vandalism"—easily, but a little too hastily, said. Actually, the Versailles troops fired from the shelter of the houses until the insurgents had exhausted their last ammunition; then they advanced on the double and shot down the defenders. It was to counter this tactic that the Federals set fire to the buildings near the barricades; thus they flushed the Versailles soldiers out into the open. Marx vindicated the Commune, which "used fire strictly as a means of defense, to keep the Versailles troops from the avenues which Haussmann had opened out expressly for artillery fire." For the Federals, it was a question of "covering their defeat, just as the Versailles troops opened their advance by shells which destroyed at least as many buildings as did the Commune."[30] Moreover, the Federals resorted to incendiarism only when Versailles began its mass execution of prisoners—which was what invested the struggle with its final and inexpiable character.

But there was something else, too. If the defense of the Rue Royale or the Rue de Lille required that the buildings near the barricades be set afire, no rationale of a military nature justified the burning of, for example, the Tuileries; we must have recourse to another explanation. Benoît Malon is the one who gives it to us: "It was permissible for the people of Paris, that magnanimous people who for a century had sacrificed the best of each of its generations for world progress, that people which, at that very moment, was being slaughtered for its republican faith—to burn the Palace of Kings."[31] Lissagaray goes further: "The angry flames seemed to rise up against Versailles, and to tell the vanquisher returning to Paris that there was no longer any place for him there; that those vast monuments of monarchy would shelter monarchy no more." And he adds the theory which makes archeologists wince, but which is justifiable if one still believes in the power of symbols: "The sovereign— whatever it be, people or king—never forgives the enemy his symbols. So it was that in the sixteenth century and in '89, neither the royalty nor the bourgeois could rest until feudalism's nests of stone had been destroyed and razed to the ground."[32]

On the sites of the fires—the Légion d'Honneur, the Rue Royale, the Tuileries—women as well as Federals were arrested. Did they play a part in setting the fires? Does the myth of the *pétroleuses* correspond to any reality? We shall discuss that later.

In spite of bitter local defenses, the Versailles troops advanced little by little. At the corner of the Rue Racine and the Rue École de Médecine, the barricade was held by women.[33] On the Rue du Pot-de-Fer, women were fighting. On the Rue Mouffetard women brought a fleeing sergeant back into the fighting.[34] In the Place du Panthéon, women prepared rifles, while the men fired.[35] The barricade on the Place du Château-d'Eau exerted a sort of fascination. An English medical student, who had set up an ambulance alongside it, tells us: "Just at the moment when the National Guards began to retreat, a women's battalion turned up; they came forward on the double and began to fire, crying 'Long live the Commune.' They were armed with Snider carbines, and shot admirably. They fought like devils. . . ." Fifty-two were killed there. Among them, a girl in her twenties, dressed like a member of the Fusilier Marin, "rosy and beautiful with her curly black hair," fought all day long: Marie M., whose first name at least we know among all these dead, anonymous women who will never be counted.[36] The English student goes on:

A poor woman was fighting in a cart, and sobbing bitterly. I offered her a glass of wine and a piece of bread. She refused, saying "For the little time I have left to live, it isn't worth the trouble." The woman was taken by four soldiers, who undressed her. An officer interrogated her: "You have killed two of my men." The woman began to laugh ironically and replied harshly: "May God punish me for not having killed more. I had two sons at Issy; they were both killed. And two at Neuilly. My husband died at this

barricade—and now do what you want with me." I
did not hear any more; I crawled away, but not soon
enough to avoid hearing the command "Fire," which
told me that everything was over.[37]

There are hundreds of similar stories on record. An enemy
of the Commune, Arsène Houssaye, tells us that a girl,
well-known in the Rue Richelieu and the Place du Palais-
Royal, was arrested, revolver in hand, in a house from
which two shots had issued. She denied it at first. And
then, suddenly: "All right, yes; I did the shooting." "Until
then," says Arsène Houssaye, "she had been thought to be
only a frowzy prostitute, bosom swaying, trailing a faded
silk dress, with cheap jewelry in her ears and on her
fingers. But this was the beginning of her transfiguration:
that proud tone in which she replied after so many days of
humiliation. 'Yes, it was me,' she answered, 'and I'd have
liked to kill all the Versailles people with one shot
because they killed my lover. And I have ony one regret:
it's having killed just one of them. And if I could start
in again, I would.' A few minutes later, they shot her
against the iron bars of the Louvre colonnade."[38]

But repression struck not only the fighting men and
women taken with weapon in hand, or those who openly
proclaimed themselves responsible for their acts; it struck
at random. Every poor woman was suspect. Even more so
if she carried a market basket or a bottle: she was a
pétroleuse, and was executed on the spot to the furious
cries of the mob. A woman recognized her husband among
some arrested Federals; she wanted to talk to him. A blow
from a rifle butt threw her onto the pavement. Her child
rolled in the gutter.[39] The husband of Marguerite
Tinayre, who had not been involved in the insurrection,
was shot without a trial. Any expression of grief alongside
the common graves in which the Federals were heaped

up was proof of complicity. Any weeping woman was an "insurgent female."[40]

As for the women who were executed, they were treated somewhat like unfortunate Arabs belonging to insurgent tribes. After they were shot, while they were still in their death throes, they were stripped of some of their clothes, and sometimes the insult went further, as in the Faubourg Montmartre or the Place Vendôme, where women were left naked and sullied upon the sidewalks.[41]

Even partisans of Versailles were arrested, like that society woman whom a deputy of the National Assembly found by accident among the women arrested as "*pétroleuses.*"[42]

Prisoners, both men and women, who were being sent to Versailles in a long line were subjected to the insults, jeers and blows of an unleashed mob. Some women dragged themselves along, exhausted, leaning upon their neighbors. But others walked with head held high, like that girl mentioned by *The Times* correspondent: "The crowd heaped its outrages upon her. She did not flinch, and shamed the men by her stoicism."[43] Society women beat the prisoners with their parasols. My great-grandmother, caught up in the crowd, cried "Those poor people!" "Be quiet, lady," someone said to her, "or they'll take you too." Even Maxime du Camp was outraged.[44] *Le Figaro* was somewhat embarrassed; but it consoled itself by thinking that these insurgent women were all prostitutes, and, as such, had no right to any pity.[45]

Having escaped her barricade in the nick of time, Louise Michel changed her bullet-rent skirt, borrowed a hooded cape to look "as bourgeois as possible," and went back to her school on the Rue Oudot, where she lived with her mother. The concierge told her that the Versailles people had come to look for her, and had arrested her mother instead. Grief-crazed, she ran to the nearest police station. "She is in Bastion 37," the chief of police told her, "but she is to be shot this very hour." Louise rushed to the Bastion, saw her mother in the courtyard, and gave herself up to take her place. She saw members of the Montmartre Vigilance Committee, the *Club de la Révolution,* and Federals from the 61st Battalion. Nearby they were shooting an unidentified man who had been mistaken for Mégy. No matter, it was just one more dead man. General de Galliffet arrived. "Galliffet, that's me," he shouted. "People of Montmartre, you think I am very cruel. I am even more so than you think." Then Louise Michel, who had lost none of her insolence, sang softly: *"C'est moi qui suis Lindor, berger de ce troupeau."* The prisoners burst into laughter. "Fire into the mob," cried the furious Galliffet. But, weary of killing, the soldiers did not fire.

The prisoners were herded into a group. Louise Michel, with her undeniably poetic temperament, described that departure and the long march in the night. "We marched, lulled by the regular pace of the horses, going off into the night lit occasionally by red fires. . . . It was really the unknown, a dream-fog where no detail was allowed to escape." The prisoners were made to go down into the La Muette ravine: "Rays of moonlight slid between the horses' hooves on that narrow path we were descending." "What are you thinking about?" a soldier asked her. "I am looking," she answered.[46] Then it was Versailles, and Satory.*

There she recognized Malvina Poulain and Béatrix Excoffon, who had been called for execution three times,

---

* The Satory Depot lay southwest of Versailles. It was a vast, fortified plateau and one of the four major prisons used by Versailles for incarcerating its *Communard* prisoners before shooting many of them.—*Trans.*

and who, for four days, had been sleeping on the cobble-
stones of the courtyard.[47] There, too, were an old nun
who had given a wounded Federal a drink of water; a
dazed woman who did not know whether she had been
arrested by the Commune or Versailles; a deaf-mute
woman who, it was said, had cried "Long live the Commune!" Each day, Louise Michel was told she would be
shot the next morning. "As you like," she answered.

Those nights at Satory were like bad dreams. The
women had been shut up in a sort of storehouse. "On the
floor were snaky, silvery little threads forming currents
between veritable lakes, large as anthills, and filled, like
rivulets, with a nacreous swarm. They were lice. . . ."[48]
In the courtyard, prisoners were crammed together in the
rain, lying in mud. From time to time, they were fired
upon at random. Sometimes names were called out and
men would get up. They would be given shovels with
which they had to dig their own graves.

Béatrix Excoffon and Louise Michel appeared before a
joint commission which interrogated them. Desperate to
have news of her children and to exonerate her mother,
Béatrix took responsibility for everything of which she
was accused. "Unfortunate woman," a gendarme said to
her, "you are going to get yourself shot."[49]

As for Louise Michel, she answered insolently. Yes, she
had been involved in the La Villette affair; yes, in the
burial of Victor Noir; yes, in the October 31st demonstration; yes, in the January 22nd one; and during the
Commune, yes, she had been in the marching battalions.
They picked out the "ringleaders" Louise Michel, Eulalie
Papavoine, Victorine Gorget, and about forty others, who
were sent to the Chantiers prison, then the Versailles
house of correction. At the end of two weeks, they had the
right to a pallet of straw for two, a package of food for
four. The recalcitrants were punished by being tied to a

stake for several hours, as we are told by a schoolteacher, Mme. Hardouin, who was arrested on hearsay evidence and then acquitted.[50]

Everyone left the prison. At the Gare de l'Ouest, there was a group of eight hundred women who had not been able to change their linen for weeks. The guards would strike them, usually in the breast. Some women had miscarriages; others went mad.[51] The forts and prison ships overflowed with prisoners. More than a thousand died of hunger and ill treatment.

It is officially acknowledged that thirty thousand Federals disappeared during the struggle. Others have said a hundred thousand. As with St. Bartholomew's Day, we shall never know the exact number of the victims of "the week in May."

CHAPTER TWELVE

———◆———

WERE THERE ANY PÉTROLEUSES?

D ID WOMEN PLAY a part in the Paris fires? Were there any *pétroleuses?* Now that I have reached the heart of my subject matter, I must admit that I do not know the answer; all I can do is present the evidence and discuss it objectively.

Enemies of the Commune accused women of having had a part in setting Paris on fire. "Everything was ready. The bottles of kerosene were at hand, and men and women were stationed to spread the oil and make a blazing mass out of the 2nd arrondissement. The arrival of the Versailles troops had been so sudden that it had upset this fine plan." A reporter asserts that he was given these details by a captain of the Vengeurs.[1] A little girl, eight years old, arrested just when (so it was claimed) she was about to throw kerosene into a cellar, was supposed to have said that there existed in Paris 8,000 *pétroleuses*, organized into a brigade by Ferré. In every quarter, they formed squads commanded by female sergeants and corporals; their responsibility was to set fires to whatever extent the Versailles troops forced their way into Paris. The Versailles press gives many other details: little stickers, bearing the notation B.P.B. (*bon pour brûler*— good for burning) and a Bacchante's head, were said to have been affixed to buildings that were to be set afire. There was talk about kerosene eggs equipped with nitroglycerine primers, and about balloons carrying incendiary material. It was said that a canteen keeper had been arrested with a keg containing a half-gallon of kerosene. On the Rue des Vinaigriers, about thirty kerosene eggs had been found in the house of two women. Soon acid was added to kerosene, *vitrioleuses* to *pétroleuses;* these *vitrioleuses* were ordered by the Commune to disfigure the officers and soldiers of Versailles.[2]

By now, verisimilitude counted for little. *Le Figaro* stated that in Montmartre, a woman and a little girl had been arrested; for an hour they had been throwing kerosene into cellars; the proof of this was that their milk-bottle was still full of kerosene.[3] *La Patrie* reported that they had found, in the Faubourg Saint-Germain, the charred skeleton of a *pétroleuse,* with a pipe in her mouth; the proof was that her clothes were still soaked with kerosene. "One assumes that it was the fire from the pipe which would have brought about this combustion," the paper explained wisely. But what it did not explain is how kerosene-soaked clothing could remain on a charred skeleton.[4]

In this mass hysteria, *pétroleuses* were to be found everywhere. In the areas occupied by the Versailles army, it was enough that a woman be poor and ill-dressed, and that she be carrying a basket, box, or milkbottle. At the corner of the Rue de Rivoli and the Rue Castiglione, a crowd gathered around a woman who had just been arrested by two artillerymen. She was accused of having thrown a bottle of kerosene at the Ministry of Finance, which had been burning for several days. Two gendarmes beat her to death.[5]

Hundreds of women—who will ever know how many?—were thus executed then and there. Maxime du Camp himself made short work of these legends. He writes:

> Since the morning of the 24th, Paris had been seized by madness. It was said that women were slipping into the neighborhoods already given up by our troops, that they were throwing sulphur wicks into the cellar vents, pouring kerosene on the awnings of shops, and lighting fires everywhere. This legend, excused and even justified by the horrible sights that people had before their eyes, was absolutely false. No house burned in the area occupied by the French army.

And he quotes the supporting statement of Colonel Hofmann, from the United States Legation, who on May 26 wrote: "Kerosene is the madness of the hour. Peaceable housewives are closing the cellar openings that come out onto the sidewalk, under the absurd pretext that gangs of women are roaming the streets and throwing kerosene into cellars, then setting fire to it."[6]

On their side, the supporters of the Commune have flatly denied the existence of any *pétroleuses*. Louise Michel: "The most insane tales have been going around about *pétroleuses*. There were no *pétroleuses*. The women were fighting like lionesses, but I saw no one but myself crying 'Fire! Fire!' in front of those monsters."[7] Lissagaray, replying in 1897 to an inquiry in *La Revue Blanche* about the Commune (his ironic and disillusioned tone is very different from that of *L'Histoire* and the *Huit Journées*), nonetheless stated strongly: "As for the *pétroleuses*, they were chimerical creatures, comparable to salamanders or elves. The Councils of War never succeeded in producing a single one."[8] And Karl Marx, in an interview for *The New York Herald* of August 3, 1871, detailing the relations between the International and the Commune, declared that although the two had worked together, since they were fighting the same enemy, it was absurd to say that the leaders of the insurrection were acting upon orders received from the Central Committee of the International, in London. On the subject of the *pétroleuses*, he adds:

> This story is one of the most abominable schemes that has ever been invented in a civilized country. I am certain that not one woman, not one child, could be accused with the slightest semblance of proof of having poured kerosene in houses or of having tried to set anything on fire; and yet hundreds were shot for that, and thousands were deported to Cayenne. Anything that might have been burned was burned by men.

The New York Herald's reporter answered, "I must say that I am convinced of the same thing. I have never met a single person who really saw a woman or a child with kerosene."[9]

What can we make of all of this? I believe that we must distinguish between two sets of circumstances: first, fire as a weapon of war, a defensive method used by the Federals against the Versailles army, which was attacking with all the resources of a regular army, and ruthlessly murdering the insurgents taken prisoner. As for the second sort of fire, attributed specifically to those famous *pétroleuses*, it certainly seems that we are dealing with a myth, of which one of the most virulent slanderers of the Commune, Maxime du Camp, himself took little account. There is no question that what is involved here is one of those manifestations of collective fear, such as we occasionally encounter in history: the Great Fear of 1789, or even more recently, the fear that the world was coming to an end which impelled crowds of Indians toward their sanctuaries.

But the Paris fires, during the course of an armed struggle, present another problem. They were lit during the fighting, and lit by fighters. There is no reason to think that the women who were helping to build and defend the barricades did not also have a hand in these fires. In the statutes of the *Union des Femmes pour la Défense de Paris et les Soins aux Blessés,* we read the following brief sentence: "Article 14: The money left over from the administrative costs will be used . . . for buying kerosene and weapons for the *citoyennes* who will fight at the barricades; should the occasion arise, weapons will be distributed according to the drawing of lots."[10] It is difficult to concede, along with certain historians motivated by I know not what sort of hypocritical daintiness, that the word "kerosene" coupled with the word "weapons" has, here, only a domestic meaning—harmless kerosene to light the family lamps. It is more likely that kerosene had already been regarded as the ultimate means of defending the Commune.

The role of the *Union des Femmes* suggested by this document is confirmed by the testimony of Barral de Montaud, in *L'Enquête Parlementaire sur le 18 Mars.* I am well aware that Barral de Montaud was a sorry specimen. An agent of Versailles, he had succeeded in being appointed leader of the 7th Legion of Federals. Through a very questionable woman, Marie Leroy, the mistress of the Commune member Raoul Urbain, he had engineered one of the most debatable measures of the Commune, the proposition that hostages be shot immediately in reprisal for the murder of an ambulance nurse.[11] But this loathsome side of the secret agent should not make us categorically reject his testimony when it corroborates the statutes of the *Union des Femmes*. According to Barral de Montaud, the International was not uninvolved in the Paris fires, "since it was acting through the *Union des Femmes*. If it did not actually give the orders to set the fires it furnished the means of doing so, for, I repeat, it was the Women's Committee, a subsidiary of the International, that did everything."[12]

That is giving much too much importance to the International, which represented only one tendency of the Commune, and to the *Union des Femmes,* which was far from controlling the activity of all the women fighting. Very rarely do the proceedings and the dossiers of reprieve mention that the accused women belonged to the *Union des Femmes*. And with only a few exceptions—Nathalie Lemel and Elizabeth Dmitrieff—we do not find the names of the accused in the lists of members of the *Union* which have come down to us. And one has the impression that the Councils of War took a great deal of trouble to turn up *"pétroleuses,"* without much success.

Let us at the outset eliminate an affair of civil law that people wanted to turn into a political case, according to a well-known process of amalgamation. This was the case of a certain Marie-Jeanne Moussu, *femme* Gourier; she was a laundress, born August 4, 1829 in Bourg (Haute-Marne).[13] "The Moussu woman is the most perfect imaginable type of these unspeakable creatures from the slums who, it is known, provided the Commune with powerful auxiliaries for the purpose of burning Paris," we read in *La Gazette des Tribunaux* for September 23, 1871. But suddenly the editor adds: "What is curious about this Moussu case is that she said she was guilty of the act of which she was accused, not at the time when the troops entered Paris, but long afterwards, on June 19, when everything was over." Curious indeed. This *pétroleuse*-come-lately must have been either very stubborn, or very fanatical, or very strange. Now she stated that she had tried to set fire to the house where she believed her lover to be living, to wreak vengeance upon him. We can well believe it. In any event, it is impossible to catch any hint enabling us to spell out any intention of a political nature. It is an affair of civil law, having no relation to the Commune; for it Marie-Jeanne Moussu was sentenced to death.

With the fire set in the Magasins du Tapis Rouge on May 25, we find ourselves concerned once more with acts of war. The Federals had sworn that they would die before they surrendered, and their commander, Brunel, had given the order to destroy the arsenal, whose flames were to erect a barrier before the enemy. Two women were accused as accomplices: a concierge, Louise-Frédérique Noël, *femme* Bonnefoy, born in Paris in 1827, and a parasol maker, Jeanne-Victorine Laymet, also born in Paris, in 1840. Jeanne Laymet was separated from her husband, a certain Roubert, and for ten years had been living with a business man, Ernest Levieux, by whom she had had a child. The two women, who got along very well, had shown great devotion to the Commune, worked at building the barricades, and had offered their windows to the Federals so that they might fire in shelter. They were also accused of having helped to set fire to the "Tapis Rouge," but the Fourth Council of War did not sustain this charge. They were sentenced to banishment to a fortress, and deprival of civic rights, for having "incited to massacre, pillage, and destruction of property, and for having participated in the construction of the barricades."[14]

A cook, Eugénie Chilly, *femme* Desjardins—called "La Picarde"—was accused of having carried kerosene, under her skirts and in her pockets, to her lover, an unskilled laborer named François Bufferne, a National Guard in the 6th Company of the 184th Federal Battalion, in order to set the Prefecture of Police on fire. She was sentenced to twenty years at hard labor.[15]

All these are small fry. There remain two much more important cases, which Maxime du Camp and other pen-pushers have bedecked with all their insults and embroidered with lyrical slander. These women were drunken Bacchantes, hysterical Messalinas dancing around a Spahi,* "the black devil"—a round of infernal witches.

After the trials of the Commune members and those of the Central Committee, that of the *"Pétroleuses"* took place on September 3, 1871. On Tuesday, May 22, Eudes and Mégy, with the 135th Belleville Battalion and the Enfants Perdus, had occupied the Rue de Lille, the Rue Solférino, the Légion d'Honneur, and the Court of Accounts. The battle with Versailles began, and as a means of defense, the Federals set fire to the Légion d'Honneur and to some of the houses on the Rue de Lille. Among the fighters were seen several women, who were arrested: Élizabeth Rétiffe, Joséphine Marchais, Eugénie Suétens, Eulalie Papavoine, and Lucie Maris, *femme* Bocquin. Two others escaped their hunt, a certain Mme. Masson, who seems to have played an important role, and a very young girl who was gathering up the wounded.[16]

These women were coming and going, serving food and drink to the insurgents. Most of them were armed and wore red scarves, or were wearing the National Guard uniform. One, very tall, fired from the barricade on the Rue de Bellechasse. Another was seen to roll a cask of kerosene against the door of the hotel at 6 Rue de Bellechasse. These women, said witnesses, made "horrifying remarks," and forced the Federals to remain at the barricades.

---

* Member of Moslem cavalry corps under the Ottoman Empire; in the French army, the Spahis were a cavalry corps of native Algerians and Senegalese, famous for their exotic dress uniforms.—*Trans.*

None of these women [added the indictment] was ignorant of the plans of the insurgents, for they were crying at the top of their voices, "Paris must be blown up." In vain did they deny any participation in rioting and fire-setting, trying to give themselves a sublime role filled with charity and dedication. What they could not deny was that they had knowingly abetted the villains of the Enfants Perdus, and of the 135th Federal Battalion, and has assisted them in their criminal exploits.[17]

The women who appeared before this military tribunal were poor, and not at all able to defend themselves.

Élizabeth Rétiffe, a thirty-nine-year-old cardboard maker, was born in Vézelise (Meurthe).[18] For seven years she had lived faithfully with a Parisian road-repair foreman, whom she left because he used to beat her. During a period of poverty, she had taken her clothing to the Mont-de-Piété. From then on, she lived alone on her meager wages. During the Siege, cardboard makers found work scarce. Élizabeth Rétiffe had to accept the relief furnished to paupers by the city of Paris: a pound of bread and sixty centimes. However, despite her poverty, she found the means to pay her rent regularly.[19] Even though she had been sentenced to twenty days in prison in 1853 for having got into a fight with a woman, and fined sixteen francs in 1855 for having insulted a policeman, she was liked in her neighborhood of the Rue du Temple "for her gentleness, her honesty, and her good relations with everyone," the police commissioner stated. Early in May, a neighbor, Eulalie Papavoine, urged her to accompany the 135th Federal Battalion of Belleville as a canteen worker. She accepted, because she had nothing to live on. But she quickly became an ambulance nurse, because "it grieved her so much to see those unhappy wounded men." Before the military tribunal, she asserted: "I would have aided a

Versailles soldier just as willingly as a National Guard."[20] At the Palais de la Légion d'Honneur she had been seen dressed in a white jacket, wearing a red scarf and carrying a rifle slung over her shoulder; but no one had seen her fire it. "She was busy taking care of food, bringing drink to the barricades," said a witness, "and gathering up the wounded." "I gave first aid before taking them to La Charité," she confirmed.

"You rolled no casks of kerosene?" the presiding judge asked her.

"No."

And indeed, the witnesses, who recognized her, "had never seen her do anything extraordinary."[21]

The seamstress Eulalie Papavoine was born in Auxerre in 1846. She had "no previous criminal record." For two years she had lived with a journeyman engraver, Ernest Balthazar, by whom she had a child. Ernest Balthazar was a member of the National Guard in the 135th Battalion, and she had followed him as an ambulance nurse to Neuilly, Issy, Vanves, Levallois-Perret, then to the Légion d'Honneur—everywhere that the battalion fought. Out of conviction? We do not know. Perhaps simply because a woman ought to follow her man, because that is an elementary rule of morality. An ambulance station had been organized in the Rue Solférino, where there were still victims of the Avenue Rapp explosion. Eulalie Papavoine gathered up the injured, took them to the ambulance station for first aid, then accompanied them to the Charité Hospital. "When the Légion d'Honneur started to burn, I was at La Charité," she said. "I stayed there, captured. I did indeed see the kerosene casks, but I did not have anything to do with them."[22]

"You certainly must have suspected that they were going to burn some buildings," said the presiding judge. "Why did you not leave those wretched people?"

"I wanted to share my lover's fate."

"Why," the presiding judge asked again, "did you stay behind when the battalion fled?"

And poor Eulalie Papavoine, seamstress, gave this utterly simple and sublime statement:

"We had dead and wounded men."[23]

There was nothing that predisposed Lucie Maris, *femme* Bocquin, born in Choisel (Seine-et-Oise) in 1843, day worker, to serve the Commune. The judges of the Council of War did not understand it at all: she was a "quiet" woman, who had married a "decent and hard-working" laborer; they had a child. Her behavior was of the most "regular" sort; in her district, she was thought of as an industrious worker, "whose character was gentle and obliging toward her neighbors."[24] Respectful of law and morality, she seemed, therefore, more like a candidate for a good-conduct award than a militant working to subvert society. But her husband left her to join the Army. She became acquainted with one Marcelin Dubois, a guardsman of the 135th Federal Battalion. The crime began with adultery. It is thus that Lucie Bocquin found herself at the Légion d'Honneur on May 22 and 23; there, on the barricade, she gathered up her lover's body.

With Joséphine Marchais and Eugénie Suétens, we find figures that conform more to reactionary stereotypes, which demand that political rebels always be habitual criminals, out-and-out jailbirds who pose no problem to the pillars of a well-made social order.

Joséphine Marchais, day worker, did not leave a good reputation behind her in Blois, where she was born; no more so in Charonne where she was living. She had been sentenced to six months in prison for theft; her mother, to five years' imprisonment and ten years' police supervision for incitement to debauchery; her sister Madeleine was put in a house of correction until she was twenty years old, then sentenced to three months in prison for theft.[25] With a family like that, we know well what to expect: these reprobates could not but join the Commune. Since the month of March, Joséphine Marchais had been a canteen keeper for the Enfants Perdus Battalion, where her lover, a butcher's boy named Jean Guy, was. "The status of canteen keeper for the Enfants Perdus indicates right away of what the said Marchais is capable . . ." the indictment declares. She was accused of having participated in the looting of the Comte de Béthune's town house, wearing a Tyrolian hat and armed with a rifle; of having said horrifying things to incite the National Guardsmen to battle ("Pack of traitors, go on and fight," she cried to them, "if I am killed, I want to kill first!"); of having led her lover Jean Guy, who wanted to desert, to the barricades. A witness stated that she seemed to him more dangerous than the Enfants Perdus themselves. But no one saw her putting any kerosene anywhere. Joséphine Marchais denied everything: she was merely going along the Rue de Lille to return some linen that she had washed for the Federals.[26]

We are rather well informed about Eugénie Suétens, laundress, born in Beauvais in 1846. Her mother belonged to a family of "decent and quiet" workers. But her father, a tailor, evinced "advanced" ideas; in 1848 he had left Beauvais to settle in Paris. With such a father, it is not surprising that Eugénie Suétens was sentenced, in 1867, to a year in prison for theft. Moreover, she had been living (true, for six years) in concubinage with a stonemason, Aubert, a quartermaster sergeant in the 135th Battalion. In the Commune's early days she had joined the regiment as canteen-worker; she had taken part in all the fighting, at Neuilly, Issy, Vanves, and Levallois-Perret, where she had been wounded twice.[27] Armed with a chassepot rifle and wearing a red scarf, she had been seen in the courtyard of the Légion d'Honneur. She was bringing drink to the fighters, gathering up the wounded, and was said to have taken part in the building of the barricades.

She admitted having received provisions: three bottles of wine, candles, sugar, butter, sardines—merely, after all, the normal rations of fighting troops. But kerosene?

"I never touched any kerosene."

"Were you given any money?"

"I was given ten francs to pay the ambulance nurses."

But the presiding judge had another idea in mind:

"On the contrary, we believe that it was to encourage you to do what you were ordered to do: that is, to set fires."[28]

This hypothesis was not confirmed.

One woman was not at the prisoners' dock: Mme. Masson, who seems to have played an important role. A Mme. Masson figures among the members of Jules Allix's committee, but not of the *Union des Femmes*. She was a blonde woman of about twenty-five, who had a German (?) accent and wore the Commune's silver-fringed red scarf and an armband. She was armed with a carbine and a revolver. It was to her that a Federal commandant had given sixty francs to pay the ambulance nurses, and she—she alone—had been seen firing.[29] We might perhaps have learned more from the interrogation of Mme. Masson, since the other women who were accused were evidently nothing but accomplices.

What can we make of all this? The witnesses for the prosecution were categorical: the accused had not been seen to roll any barrels of kerosene. They limited themselves to cooking and caring for the wounded. "After administering first aid," said a tavernkeeper, "they came to my place and I gave them something to eat." Yet it was he who had had Élizabeth Rétiffe arrested. Did he, then, believe that she was guilty?

"Of what?"

"Of insurrection."

" . . . ."

"And of the fires too?"

"Certainly not."

"Who set the fires?" asked the presiding judge.

"I don't know. To me, they're not guilty of that."

"I'm aware that you didn't see these women with torches in their hands. But I am asking for your impression. You saw no kerosene?"

"No."[30]

A dressmaker recognized the five accused women. She had seen them passing with rifles slung over their shoulders. But they had done nothing "unusual." They had been cooking and tending the wounded.[31]

All of this was not at all satisfactory to the presiding judge. "It is extraordinary that it should be so difficult to make the witnesses talk," he declared. Well, no matter. It was necessary to set examples: he would set examples.

Captain Jouenne began his indictment, immediately elevating the proceedings to dizzying heights. Civilization itself was at stake.

The horrible campaign against civilization begun on last March 18, by people who believe in neither God nor Country, as Jules Allix, one of them, proclaimed, must bring before you not only men forgetful of their most sacred duties, but also—and, alas, in great number—unworthy creatures who seem to have taken on the task of becoming an opprobrium to their sex, and of repudiating the great and magnificent role of woman in society.

And what, then, was this magnificent role? That of "legitimate" wife, the object of our affection and respect, entirely devoted to her family whom she served as guide and protectress—she must exercise her influence over man, to maintain his respect for his social duties.

"But if, deserting this sacred mission, the nature of her influence changes, and serves none but the spirit of evil, she becomes a moral monstrosity; then woman is more dangerous than the most dangerous man."

Even though these seamstresses, cleaning women, and laundresses could scarcely be mistaken for victims of culture, what Captain Jouenne was putting on trial was education for women.

If they were illiterate, one might perhaps grieve as one damned them; but, among these women—and I blush to give them the name of women—we find some who are unable to summon to their aid even the paltry resource of ignorance. . . . While lofty minds (and we must cordially second them) call for that important benefit of education for the people, what a bitter deception is this for them and for us! Among the accused, we see schoolteachers. These women cannot pretend that the idea of good and evil was unknown to them.

All this was the fault of the emancipation of women.

"And look where we are led by all the dangerous utopias," continued Captain Jouenne, "the emancipation of women, preached by the scholars who did not know what power had been given them to exercise, and who, at the moments of uprising and revolution, wanted to recruit powerful auxiliaries for themselves."

Indeed, what ridiculous fantasies had not been proposed to them?

"Have they not held out to all these wretched creatures bright prospects, incredible chimeras: women judges, women as members of the bar! Yes, women lawyers; deputies, perhaps, and—for all we know—commandants? Generals of the Army? Certainly, faced with these miserable aberrations, we believe that we are dreaming!"

After having appropriately stigmatized these pernicious doctrines and unlikely prognostications, the Captain called all the women of the Commune to account: the speakers of the Clubs ("those heroines of immorality, theft, and arson, who, from the pulpits of our churches, have substituted criminal propaganda for the word of the Gospel"); the secular schoolteachers ("who, desecrating the purity of childhood, have, in the schools, usurped the venerated functions of the Sisters of Charity"), and particularly that "Michel woman," who replaced hymns by *La Marseillaise* and *Le Chant du Départ,* and whose trial would be of extreme importance.

But let us leave these generalities to return to the facts, to those unfortunate women who have been somewhat forgotten in their dock, and who scarcely seemed to have been contaminated by the principles of women's emancipation or by an excess of education. In all the testimony he heard, Captain Jouenne found the proof of their having been present among the insurgents (which was true), of the active part they took in the insurrection (which was probable), of their participation in looting (of butter and sardines), and in the fires (which was not at all proven).

The lawyer Thiroux pleaded for Élizabeth Rétiffe:

> I look for an insurgent, I find a woman covered by the neutrality of Geneva. I look for a thief, I find a woman who pays her rent, even during the Siege: a small proof of a great honesty. . . . I look for an accomplice in murder, I find an ambulance nurse leading away the wounded. I look for a *pétroleuse,* and I see in her hands neither fire nor kerosene.

As for Eugénie Suétens, Sergeant Bordelais, who replaced the defaulting lawyer, "relied upon the wisdom of the Council." Joséphine Marchais, too, was defended by a military man, Lieutenant Guinez, who took "the place deserted by the members of the bar." They had refused to "extend their hand to these outcasts of society," he declared. Lieutenant Guinez was really an honorable man, and did what he could to save the accused woman whose defense he had undertaken: poverty was the cause of everything.

"I wonder, in our corrupt times, where a poor woman goes when she has no more bread?" What jobs, what work could she find? "Young people not strong enough to carry a musket, men whom I accuse and scorn, hold a lot of jobs which might advantageously be filled by women, and do not hesitate to wrest from them their daily bread." It was poverty, then, that impelled women to join the insurgents. "Have pity, gentlemen," he concluded, "these are women. . . . Hearken to my plea: it is the plea of a soldier."

These few words "spoken with a simplicity and warmth that were entirely military, aroused murmurs of approval in the audience," noted the editor of the *Gazette des Tribunaux*.

Haussmann, who pleaded for Eulalie Papavoine, held against his client only her presence at the barricades and her filching of three handkerchiefs. In her case, he found no proof that she had participated in arson. For Lucie Bocquin, whose absent lawyer he was replacing, he simply asked for acquittal.

But this was not the opinion of the Council of War. The judgment was a terrible one: Élizabeth Rétiffe was condemned to death; Joséphine Marchais, to death; Eugénie Suétens, to death. Eulalie Papavoine, to banishment to a fortress; Lucie Bocquin, to ten years in solitary confinement.

Eugénie Suétens and Joséphine Marchais wept. Élizabeth Rétiffe remained impassive.[32]

Victor Hugo raised his great voice to defend the insurgents, whom he considered as revolutionary combatants and not as civil criminals.[33] Therefore he asked for the lives of Rossel, Ferré, all the insurgents of the Commune, and those three unfortunate women Marchais, Suétens, and Papavoine: "One of them is a mother, and before her death sentence, she said [Hugo is lending her his words]: 'It's all right, but who is going to feed my child?' " And the author of *Les Misérables,* who was not only a great writer but also a man of goodness and magnanimity, went on: "The entire social malady is in this statement. . . . Thus, here is a mother who is going to die, and there is a little baby who is also going to die, in consequence. Our justice sometimes has these results. Is the mother guilty? Answer yes or no. Is the child? Try and answer yes."[34]

Was Hugo's intercession decisive? Either that, or the judges on the Commission for Pardons hesitated before the lack of evidence; at any rate, those death sentences were commuted to hard labor for life, and deportation to Guiana.[35]

A second *"pétroleuse"* affair attracted public attention on April 16, 1872, just as the public had begun to grow weary of the whole thing. This time it involved three women who were accused of having taken part in the fires at the Rue Royale, the Place de la Concorde, and the Tuileries.

Once again, Maxime du Camp has left us fevered descriptions of Florence Wandeval, Anne-Marie Menand, and Aurore Machu. "Three sinister females had been inspiring and inflaming the men, embracing the artillerymen, and displaying an immodesty unshamed by broad daylight."[36] He accused them of having poured kerosene and of having indulged in obscene bacchanals in the midst of burning houses. "Machu, Menand, and Wandeval, sweating, with their clothing undone, their bosoms almost bare, passed from man to man, sometimes screaming: 'Drink!' " . . . etc. Such is his tone. To this, Brunel, commandant of the Federals, calmly replied:

> The appearance in our ranks of shameless slatterns, half-naked women, *pétroleuse*-Messalinas who, like the mythological Furies, kindled courage and

breathed life into arson, is an invention which, when all is said and done, can be accounted for. With such means, the picture is muddied, and the reader, beside himself, retains in his mind fantastic figures which prepare him to welcome the return to a monarchy.[37]

Let us, however, try to see things a little more clearly. The dossiers of the Councils of War and of the Commission for Pardons, in their aridity, may perhaps permit us to do so.

On Monday, May 22, 1871, the Federal Battalion led by Commandant Brunel attempted to join General Eudes at the Corps Législatif. With their cannons, they reinforced the barricades of the Rue Royale and the Faubourg Saint-Honoré. The battle lasted until Tuesday noon. Then, afraid they would be surrounded, the Federals raised a barrier of flames between themselves and the Versailles army. There were women among the fighters. Some were dressed in naval or National Guard uniforms, and armed with rifles; others wore the armband of the Geneva Convention. They fought, or else gathered up the wounded. "The women who followed the Federals must have helped them in all the crimes that were committed, for they were more fanatic than the men," said a witness.[38] Three of them were arrested: Aurore Machu, Florence Wandeval, and Anne-Marie Menand. Had some *pétroleuses* finally been captured?

Let us dispense with Aurore Machu immediately. For her "there was no alleged crime of arson."[39] Dressed in a naval uniform, this woman pointed and fired a cannon in the Place de la Concorde. When she was not by her weapon, she was seen calmly seated under the dome of the Naval Ministry. It was said that her comrades bore her in triumph to the Hôtel de Ville, where she was commended for her skill and courage.[40]

In Florence Wandeval and Anne-Marie Menand, we

find women who were, perhaps, more closely mixed up with the fires.

Florence Wandeval was born in Berchem, Belgium, in 1848. She came to France at a very young age, and first lived in Angers, which she left at seventeen to settle in Paris. She married someone named Baruteau, was separated from him, and lived with a lover, Bled, in the Rue Boulard, under the name of Amélie Maison. A day-worker, she had good references and had never been convicted of any crime. Then came the war and the Siege. Florence Wandeval joined the 107th Marching Battalion where her lover was a sergeant, as an ambulance nurse. She remained there during the Commune. Before the Council of War, she stated that she tended the wounded, and had never had a part in any fires:

> Lightly wounded in the leg, on Tuesday, May 23, I was awakened during the night when the remnants of Lieutenant Brunel's battalion were going to beat a retreat. We went back onto the embankments. At that time the fire was at the Tuileries, and columns of flame were rising from the Palace. I cannot tell you who set the fire. I thought then, as I do now, that it had been started by the shells that were falling on every side.

She tried to exonerate not only herself, but her comrades as well: "I swear in any case that nothing can make me suspect the Federals of being the cause of that calamity." She told further how their little band got as far as Les Halles, and then dispersed. She went alone with a wounded man and looked for a doctor to care for him. Along the way, she was hit in the right breast by a bullet.[41] But the witnesses contradicted her, and their accounts were in agreement with each other. She was said to have been heard saying, "I've just set the f . . . Tuileries on fire. Now a king can come; he'll find his palace in ashes."

And again: "We've come from setting the Tuileries on fire, and from tonight on, many others will burn. No one but the people will rule." She was said to have been injured leaving the Tuileries, as she went through the railings. "You're a brave girl," one of her comrades was supposed to have said to her. "Ah," she replied, "we'll see many others!"[42] It must be conceded that these words have an unmistakably authentic ring. It does seem that Florence Wandeval was among the Federals who set the Tuileries on fire.

As for Anne-Marie Menand, called Jeanne-Marie (could it be Rimbaud's?*), she was known in the area around La Madeleine as "the woman with the yellow dog." She was a poor creature, an easy target for Maxime du Camp's persecution: "I have never seen such ugliness. Dark-skinned, with staring eyes, dull and dirty hair, her face pocked and freckled, thin lips and a silly laugh, she had some wild quality about her, which reminded one of the panic of nocturnal birds suddenly put into the daylight...."[43] We know the process: physical defects (including freckles) indicate a corresponding moral ugliness, and become a sign of predestination to evil. In the same way, but conversely, people like Vuillaume and Vallès never saw anything but beautiful, young, joyful, healthy girls among the Commune fighters—which is equally absurd.

But in any case, everything that we know of Anne-Marie Menand scarcely conferred upon her the ideal aspect of a revolutionary militant. She came from Brittany, and was born in 1837, in Saint-Séglin (Ille-et-Vilaine). She said that she was a cook, but had left her last job in 1867 to go sell newspapers in the kiosks along the Rue Royale and the Place de la Madeleine. In October, 1870, she went to Vincennes to sell brandy to the soldiers. But she was her own best customer, and was often seen drunk. Also, she

* See pp. 229–30.—*Trans.*

was sentenced to six days in prison for having bought military clothing. After the armistice, she went on selling brandy, this time to the Prussians, as she had to the French soldiers, and worked occasionally as a prostitute. A few days after the Commune, she returned to live in Paris, on the Rue Saint-Honoré, and worked for her sister-in-law, who had a canteen on the Avenue de Wagram. Thus Anne-Marie Menand had nothing militant about her. She had been seen at neither the Clubs nor the *Union des Femmes*. And when she found herself mixed up in the battle, it was because they were fighting in her neighborhood. She helped to tend the wounded who were being carried in makeshift ambulances, to 15 and 25 Rue Royale. Accompanied by a Federal, she requisitioned linen, searched for food, and tried to find "bourgeois-looking" clothes for the Federals so that they could escape. But she also had another role. She went into the houses that were to be burned.

"They've sent me to tell you to get out."

"But why?"

"Because they're going to burn it."

At the Rue Boissy-d'Anglas: "I've come to save you, because they're going to set a fire here. Follow me."

And to another witness who took refuge in the Rue Saint-Florentin: "Don't be afraid of anything; I'm with you."[44]

All of this proved to the Council of War that Anne-Marie Menand knew the intentions of the Federals. From that to admitting that she herself had set fires was only one step, quickly taken. Especially since she had been heard to say: "It's a good thing that this church (La Madeleine) is being looted. They deserved it." And again, "We're going to win, and we'll burn all the rich people's shanties."

Therefore she was condemned to death, but her sentence was commuted to hard labor in Guiana. Florence

Wandeval and Aurore Machu were sentenced to hard labor for life.[45]

Another woman, Marie-Jeanne Bouquet, *femme* Lucas, who was president of the *Club Saint-Nicolas-des-Champs,* was said to have shown the Federals how to make the Molotov cocktails of that day: a bottle of kerosene fitted with a wick. Twenty years of hard labor.[46]

From prison, Anne-Marie Menand wrote to the curé of the Saint-Malo parish at Dinan, to clear herself of the accusations that hung heavily upon her: "I was arrested like everyone, because they *were* arresting everyone, in the houses and everywhere. . . ." As for the director of the Auberive prison, he did not see Aurore Machu as the Messalina that Maxime du Camp described. She was "an indefatigable worker" and a good student at school; she had a timid disposition: "Machu lets herself be led easily. Also, this unhappy woman bitterly deplores her weakness, which was the cause of her sentence." Therefore the Auberive director interceded for her: she was a widow and the mother of two children without support; several times he asked that her sentence be reduced. But in vain.[47]

What, then, is there left to say about the *"pétroleuses"*? women who, shoulder to shoulder with the Federals, struggled for the defense of the barricades, and took up the wounded. Among those whose names have been preserved by the judicial records, only Florence Wandeval and Anne-Marie Menand may have taken part in the fires. But certainly not Élizabeth Rétiffe, Eugénie Suétens, Joséphine Marchais, Eulalie Papavoine, or Aurore Machu—all of whom were, nonetheless, condemned as *"pétroleuses,"* because someone had to be guilty and no one could be found. But neither Florence Wandeval nor Anne-Marie Menand appear to be Commune militants. We find them neither in the Clubs nor in the *Union des Femmes.* They were individual women, involved in the battles by accident.

How, then, did the *Union des Femmes* participate in the Paris fires? Did it, indeed, play any role? Only the little sentence in the statutes, putting weapons and kerosene on the same level, might indicate so. But we have no evidence that the plan became fact. The women of the *Union* who died on the barricades of Les Batignolles or the Place Blanche have taken their secret with them.

CHAPTER THIRTEEN

THE EXECUTION OF HOSTAGES

ON APRIL 5, as a counter to the Versailles army's execution of Duval and Flourens, and as an attempt to stop the executions of prisoners, the Commune passed a decree concerning hostages, which resolved that any person accused of complicity with the Versailles government would be arrested, and that a grand jury would be formed and would pronounce judgment within forty-eight hours. Every accused person who was judged guilty would be considered a hostage. Any executions of prisoners of war or supporters of the Commune would be answered by the execution of three times as many hostages.[1] This decree was not enforced, not even when the Commune learned, on May 17, that Versailles had summarily shot an ambulance nurse under particularly revolting circumstances. However, a member of the Commune, Urbain—submitting unawares to the pressure of the Versailles agent Barral de Montaud, and his mistress Marie Leroy—had insisted that the April decree immediately be administered. But nothing came of this: the Commune members were not in the least bloodthirsty and feared the shadow of any illegality; moreover, they understood that it was to the Versailles government's interest that the Commune's hands be stained with blood.[2]

When the soldiers of the regular army entered Paris, the massacre of Federals began immediately. As early as May 23, to avenge the memory of Generals Lecomte and Clément Thomas, the soldiers shot 42 men, 3 women, and 2 children chosen at random along the Rue des Rosiers. Forty-seven victims propitiating the shades of two generals: so heavily did they weigh. One woman refused to kneel: "Show these wretches that you know how to die on your feet," she said.[3]

At Les Batignolles, in the Place Clichy, on the outer boulevards, on the Place de l'Hôtel de Ville—everywhere —the butchery went on. A passerby who was particularly hostile to the Commune tabulated how many murdered bodies he had encountered on May 24. At the Quai d'Orsay, across from La Bourdonnais, 47 shot (9 women and 38 men); at the Alma hill, 16 shot (5 women, 11 men); at the Pont des Invalides, in front of the tobacco factory: 8 shot (2 women, 6 men); at the Invalides esplanade, 12 shot (1 woman, 11 men); at the Pont de la Concorde, 2 shot; at the Cour du Télégraphe, ten delivery vans, with 40 shot in each wagon: 400 bodies; at the Place de la Concorde, 2 women, for having killed an officer; opposite the Conseil d'Etat and the Légion d'Honneur, 60 shot (10 women, 50 men). And this only took care of a tiny fraction of Paris, during a single day.[4]

During the course of this dreadful bloodshed, the Federals executed, for their part, 84 hostages.[5] But the execution of the Archbishop of Paris, the execution of Jesuits, of Dominicans, and of the Comte de Beaufort, who was considered to be a traitor—these weigh more heavily in history than the thousands of nameless murders perpetrated by the soldiers of order: bootmakers, stonecutters, carpenters, masons, day laborers, or seamstresses—small fry, neglected by history. Mme. de Lamballe's head on the end of a stick weighed much more in the traditional balance of history than the sacrifice of thousands of unknown people. Right-thinking people were indignant at the former, but considered the latter insignificant. The masses form the vile matter of history. A hundred thousand infantrymen are not worth the death of a general.

Women were mixed up in these executions. Maxime du Camp, once more, accused them of having driven and excited the men, of having sometimes delivered the first blows. One of the men active in the Commune, Da Costa, expressed the same opinion.[6] Thus, by means of a sort of latent antifeminism, the enemies and the supporters of the Commune shifted the responsibility for the summary executions onto women. But in this matter too, the fact seems to be that they had only walk-on roles; they were neither better nor worse than the men around them, neither more pitiable nor more ferocious.

On June 29, 1872, the Sixth Council of War sentenced a girl, Marceline Expilly (*femme* Adolphe) to death. She had been an abandoned baby, left at the Auxerre foundling hospital in November, 1848. She was brought up among various people, and married a man who, like herself, had been illegitimate and a foundling. However, she left him after six months. It was under the name of one of her friends, Amélie Célestine Clairiot, whose identification card she had borrowed—to find, she said, a job as a housemaid—that she was arrested and sentenced. On May 26, 1871, a man dressed in a white shirt (there was a rumor that the policemen were dressed that way) was arrested in the Place de la Bastille and taken to La Petite Roquette. A summary trial condemned him to death, and he was led in front of the Grande Roquette wall to be shot. Marceline Expilly, rifle slung over her shoulder, was in the courtyard beside the fountain where she was playfully throwing water onto some Federals' faces. Did she really ask to command the firing squad? We do not know, and the court proceedings do not clear things up. She herself claimed that she had gone into La Roquette only to meet her lover. However that may be, she was condemned to death under the name of her friend Amélie Clairiot, then transferred to Guiana to do a sentence of hard labor.[7]

The canteen worker Marguerite Lachaise—admired, as we have seen, by her comrades in the 66th Battalion for her courage—was also tried in January 1872. She was accused of having taken part in the murder of the Comte de Beaufort. This authentic count, who became a captain of the Federals, was a strange person. There were hovering suspicions about his loyalty to the Commune.[8] The 66th Battalion held him responsible for the losses it had suffered during the course of various sorties. After an undisciplined action—so common in the Federal army—he had been heard to say, "I must purge this battalion." On May 24, Beaufort was arrested, at the instigation of Marguerite Lachaise, by the guards of the 66th Battalion. He was taken to the office of Commander Genton. Listening to his explanations, Genton stated that he was not qualified to continue the interrogation (the Versailles officers, at that very moment, were not being so careful about their prisoners). Someone said: "You can't shoot a man for a remark he made." Old Delescluze, supported by two or three members of the Commune, also intervened on behalf of the prisoner. Three times he tired to get upon a bench to appease the mob. But the cries continued: "Death, death! He's a traitor. He's a nobleman and a count. He

could only be among us to betray us. He has to be shot."
Marguerite Lachaise was supposed to have said to Delescluze: "If you don't have him shot, I'll shoot him myself."
Finally the mob took Beaufort into a vacant lot at the
corner of the Avenue Parmentier and the Rue de la
Roquette. A witness claimed to have heard Marguerite
Lachaise say, "That's good . . . there aren't enough like
that. . . . I'm so happy I could die." But another asserted
that she added her pleas to those of Delescluze, that she
asked for two hours' respite to examine the charges weigh-
ing upon Beaufort, and that she began to cry when she saw
the mob leading him off to be shot.

Confronted with these contradictory accounts, one hesi-
tates to delineate the features of Marguerite Lachaise. It
is certain that she was brave; she showed that at Issy and
Meudon, and her comrades in the 66th Battalion admired
her and asked that she be cited for bravery. But then courage can be found in a harpy. However, there are indications that Marguerite Lachaise was not the shameless
shrew that a witness thought he recognized her to be. On
the afternoon of May 24, at La Roquette, Commandant
Genton asked for men from the 66th Battalion, in order
to execute the Bishop of Paris and other hostages. Marguerite Lachaise went into La Roquette, despite the
opposition of a captain of the 207th Battalion:

"You know very well that women do not come in here."

"I'm not a woman, but a man, because I'm a canteen
worker."

And she opposed "her" battalion's participation in the
execution of hostages:

"Already this morning they have shot a Federal officer,"
she explained. "This is too much. I don't want 'my' battalion being called murderers."

And she left La Roquette, taking with her the guards of
the 66th Battalion. Yet Marguerite Lachaise was condemned to death for having taken part in the Comte de

Beaufort's execution, whereas this had not really been proved. She, too, was deported to Guiana.[9]

A girl was said to have participated in the murder of some Arcueil Dominicans (May 25) who had been accused of having surrendered Le Moulin-Saquet to Versailles.[10] Among the fourteen accused, only one woman, Pauline Octavie Lecomte (*femme* Buffo), figured in this trial. She was a seamstress, the wife of a stonecutter who was a guard in the 101st Federal Battalion. No other charge was sustained against her except that some little spoons had been found in her lodgings with the monogram of the Pavillon de l'Horloge. She replied that she had been given them by her daughter, a year before, and that she did not think they had any value. Pauline Buffo was acquitted.[11]

On May 26, driven to despair by the ruthless murders committed by Versailles, a mob executed forty-seven hostages on the Rue Haxo, despite the intervention of members of the Commune. There too, women were involved and witnesses accused one of them of having been the first to fire.[12] Vallès gives us an account of the conversation he had with one of these women who was shouting "Death!" in the crowd. She had a sister who had been seduced, and then abandoned pregnant, by a curate. The canteen keeper who gave the signal to fire was the daughter of a man arrested during the Empire, denounced by an *agent provocateur;* he had died in prison. Vallès said that these women had no ideas about "the Social State"; rather, they were there because they had suffered under the established order.[13]

One woman sentenced to hard labor for life, for complicity in the Rue Haxo massacre, was Pauline Lise Séret, wife of a sculptor, Bourette, born in Paris in 1825. She was charged with having propagandized for the Commune, gone looking for draft dodgers, threatened a man who was hiding two policemen, and incited the mob to the murder of the hostages. The Government commissioner even

added that she "had outraged the corpses of the victims."
Even though she had "no previous criminal record," and
even though the information obtained about her by the
police commissioner was favorable, she was considered a
"dangerous woman." Later, at Auberive, she proved to be
hard-working, obedient, and "worthy of interest," according to the prison director. Her husband, who had not
participated in the Commune, was nevertheless arrested,
and went mad on the prison boats.[14]

By May 27, all was lost. Taking advantage of the dis-
order, the La Roquette prisoners fled. Four of them, Mon-
signor Surrat (the vicar general of the archdiocese), the
Abbé Bécourt, Father Houillon, and a policeman named
Chaulieu, were arrested at a barricade on the Boulevard
Voltaire, where the Federals were still fighting doggedly.
They were led to La Roquette. An ambulance nurse,
Marie Wolff, *femme* Guyard, took part in their execution.
She was a character out of *Les Mystères de Paris*. Born in
Bar-le-Duc in 1849, the ragpicker Marie Wolff had been
sentenced for theft and for vagrancy. What misery, what
rancor, what despair was she avenging when she shouted:
"If you don't shoot them, I'll make it my business to."[15]
A washerwoman in her neighborhood, called as a witness,
formally identified her:

> She was carrying a red banner and wore a belt with
> weapons stuck into it. She was dressed in a grey skirt
> and jacket, and a very faded blue apron. She wore her
> hair braided on her head, with a band around it; and
> wore hobnailed boots which she later threw away at
> Saint-Lazare, when she saw that I recognized her; for
> I had done her laundry three or four times during the
> Siege. I said that what she was doing was no good, and
> that she would get into trouble because of it. She
> replied, as she went back down the street, by threaten-
> ing to do me in.[16]

She was condemned to death on April 24, 1872; her sentence was commuted to hard labor for life.[17]

A tavern waitress, Marie Cailleux, was implicated in the same affair. But nothing could be sustained against her except that she had worked at building the barricade at Père-Lachaise, and that she had fired her rifle, She was sentenced to deportation to New Caledonia, where she married another deportee of the Commune.[18]

————◆————

CHAPTER FOURTEEN

THE MAJOR TRIALS

THE TRIAL OF LOUISE MICHEL—called "the new Théroigne," "the Inspirer," "the revolutionary breath of the Commune" by the newspapers—was awaited with interest.

On December 16, 1871, she appeared before the Sixth Council of War. The spectators' hopes were not let down. More courageous than most of the Commune members, Louise Michel assumed total responsibility, before the tribunal and before history, for her acts. Dressed in black, she lifted back her veil; beneath her magnificent forehead her large dark eyes looked steadily at her judges. She seemed to be the very incarnation of the vanquished insurrection, of eternal revolution. The lawyer Haussmann was in attendance, but she wanted to handle her own defense on all of the counts of which she was accused: complicity in the arrest and execution of Generals Lecomte and Clément Thomas; the plan to assassinate Thiers; having organized both the *Union des Femmes* (which was false) and the Vigilance Committees (which was true); the drafting of the famous appeal "In the name of the Social Revolution that we hail . . ."; being president of the *Club de la Révolution*; the profession in front of her students of doctrines of "free thought"; fighting in the front lines at Issy, Clamart, Montmartre; rallying the deserters; membership in the International, and so on. In all of this, the prosecutor saw only one motive: pride. They evoked her hardheartedness (those who knew her called her "the good Louise"): "Her mother may, perhaps, have gone without bread; but what matter?" (we know how Louise Michel loved her mother, and that she turned herself in to save her). "As guilty as Ferré, whom she is so strangely protecting, and whose mind, to use one of her expressions, is a challenge flung to conscience and her answer, a revolution," she stirred up the passions of the mob, preached ruthless war, and, a "she-wolf hungry for blood," provoked the execution of the hostages "by her infernal machinations."[1]

This time it was no poor, trembling, unaware woman, brutalized by poverty, whom the officers of the Council of War had before them, but an intelligent, ardent woman, in harmony with herself. No chasm between her action and her thought: everything that she had done, she had fully desired to do.

I do not want to defend myself; I do not want to be defended. I belong entirely to the Social Revolution, and I declare that I accept full responsibility for all my actions. I accept it entirely and unreservedly. You accuse me of having taken part in the execution of the generals? I should answer yes to that, if I had been in Montmartre when they wanted to have the people fired upon; I would not have hesitated, myself, to fire at men who gave such orders. But I do not understand why they were shot when they were prisoners, and I regard that action as arrant cowardice.

As for the fires in Paris, yes, I took part in them. I wanted to set up a barrier of flames before the invaders from Versailles. I have no accomplices in that act.

It does not seem that Louise Michel actually took part in the burning of Paris; but she wanted to take upon herself all the charges that were made against the Commune.

I have been told that I am an accomplice of the Commune. Certainly, yes; for the Commune wanted, above all else, the Social Revolution, and the Social Revolution is the dearest of my desires. Even more, I am honored in being one of the supporters of the Commune.

But, Louise Michel asserted, the Commune had had no hand in the executions and fires.

Why should I defend myself? I have already announced that I refuse to do so. You are men who are going to judge me. You are before me; your faces are revealed. You are men, and I am only a woman; yet I look you in the eye. I know very well that nothing I might say to you will change your sentence in any respect.

And, proudly, she flung into the military judges' faces:

We never wanted anything but the triumph of the great principles of the Revolution. That I swear, by our martyrs felled on the Satory Plain; by our martyrs whom I hail aloud here, and who, one day, will surely find an avenger. Once more: I am yours. Do with me what you want. Take my life, if you want it. I am not the woman to argue with you for an instant.

Then the interrogation began. When she had heard of the execution of Generals Lecomte and Thomas, she said: "They have been shot. That's good." Did she, then, approve of these executions?

"That is no proof," she replied. "The words I uttered were for the purpose of not stemming the tide of the Revolution."

She had contributed to newspapers that called for the confiscation of the clergy's goods, and other subversive measures.

"Of course. But we never wanted to take those goods for ourselves. We had no thought but that of giving them to the people, to increase their well-being."

She had demanded the abolition of the magistracy.

"That's because the examples of their mistakes were always before my eyes."

She acknowledged having wanted to assassinate Thiers.

Her answers aroused the indignation of an audience made up of Versailles partisans. (The Commune partisans had been arrested, hidden, or terrorized.) But Louise Michel did not seem to notice this; once or twice, however, she turned around and smiled scornfully.

The witnesses did not add any information that was not already known, for Louise Michel avowed everything of which she was accused, and more besides. Captain Dailly, delivering the indictment, demanded that an accused woman who represented a permanent danger to society be cut off from it. Her lawyer declined to plead, since Louise Michel did not want to be defended, and threw himself "onto the wisdom of the Council." Then, one last time, Louise Michel spoke out:

What I demand of you, who call yourselves a Council of War, who sit as my judges, and who do not disguise yourselves as the Commission for Pardons; you, who are military men, and who deliver judgment before the eyes of everyone: what I demand of you is the Satory Plain, where my brothers are already fallen. I must be cut off from society; you have been told to do so. Well, the Commissioner of the Republic is right. Since it seems that every heart that beats for freedom has no right to anything but a little slug of lead, I demand my share. If you let me live, I shall never cease to cry for vengeance; and I shall avenge my brothers by denouncing the murderers of the Commission for Pardon. . . ."

The presiding judge interrupted her: "I cannot allow you to speak if you go on in that manner." Louise Michel: "I have finished. If you are not cowards, kill me."

The room, so hostile at the outset, was caught by emotion. Louise Michel was sentenced to banishment to a fortress. When the court clerk informed her that she had at her disposal twenty-four hours during which to lodge an appeal, she merely answered:

"No. There is no appeal. But I would have preferred death."[2]

Sophie Poirier, the president of the 18th arrondissement Vigilance Committee and the *Club de la Boule Noire,* was also sentenced to banishment to a fortress. In society's eyes, her past was irreproachable. She does not seem to have voted for the death of the Archbishop of Paris, at the time when the Versailles government would not hand over Blanqui. But she had signed up ambulance nurses. "And," details the indictment, "it is known that these ambulance nurses were willing to turn into barricade-fighters and *pétroleuses. Citoyenne* Poirier, then, in this situation, was doing nothing but carrying out the plan of the *Union des Femmes pour la Défense de Paris.*" To obtain quarters for the *Club de la Boule Noire,* she had had an occupied apartment requisitioned in the Rue des Acacias. She had transmitted to the Commune's Police Commissioner information that would allow him to proceed with requisitions and arrests. She had organized an assembly of more than twenty persons, and had incited to civil war.

Sophie Poirier defended herself circumspectly. It was not she who had signed the documents attributed to her. It had been for the Government of National Defense, and with the authorization of Clemenceau, the mayor of Montmartre, that she had organized a sewing workshop of seventy-five or eighty working women. And she had sought to turn them into ambulance nurses because those women had no more work under the Commune. The Vigilance Committee, she said, had no purpose but that of allocating work, giving welfare aid, and visiting the sick and poor. As for the *Club de la Boule Noire,* it was not she who had founded it; she had only used it as a place to meet her workers. But the Council of War did not admit any of these explanations. Its opinion was that she had exerted a "deplorable influence upon that portion of the feminine population of Paris which later found itself disposed to lend its incendiary support."[3]

Béatrix Excoffon, the vice-president of the *Club de la Boule Noire,* also appeared before the Council of War. It was she who had requisitioned the apartment in the Rue des Acacias, and she had played an important role in the Vigilance Committee and the *Club de la Boule Noire.* Béatrix Excoffon used the same method of defense as had Sophie Poirier. The Vigilance Committee's sole purpose was to provide jobs for women who were out of work. Certainly, she had attended almost all the Club's meetings, but she had spoken there only three or four times, and always to exert a moderating influence. But Béatrix

Excoffon, by way of her family and that of her "companion," belonged to a revolutionary background. In her neighborhood she was called "La Républicaine"—a serious charge in the eyes of these "republican" judges. Therefore, on October 13, 1871, she was sentenced to banishment to a fortress.[4]

Imprisoned at Auberive, she was at first considered "a dangerous woman, having a bent for rebellion, and pushing others into it."[5]

But she seems gradually to have come around to "more wholesome" ideas. And soon the Government Commissioner was of the opinion that her sentence could be reduced. On March 28, 1872, it was lightened to ten years' imprisonment. Indeed, Béatrix Excoffon wrote some remarkably platitudinous letters from the Rouen prison. She expressed her sincere repentance "for everything I might have done, being too young to be able to distinguish good from evil, and not to have wanted to take into a count [sic] the advice of my parents, as well as M. Excoffon's." She painted the situation: her widowed mother, the deaths of her only child and of a little brother-in-law that she had brought up. Her lover, whom she had been about to marry, had been subjected to such psychological blows that he was mentally deranged for eight months.[6] On September 28, 1874, in another letter to the President of the Republic, she fell back upon the same tone:

> I was only twenty-one years old when I was arrested; knowing nothing and not believing I was doing wrong, I threw myself into the whirlwind that was carrying Paris to its ruination, not having cared to listen to the advice of the father of my children, who had never wished to get mixed up in it, and who wanted me to do likewise. But I, child that I was, without understanding anything, did not pay attention to him, and I went right on.

But now she had returned to a more wholesome vision of the world. In another letter, to Mme. de Rémusat, who had already intervened in her behalf, the atheistic "République" wrote: "I should, at the time of that ordeal, have thought of my great, God-given duty of motherhood. Alas, I did not do so. Every day I ask God to pardon me for this, and I thank Him for having, in His bounty, put generous hearts along my path."[7] And so on. The director of the Rouen prison voiced some doubts about the sincerity of this conversion.[8] But the Vice-President of the Chamber of Deputies, the deputy from the Eure-et-Loire, and Clemenceau intervened on her behalf. Was it as a result of all these interventions that the prison director changed his mind? Béatrix Excoffon gave the other prisoners an example of submissiveness. She seemed to have returned to "the good path." As the overseer of the workshop, she gave "good advice" to her companions. Her correspondence with her family showed that she now understood "the duty of women in society." She showed great respect for the nuns, whose exhortations seemed to have had "the best possible influence" upon her. In short, the *Communarde* apparently turned into a model of virtue: the rest of her sentence was remitted on November 26, 1878, as an encouragement to the other prisoners.[9]

On December 29, 1871, another member of the Montmartre Vigilance Committee, Jaclard's wife, Anna Korvina Krukovskaya, was sentenced *in absentia* to hard labor for life. Her political activity was not in the least emphasized; instead, oddly enough, this general's daughter was accused of "complicity in the fraudulent removal of various objects, at the expense of M. de Polignac."[10] Commune partisans always had to be put on the same footing as civil criminals.

After the insurrection, Victor Jaclard stayed hidden for some time, and was then arrested. Anna's sister and

brother-in-law, Professors Sophie and Vladimir Kovalevsky—the three had been reunited during the Commune[11]
—had General Krukovsky come to Paris. In fact, they had
remembered that the General had formerly met Thiers,
at some watering spot. They were all upright people. The
General obtained an audience with the statesman concerning this rather compromising family. But Professor
Kovalevsky made a more radical decision. He helped his
brother-in-law escape, and sent him into Switzerland with
his own passport. Accompanied by her father, Anna went
to the Jura, near Bern, to rejoin her husband. In 1874,
the Jaclards arrived in Russia, where Anna took up her
pen once more. She wrote several more short stories. But,
undermined by the privations of the Siege and the Commune, she died in Paris in 1887 at the age of forty-four.
Louise Michel was present at her funeral. At her request,
no speeches were made over her grave. A friend quietly
recalled "her qualities of courage and devotion," and the
intelligent support that she constantly gave her husband
and her friends during "their political tasks and struggles."[12]

Paule Minck and André Léo also took refuge in Switzerland and returned to their propaganda in behalf of the
defeated Commune. They tried to make its meaning and
its grandeur understood to ears numbed by the prose of
the Versailles press. André Léo was invited to the Peace
Congress being held in Lausanne in September, 1871.
She tried to open the eyes and ears of those placid Swiss
who were so far removed from revolutionary struggle.

Who is so deaf that he has not heard the cannons of
Paris and Versailles? And those firing-squads in the
parks, the cemeteries, the vacant lots, and the villages
around Paris? Who is so blind that he has not seen
those wagonloads of corpses being taken off, first
during the day, and then by night? Those prisoners

—men, women, children—being taken to their death by the hundreds, under the fire of artillery and *mitrailleuse?*

Certainly André Léo would not defend the "blindness" and "incompetence" of most of the men of the Commune, whom she never ceased to denounce. But "these mistakes became honorable by comparison with the orgy of infamy that followed them." She explained things and brought them back to focus. The law concerning hostages was administered by the mob only after May 23, when the Commune no longer existed and when Versailles had begun its mass slaughter. The fires had been caused by the Versailles shells, as much as by the need for defense. The Commune had killed sixty-four; the number of murdered *Communards* mounted to fifteen or twenty thousand (and here André Léo, always scrupulous, estimates far lower than the actual figure). Thus, it was the murderers who were making the accusations. On the one side were all the defenders of privilege; on the other were the democrats. But the latter remained divided, for, as André Léo explained, some preferred liberty, and others equality. Well, "there can be no equality without liberty, nor any liberty without equality." And it was that which separated the socialists from the liberal bourgeoisie. But André Léo noted—and it is even more true today—that the middle- and lower-income bourgeoisie suffered as much as the common people from a capitalist government. "The law of capital is aristocratic by nature," she went on. "It tends increasingly to concentrate power in the hands of a few; it inevitably creates an oligarchy, which is master of the nation's power. . . . It pursues the interest of a few as against the interest of all. . . . It is opposed to the new conception of justice. . . . It holds in servitude, not only the poor, but the great majority of the bourgeoisie who live by their work and their ability"—and who, perhaps even more than manual laborers, were dependent upon the whim of the capitalists. Therefore it was to the interest of the working class, and also a great portion of the bourgeoisie, to abolish the law of capital; and it was necessary to find a way to do so. The March 18th Revolution had been guided, not by the socialists, but by "bourgeois Jacobinism." André Léo wanted all factions of democracy to unite so as to establish a common program that would include all freedoms (press, assembly, etc.), communal liberties, a single and graduated tax, the organization of a citizens' army, and a free, democratic and universal education. "As long as a child is poor . . . as long as he grows up with no ideal but the tavern, no future but the day-to-day work of a beast of burden, most members of humanity will be deprived of their rights . . . equality will be only a decoy, and war—the most horrible, the most desperate of all wars, be it unleashed or latent—will desolate the world and dishonor humanity."

This explanation, this perspective on civil war, provoked violent interruptions; the president of the Congress for Peace forbade André Léo to go on with her speech. "I had come to this Congress with one hope, and I left it with profound sadness," she concluded. The bourgeoisie, even the liberal bourgeoisie, could not permit itself to be reminded of the existence of the "class struggle."[13]

The women who had guided the _Union des Femmes_ also came to different fates. Nathalie Lemel, before the Council of War, assumed entire responsibility for her actions. After the defeat of the Commune, she had tried to kill herself out of despair. She was arrested the next day (June 21, 1871), and appeared before the Fourth Council of War on September 10, 1872.

Like Louise Michel, she acknowledged all acts of which she was accused.

Yes, she and Varlin had founded the cooperative _La Marmite_, "for the purpose of removing ourselves from the demands of hash-house cooks, and meeting to eat together like a family." Yes, she had been active in politics, but until the Siege of Paris she had been concerned solely with the problems of working women. Yes, under the Commune she had taken part in the insurrection: "I drew up a manifesto with four other women. I drafted an appeal to working women. I cooperated in building the barricades. I spoke in the clubs. . . ."

She acknowledged having run the *Union des Femmes,* along with Elizabeth Dmitrieff. She acknowledged the document: "In the name of the Social Revolution that we hail . . ." She acknowledged that she had gone, on the orders of the Commune, with about fifty women to defend the barricades of Les Batignolles and the Place Pigalle. But she had not been armed:

"I was satisfied with passing ammunition to the fighters, and giving first aid to the wounded."

A bookbinder, Mme. Clémenceau, witness for the prosecution, stated that she had heard the accused speaking in the Clubs, calling upon women to defend the barricades and to care for the wounded. She had run into her in the street, when the fires were burning:

"That's nothing," Nathalie was supposed to have replied to her. "That's only the Tuileries and the Palais Royal. Since we don't want any more kings, we don't need any palaces."

Another bookbinder, Mme. Hubert, came to testify in her behalf:

"For six months I saw her eating nothing but bread and cheese, so that she could feed her children."

But the Police Commissioner remarked that Nathalie Lemel read nothing but "bad newspapers," about which she had spoken in the workshops before her comrades. Despite her "frank and unaffected" attitude, which was emphasized by Joly, who was defending her, Nathalie

Lemel, like Louise Michel, was sentenced to banishment to a fortress.

She refused to lodge any appeal. Upon learning that the director of the La Rochelle house of detention, where she was imprisoned, had decided to postpone her deportation because he had heard no news of her petition for reprieve, she proudly wrote to the prefect: "I declare formally that not only have I made none, but I disclaim that which was made unbeknownst to me, as well as any which might be made in the future. My sentence is irrevocable. . . ."[14]

Elizabeth Dmitrieff was more fortunate. She succeeded in escaping, and the police searched for her in vain. At the *Union des Femmes,* they had found papers signed by her: a commendation for good citizenship for *citoyen* Henri Colleville; a request addressed to the municipal council of the 11th arrondissement, for obtaining chairs, candelabra, and candles from the Saint-Ambroise church, to be used for a meeting; the order to muster the women of the committee to go to the barricades. But what was she doing before March 18? The police did not know. And, after the "Week in May," they were unable to lay their hands on her. Therefore, the Sixth Council of War sentenced a specter *in absentia* on October 26, 1872, to banishment to a fortress "for incitement to civil war." This specter, who seems not to have had "any previous criminal record," was, moreover, later pardoned, under the terms of a deportation order.[15]

Elizabeth could not have cared less; she had taken refuge in Switzerland. Lissagaray, in *Les Huit Journées de Mai,* spoke admiringly of the Russian revolutionary: "Tall, golden-haired, wonderfully pretty, smiling, she supported the wounded man [Frankel], whose blood flowed onto her elegant dress. For several days, she had worked unstintingly at the barricades, caring for the wounded,

finding unbelievable strength in her noble heart. . . ."[16]
But much later, in 1897, in an interview for *La Revue
Blanche,* the old *Communard,* bitter, disappointed, out
of touch with his youth, affected an irony which would
not have been displeasing to Maxime du Camp:

> Another, who was called Dmitrieff, had an imagina-
> tion with a sense of tragedy. She came from Russia,
> where she had left her husband in the lurch. . . . One
> saw her, during the Commune, dressed in a magnifi-
> cent red gown, her belt crenelated with pistols. She
> was twenty years old, and very pretty. She had ad-
> mirers. Whether it was that "the bare-armed people"
> were not, *in camera,* very pleasing to her, or that love
> was, for her, an exclusively feminine sport, nothing
> could melt this iceberg. And when, at the barricades,
> she took the wounded Frankel into her arms, she did
> so chastely. For she was at the barricades, where her
> bravura was charming. Mark the outfit, entirely of
> black velvet. . . .

He continued in the same bantering vein, describing the
residence of the beautiful "Russian princess" in Switzerland.

> She was very rich, and kept a house at the lakeside,
> where she extended her hospitality to refugees; in her
> salons there was a brilliant society of "hard labor,"
> with a sprinkling of death sentences, and other
> exotica. Then she went back to Russia to rejoin her
> husband; he died shortly thereafter. There was a trial,
> where she appeared as a witness. It seems that milord
> had been poisoned. The steward was sent to Siberia,
> where she hastened to join him. There has been no
> news of her since.[17]

All this information is as dubious as it is spiteful. Elizabeth Dmitrieff did indeed go back to Russia, and she was

involved in a trial. Marx used his influence with Professor Kovalevsky to help her find a lawyer. "I have learned that a Russian lady who has given great service to the Party cannot find a lawyer in Moscow, because she has no money."[18] Elizabeth married a deportee in Siberia, where she died, but nothing indicates that this deportee was the murderer of her husband, as Lissagaray rather snidely asserts. Time passes, youth dies, and political solidarity does not operate to women's advantage.

What became of the other women of the *Union*? Doubtless many, like Blanche Lefebvre, died at the barricades; but the others? Neither the Archives of War in Vincennes, nor the National Archives, preserved complete files on the sentenced *Communards*. How was the choice made? What criteria were applied for those that were destroyed? Historians always work with only a fraction of the material, left to them by chance or by arbitrary choice.

Louise Michel had been sentenced, not as a teacher, but as a fighter. But Marguerite Tinayre was sentenced as a schoolteacher, for having had a job under the Commune. She had been appointed Inspector of Schools in the 12th arrondissement, and, as we know, had taken part in the secularization of the neighborhood schools. This was all that could be sustained against her. Her previous conduct had given no cause for any unfavorable attention, but she had always manifested revolutionary ideas and, it was said, was affiliated with the International. Arrested on May 26, and then released, she was sentenced *in absentia* to banishment to a fortress, "for having been in communication with the leaders of insurrectionary groups, and for having involved herself in public functions with no right to do so." Her brother, Antoine Ambroise Guerrier, manager of a tobacco factory at Reuilly, was given the same sentence, also for having held an office under the

Commune.[19] He was able to take refuge in London, where he died. As for Marguerite Tinayre's husband, the peaceable notary clerk who was never interested in politics, he made the mistake of going to look for his wife, in the midst of the turmoil, and was therefore, as we saw already, shot at Le Châtelet, without any further trial.

Accompanied by her five children, Marguerite Tinayre went first to Geneva, where she continued to fight her battle: she was seen presiding at a "civil baptism."[20] But she had to keep her five children alive. First, in Saxony, she held a position as governess for a large family, then— exile upon exile—reached Budapest where she was able to gain acceptance by virtue of her conscientiousness and her industry. The French ambassador wrote concerning her that the exiled woman had "the most perfectly honorable outward behavior one might find." Her irreproachable bearing and conduct earned her everyone's respect. In 1879, she learned that women who had suffered under extraordinary tribunals could return to France. But she was excluded from this ruling because, at Geneva, she had been involved in "socialistic and internationalistic intrigues." This was, for her, a catastrophe: it would make them believe in Budapest that she was a common criminal. She would lose her students—her own and her children's means of support. On October 15, 1879, she wrote a letter to *La Marseillaise,* in which she drew the attention of the public to the punishment which her country's justice had a second time imposed upon her:

> I am a schoolteacher, that is, I am in that peculiar situation where it is indispensable to have a good name. Not wanting to take advantage of anyone's good faith, I declared openly that I was banished (in this country, no one is shocked by that). Hungarian society accepted me, therefore, as a woman who had perhaps been led astray into extreme causes, but

definitely as a respectable woman. Families and schools opened their doors to me, my classes were attended by girls belonging to what is conventionally called "the best society." In short, I earned enough to pay for the upbringing of my four sons and my daughter. Now, the Government's proclamations class me among the worst criminals. . . .

Six years' efforts were destroyed. "You can imagine the retrospective horror that the mothers of my students felt, thinking that they could have entrusted their daughters to an habituée of magistrates' courts or even to a woman sullied by 'vile crimes.' " What could she do? She still had two children to bring up, and two to support until their studies were completed. Her oldest son had begun to work, but the draft could take him from her. She was a widow in fact, but not in law; for "the Council of War which executed my husband no doubt forgot (we can't think of everything) to ask him his name. Neither I nor his family have been able to obtain any statement of his decease." Should she ask to be pardoned?—but that would be to admit that she had been guilty. "And guilty I was not, nor can I desire to appear so before children to whom I owe the example of strength and constancy in the face of ill fortune." And besides, would they restore her civic rights, without which she could not teach in her own country?

But it seemed that Marguerite Tinayre was worried for no reason (administrative mail travels slowly). On September 3, 1879, the Head of the Sûreté Générale had authorized Marguerite Tinayre to return to France for three months. On November 29, the rest of her sentence was remitted.[21]

Other women, like Marguerite Tinayre, suffered for having accepted teaching jobs under the Commune. Thus it was that a "young and pretty person, nineteen years old, with soft eyes," appeared before the tribunal on December 16, 1871. Anne Denis and her mother ran a bookstore on the Rue Monge. One of their clients, Stanislas Blanchet, a Commune member, had offered her a position as teacher in the convent school on the Rue Gracieuse, which had been taken in charge by Mme. da Costa. Anne Denis demurred that she had no diploma. But Blanchet answered that that was not necessary for teaching six-to-eight-year-old children.

"And your method of instruction consisted of teaching little girls patriotic songs?" the presiding judge asked her.

"They used to sing *La Marseillaise,* the young woman answered sweetly. "But they knew it already: I did not have to teach it to them."

Therefore she was accused of having solicited funds for the *Union Pour la Propagande Républicaine.* She had praised the Commune, and her "fanaticism" had earned her a position as schoolteacher: six days in prison.[22]

Anne Denis got off easily.

Other women—women against whom nothing could be sustained except that they had proclaimed aloud their sympathy for the Commune—were severely punished. To Marie Ségaud, deportation. She was a humble seamstress, born in Cronat-sur-Loire, Saône-et-Loire, in 1828. She had married a Pole, Jean-Édouard Orlowsky; since 1849 he had been a mechanic for the *Chemins de Fer de l'Ouest.* He was a hard worker, earning five francs a day. A member of the National Guard during the Siege, he remained in the 91st Battalion during the Commune, but concerning him there were no grounds for prosecution. His wife, on the other hand, was an ardent *Communarde;* she was called "La Mère Duchêne" in the neighborhood. In her house were found Commune newspapers, a red sash, and a rough draft of a denunciation of Versailles agents. Marie Ségaud affirmed her convictions aloud:

"I wanted the Republic more than anything, and I thought that only the Commune could give it to us."

She was accused of having read Commune newspapers aloud.

"No; I don't read well enough."

She was further accused of having denounced two neighbors, of having urged men to fight and women to build barricades, and of having hung out at the *Club Saint-Michel*. In short, "the accused seems to us to belong to that category of dangerous women who, without taking an active part in the fighting, definitely helped to give it the odious character that it had, particularly during the final days." (But who threw the first stone? The Council of War preferred not to mention that.) Marie Ségaud was sentenced to banishment, therefore, for nothing more than having propagandized for the Commune.[23] The same thing happened to Anne Collot, *femme* Gobert, who had insulted the soldiers of the Versailles army, and had "incited the insurgents," "including her husband, a sergeant under the Commune, who by now has disappeared"[24]—a euphemism meaning that he was probably shot without a trial.

Five years in prison for Jeanne Petit, widow of Gauthier, born in Heines-les-Plates, Nièvre, in 1831, because her tavern had been a sort of revolutionary Club.[25] The same for Agathe André, *femme* Joliveau, who belonged to a family of insurgents—her husband had been taken prisoner by Versailles on the Châtillon Plain; her father had been shot at the Butte-aux-Cailles barricade. Driven to despair by the arrest of her husband, she had drafted a petition the gist of which was that policemen's wives were to be forced to march in front of the National Guards who were about to enter battle. Five years in prison, therefore, although the petition had had no effect.[26] Two years in prison for a laundress, Marie Mortier, born in 1818 in Monterne-Silly, Vienne. She was the wife of Régent Cretin, a captain of the Federals, 260th Battalion, who had been sentenced to banishment; she had insulted Versailles supporters, and tried to drag two Federals back into the fight, when, on May 22, they were running away on the Rue Royale.[27] And again, two years in prison, augmented by a two-hundred-franc fine, for the tailoress Rosalie Kosakowska, *femme* Niemic, who had turned her lodgings into a meeting-place for Polish refugees.[28]

The military tribunals of the Third Republic dealt harshly with these minor female members of the Commune. In an appendix I have added an account of some further trials and sentences.

CHAPTER FIFTEEN

---◅◈▻---

FROM AUBERIVE TO NEW CALEDONIA

I N MY MIND'S EYE, I see Auberive, with its narrow walks winding under the fir trees, its large dor-
mitories where the wind whistled as if on shipboard,
headdresses and their kerchiefs folded about their necks—
seemed like peasant women of a hundred years ago."[1]

Thus Louise Michel described the prison where, one
by one, the other sentenced women joined her: Nathalie
Lemel; Sophie Poirier; Béatrix Excoffon; Mme. Richoux;
Mme. Bruteau, "who looked like a marquise, with her
white hair sweeping back from her young face"; Marie
Chiffon who, as she put her prison number on her arm,
cried "Long live the Commune!"; and old Mme. Delettra,
"who had already fought at Lyon, during the period

when the workers in the silk factories wrote "Live working, die fighting."[2]

To the prison situation imposed upon her, Louise Michel's response was that of a poet. She wrote poetry about Ferré—whom she may have loved, and who was shot—about her dead friends, and about the defeated Revolution:

> Blow, O winter winds; and fall yet more, O snow,
> Beneath your icy veils we're closer to the dead,
> Endless be the night, and shortened be the day,
> In winter we're as one with the cold friends we
>   mourn. . . .

In August, 1873, Louise Michel and nineteen other women left Auberive for New Caledonia. They went aboard an old sailing frigate, the *Virginie*. The prisoners were locked up in iron cages, but they were permitted to take an occasional stroll on deck. The sea enchanted the landlocked, captive Louise Michel, offering her an escape from the iron cells. She who had known nothing but Chaumont, Paris, and the countryside of her childhood, passionately discovered the savage grandeur of the ocean. They were passing then by way of Cape Horn: "We saw the southern polar sea, where, in the dead of night, the snow was falling on the deck."[3] Here Louise Michel approaches the same experience as Melville's.

Rochefort was along on the trip, and exchanged poems with Louise Michel—a strange flirtation between prisoners.

From Rochefort:

> When today we saw that seal,
> I was reminded of the Past:
> Bald Rouher with his greasy hands.
> And those sharks they were fishing for
> To me seemed like the lopped-off members
> Of the *Commission des Grâces*. . . .[4]

Louise Michel answered this in a loftier tone:

The sight of these abysses makes me drunk.
Higher, O waves, and stronger, O winds,
Life itself becomes too dear
So vast, here, are one's dreams. . . .[5]

At the very depths of destitution, Louise Michel gave the little that she possessed. The captain, seeing her barefoot, sent her a pair of slippers by way of Rochefort, assuming that from Rochefort she would accept them. But three days later she had given up her footwear again, and was once more running barefoot on the deck. Forgetting that she was a prisoner, she was outraged at seeing sailors catching albatrosses with a hook, and made them stop that cruel form of hunting.

Finally they arrived at New Caledonia. The prison director wanted to send the women to a penitential colony run by nuns. But Louise Michel protested: since they had been sentenced as men, it was right that they should suffer the same penalty.

Therefore Louise Michel and Nathalie Lemel, like Rochefort, were sent to the Ducos peninsula. The deportees had straw huts for shelter; the food was bad and the water brackish. The food was cooked in the Polynesian style: a hole dug in the ground, and stones heated to a red-hot intensity in the fire; no soap; clothes shredded to tatters; chains and the whip for punishment. Many prisoners died from their privations.

Since they had demanded that the civil law be applied to them, the women were subject to the same regulations. But they had furthermore to submit to the policemen's abuses and the commandant's insults. Several were young and pretty, but never, one of their companions tells us, were these women who were imprisoned with eight hundred men "a cause of scandal or of brawling or of dispute."[6]

Louise Michel, Nathalie Lemel, Marie Schmitt, Marie Cailleux, and two other women received the order to leave the Numbo Camp for the West Bay. Nathalie Lemel protested. She did not refuse to live in the hut assigned to her, but she called attention to the fact that she was ill, in which state it was impossible for her to do her own moving, or to gather and cut her own wood; that she had built two henhouses and tilled a portion of land; and that, finally, "pursuant to the law concerning deportation which says that deportees may live in groups or in families, and which leaves them the choice of the people with whom they please to associate, Deportee Duval, *femme* Lemel, refuses community life, unless it be under these conditions."[7] Louise Michel protested, in her turn, and asked if this was to be a new outrage inflicted upon them. The transfer of the women prisoners took place notwithstanding, and they obtained permission to divide the large hut provided for them into smaller cabins, so that they could live with what women they chose.[8]

Because of the richness of her personality and the strength of her character, Louise Michel bore up better than the others under the conditions of exile. For one thing, the beauty of the land accorded with her romantic soul. Cyclones sent her into transports of wonder:

Sometimes a huge red lightning-flash rends the darkness, or reveals a single purple glow upon which the black waves float, as if in mourning. The thunder, the roughness of the sea, the alarm gun in the harbor, the noise of the water pouring down in torrents—it is all one single, immense, superb sound, the orchestra of savage nature.

And also, this woman who had studied natural sciences, who had once taken up the discipline of Claude Bernard, studied the Caledonian flora and fauna and the camouflage devices of insects. She tried to apply the principle of

vaccination to diseased papaw trees. An intelligent governor, M. de la Richerie, authorized her to experiment on
the trees in the area.

Finally, and particularly, there were the people.
Whereas many of the deported *Communards* shared the
other whites' scorn of the natives, Louise Michel made
friends with a Polynesian employee of the penitentiary
administration, "who wanted to learn the things the
whites know." She gave him lessons; in exchange, he
taught her the rudiments of the Polynesian dialects. Then
she plunged deep into the jungle to look for tribes still
practicing cannibalism; she succeeded in gaining the confidence of one of these, and collected its legends and its
music. She did not share Rousseau's theoretical admiration
for the "noble savages," but neither did she take part in
"civilized" scorn for them. She studied them as an eth-
nographer, and loved them because they were a part of
humanity. When, in 1878, a native revolt broke out,
some of the *Communards* joined the army of repression;
but Louise Michel took the part of the Polynesians and
secretly aided them. The insurrection was drowned in
blood. As for the Arab deportees from Algeria, "they were
simple and good, and of great justice," remarked Louise
Michel.

But at the same time, she fought for the well-being of
the deportees, wrote to an Australian magazine to make
known the punishments to which they were subjected, and
demanded that she, as well as her companions, be treated
with dignity.[9]

In 1879, those deportees who had a trade obtained permission to settle in Nouméa. There Louise Michel resumed her profession as schoolteacher. At first her only
students were deportees' children, but the mayor soon
entrusted her with teaching music and drawing in the
girls' schools.[10]

There had been marriages among the sentenced men

and women. Henri Place married Marie Cailleux, and Langlois, Élizabeth Deguy.[11] Most of these women behaved "well" according to the rules of bourgeois, penitentiary morality. At L'Île-des-Pins, Lucie Boisselin (Mme. Leblanc) worked hard, took good care of her children, "behaved well," and had "right ideas."[12] So, too, did Marie Braun (Mme. Testot), who lived with her husband and worked as a laundress.[13] Anne Collot, *femme* Gobert, was able to save, from her work, a sum of 600 francs.[14] Marie Gaboriaud lived with her husband Jules Chiffon, who manfully tilled his land grant. She washed the linen of the staff, and "behaved well."[15] Victorine Gorget, despite her "fanatical" nature, proved to be submissive and directed by a "good spirit."[16] Jeanne Petit, a houseworker at Nouméa, did not associate with the prisoners, and had "very good behavior," but her "fanaticism"—that is, her loyalty to the ideas of the Commune— did not cease to trouble the penitentiary administration.[17] Suzanne Preu, *femme* Dutour, lived "on very good terms" with her son, and displayed "good morality."[18]

On the other hand, Marie Cailleux had only "passable behavior," and "bad opinions."[19] Marie Schmitt, *femme* Gaspard, was directed by a "bad spirit." Her conduct and morals were dubious, and she spent her time with a male deportee (with whom, moreover, she had been living since she had arrived there).[20] As for Louise Desfossés, *femme* Boulant, she was often drunk, and had "disgusting morals."[21] Marie Leroy generally suspect, had married a third husband, and was unfavorably regarded even by the deportees.[22]

Here too, the characters of this story retain their individuality. The women of the Commune were of every description.

Those women who were sentenced to death and whose sentences had been commuted, were sent to Guiana, whose climate was known for its unhealthiness. There we find the canteen worker Lachaise, Marceline Expilly, and the "*pétroleuses*" Joséphine Marchais, Élizabeth Rétiffe, and Eugénie Suétens, as well as Anne-Marie Menand and Marie-Jeanne Moussu. In 1871, the Governor of Guiana complained that these women produced "incessant demands" on the penitentiary personnel, and created "perpetual complications." But since they had to serve their sentences in Guiana, it was impossible to send them back to France into local jails. The Governor of Guiana therefore asked the Naval Minister for permission to give them a conditional release, as was done for the native women.[23] The Governor of Guiana's "complications" were not to last much longer. A partial amnesty was passed in 1879; the full amnesty for all the sentenced men and women of the Commune—at least, those who were still alive—was passed in 1880.

A report by Captain Briot, Deputy Public Prosecutor of the Fourth Council of War, tried, in its own way, to give an outline of women's participation in the Commune.[24] There were 1,051 women brought, he said, before the Councils of War. In 850 cases there were no grounds for prosecution. The others, as we have seen, suffered penalties ranging from the death sentence (which was always commuted) to prison terms. Seeking the causes which led women to participate in the Commune, Captain Briot indiscriminately listed: the state of concubinage, depravity, and dissolution; the flaws in the regulation of prostitution; the lack of surveillance by special police squads; the admittance into Saint-Lazare, and consequent maintenance in the capital, of persons whose past history and whose corruption posed a permanent danger to public peace and morality; socialistic theories, which led to dissoluteness; the meetings and the Clubs; immoral and obscene publications; the machinations of the International; and the organization of the Central Committee of the *Union des Femmes.*

The number of prostitutes or former prostitutes (still according to Captain Briot), was said to have 246, out of 1,051 women arrested. This ratio, which seems very high, is not borne out by the files that have come down to us. However that may be, low wages were, as we have seen, the primary cause of prostitution in the nineteenth century. For many women, such work was the sole means society offered them of "earning a living," or of compensating for wages that were often uncertain, and always inadequate. Yet it is understandable that women, who are the first to suffer under the social order, would have a hand in a revolutionary movement aimed at changing that order. A prostitute taking part in a revolutionary movement is performing an act of human dignity. However, we must admit that most of them, degraded for good by their "profession," much more often collaborate with the police, and are "respectful" of the established order. And it is of course only too obvious that the virtuous indignation of the Councils of War with regard to prostitution is simply one more social hypocrisy.

Captain Briot put socialist and revolutionary propaganda on the same level with "immoral and obscene publications"—a juxtaposition that does not seem worth discussing. In general, socialist morality bears the stamp of puritanism, as the motions made in the Clubs indicated on several occasions.

Many women who joined the ranks of the Commune did not seem to be motivated by ideological impulses. Some of them were content to go along with their husbands or lovers in the ranks of the Federals. But others, on the contrary, were for the first time performing a political act, were for the first time participating in political life, from which they had always been excluded.

From this viewpoint, the *Union des Femmes,* which implicitly defended the equality of men and women in society and demanded an equal salary for the same work, was obviously a scandal—as the Government Commissioner strove to demonstrate in a patently ridiculous manner during the trial of the *"pétroleuses."*

Like the Federals themselves, these women of the Commune were recruited primarily from the working class. The Parisian working and artisan class claimed 756 of them: seamstresses, embroiderers, cleaning women, laundresses, linen-drapers, dressmakers, bookbinders, and so forth. We find only one landlady, four schoolteachers, thirty-three proprietors of hotels or cafés, eleven shop- or workroom-owners; 246 are "without profession."

But, apart from a few exceptions, the women who played a real role during the Commune—such as Louise Michel, Marguerite Tinayre, André Léo, or the Russian women Elizabeth Dmitrieff and Anna Jaclard—came from comfortable backgrounds and embraced the cause of socialism because of intellectual motives. They furnish proof, once again, that although opinions and attitudes are most often conditioned by social affiliation, there exists a margin of freedom which allows *the choice of a cause* to each man or woman. Now whatever were the mistakes and shortcomings of the Commune and its supporters, the cause remained—that of a society in the process of transformation, a society in which equality, freedom, and justice were no longer to be words devoid of meaning. However mediocre they may often have been, the *Communards* nonetheless embodied a hope which transcended them, a hope of which they were the agents, the witnesses, and the martyrs.

We shall leave the task of turning the women of the Commune into chaste heroines to the hagiographers of revolutions. But it would be equally untrue to make them into the despicable harpies described by Maxime du Camp and other reactionary historians. At the level of the masses, as at the apex, history is composed of individuals, whose essential natures are difficult to grasp. Good or bad, as Diderot would have said, cowardly or brave, who knows? We can try to grasp them only through their actions, and they constantly elude us, for their actions are ambiguous and capable of various—and contradictory—interpretations. Nonetheless, "mass movements" are achieved by men and women, each one unique, each one different. Angels and devils, models of virtue and harpies, all rub elbows in the crowds of the Commune, no more and no less so than in the courts of kings. The historians who lean toward sociology, of course, are interested only in the totality. For my own part, I have tried to do something else—probably not entirely successfully: to break up the masses into their elements, to reach the individual cells that compose them. The documents are incomplete, sketchy, and inadequate. I have come across names and deeds, but who were Élizabeth Rétiffe, Eugénie Suétens, Eulalie Papavoine—those humble women hurled into a great cause? In the end, no one will ever know.

And it is at this point, perhaps, that myth is closer to truth than is history—the poetic myth that Victor Hugo, Rimbaud, and Verlaine helped to forge.

Jean-Baptiste Clément's *Le Temps des Cerises,* which for so long was sung by all the boys and girls in Paris, and which became the melancholy refrain of the last barrel-organs, was dedicated to a Commune ambulance nurse.

And the women of the Commune also cropped up in other popular songs. In Emmanuel Delorme's *Pimprelette:*

> One day they put up the barricades,
> The two of them went down the stairs . . .[25]

Eugène Pottier was the composer of the most famous and widespread song, *L'Internationale:*

Even in their mothers' wombs
The kids are *pétroleurs* already,
To put an end to thievery
No methods are too arbitrary.
. . . Even a pregnant girl was taken,
And so we had to shoot for two
Give it a shot,
Give it a shot,
For the love of God, give it a shot.[26]

Trohel, a Blanquist, and the typographical worker Achille Le Roy honored Louise Michel:

You won't forget that modern Joan . . .[27]

or:

She stood and faced the troops of Versailles . . .[28]

But we are indebted to Hugo, Verlaine, and Rimbaud, for having offered the greatest tribute.

Victor Hugo, who never made any distinctions between his poetic and his civic activity, did not limit himself to interceding for the Commune supporters condemned to death. He put his pity and his genius at the service of the vanquished, as he had already done in *Les Châtiments*. For him, the use of words was no empty game; his poetry was at the service of "practical truth." Therefore, he put into (alas, not always good) verse the news that reached him at Brussels. He drew the world's attention to the terrible repression that followed the Commune:

The prisoner passes, she's wounded, her brow
Bears the mark of who knows what confession.
And now
She's reviled . . .

What, then, impelled her to ally herself with the insurgents? Hunger, no doubt, or the love of a man.

And Hugo contrasts the wounded woman's misery with the obscene delights of the men of Versailles, and of their wives who, "with the carved handle of their silk parasols," poke about in the wound of the captive woman.[29]

In his poem to Louise Michel, he is no longer describing poor, wretched, helpless women, but a lucid and courageous revolutionary who totally accepted the fate that she had chosen:

> Because you had seen the vast slaughter, the
>   battle,
> The People crucified, Paris reduced to tatters,
> An awe-inspiring pity was in the words you said.
> What all the great, wild spirits do, you did:
> You fought and dreamed and suffered. "I have
>   killed," you cried,
> For, weary of all these, you wanted now to die.

Hugo evokes the whole trial of Louise Michel, the accusation of the Paris fires, which she admitted to:

> Terrible, more than human, you lied against
>   yourself . . .
> "I burned the palaces," you said for all to hear,
> You glorified all those downtrodden and accused.
> You cried, "Since I have killed, kill me . . ."

And the judges were hesitant, looking at the "severe, guilty woman."

Then the poet brings his personal evidence to bear. He had known her since her youth, in the far-off time when, at Vroncourt, she still called herself Mlle. Demahis. Thus he recalls

> Your days, your nights, your cares, the tears you
>   shed for all,
> Your self-forgetfulness in giving others aid,
> Your word that was akin to the Apostle's flame,

and also her poverty, her goodness, her pride in being a
"woman of the people."

> You were so high, you seemed estranged from all
>   these quarrels;
> For all the creatures here are trivial and squalid,
> And nothing irks them more than two com-
>   mingled souls,
> The holy turbulence of things that are bestarred
> Reflected in the deeps of a great, starry heart,
> A ray of light seen bursting, blazing to a
>   flame. . . .[30]

Much later, in 1886, Verlaine, too, paid tribute to
Louise Michel, in a ballad reminiscent of Villon:

> Madame and Pauline Roland,
> Charlotte, Théroigne, and Lucile,
> Almost Joan of Arc—a jewel
> In the idiot rabble's crown;
> Heavenly name and heart, exiled
> By bourgeois France of supple spine:
> Listen, good-for-nothing wretches,
> Louise Michel is doing fine.[31]

And Rimbaud exalts the struggle of the entire working
class, in Les Mains de Jeanne-Marie:

> The hands of Jeanne-Marie are strong,
> Dark hands tanned by summer's heat,
> Hands as pallid as the dead.
> —Are these the hands of Juana?

> . . . At Madonnas' ardent feet
> Have they scattered golden blossoms?
> Within their palms there bursts and sleeps
> The black blood of belladonnas.

... A miracle: they have gone pale
Under the sun of burdened love,
Upon the bronze artillery
Throughout the town risen to arms.[32]

Hugo, Verlaine, and Rimbaud have woven crowns for the seamstresses, laundresses, cleaning women, and school-teachers of the Commune. Is there any queen who can boast of having gathered such court poets about her?

APPENDIX

---◄◆►---

FURTHER SENTENCES

AMONG THE DOSSIERS that have come down to us, we find those of several canteen workers of the Commune. Various sentences were meted out to them, ranging from hard labor to a year in prison.

To one canteen worker, Élisa Rousseau, *femme* Cabot, born in Louviers in 1832, fifteen years of hard labor: she had gone with the 84th Battalion, and had brought about the arrest of a member of the National Guard, who was executed for treason. And finally, she was alleged to have stated that she had fired fourteen cannon shots.[1] Adèle Desfossés, *femme* Boulant, born in Péronne in 1832, was sentenced to banishment to a fortress. She had been a canteen worker for the 238th Battalion, and had taken part in the fighting at Issy. But she had also been accused of looting, for among her things they had found a stuffed otter and stuffed birds, a dressing case, and a slop-basin, all of which had come from the Couvent des Oiseaux, where her battalion had been quartered.[2]

Marie Schmitt, born in Obreck, Moselle, in 1837, was the wife of a manufacturer of military equipment. She followed her husband, Gaspard, who was in the National Guard, to the 101st Battalion. She had been seen dressed in a uniform and carrying a rifle, firing in the defense of La Butte-aux-Cailles. She was a former prostitute, and her brazen attitude toward the audience antagonized the Council of War:

"I am sorry," she said, "that I did not do everything I am accused of."

She, too, was sent to New Caledonia.[3]

Sentenced to simple deportation, Marie-Delphine Derviillé, *femme* Dupré, was also exiled to New Caledonia. She had been a canteen worker in the 73rd Battalion, where her husband was, and had gone along with the Federals in their sorties. But she was also accused of having illegally confined two nuns who had been removed from the Picpus convent. "She was fanatically devoted to the Commune."[4]

The linen-draper Célestine Gallois, wife of the manual laborer Jean-Baptiste Vayeur, was born in Naives, Meuse, in 1830; she was sentenced to simple deportation, and, moreover, loss of her civic rights. (Her police record was rather lengthy.) At Courbevoie she had boasted of having "forced her milksop commander to lead back the Federals under fire coming from Mont-Valérien." She had brought about the arrest of her neighbor, a former policeman who was released three hours later. "She is a dangerous woman, whom it is important to keep at a remove from society." But at Auberive, as in the Rouen prison, she displayed "good conduct" and also "right opinions." Her sentence of exile was commuted to ten years' imprisonment, in November 1875, then reduced by a year in 1877, and by six months in 1879. She wrote to the minister on January 29, 1879, to ask him for a full pardon:

> I am writing, Monsieur le Ministre, to present my apologies to you, and to place at your feet the mistakes that I made in being involved with the Commune, begging you to grant pardon to a poor forty-nine-year-old woman, who has become a widow since entering prison (my husband died at Belle-Isle, at sea, also a prisoner, leaving a sixteen-year-old son without support), and who has a very old mother whom she wants to see again, since she is always ill. . . .[5]

The laundress Marie-Virginie Vrecq, *femme* Bediet, born in Bougival, in 1846, was known by the name of her lover Captain Vinot of the 170th Battalion, who soon became colonel in the *Vengeurs de Paris*. "La Colonelle" went with her lover to the barricade near the church of Saint-Ambroise, and when he was wounded, helped him to escape from the Versailles soldiers. She was unwarrantedly accused of being mixed up in the Rue Haxo executions, but in the end nothing was sustained against her except that she had taken part in the insurrection: she was sentenced to simple deportation.[6] If "La Colonelle" seemed energetic, violent, awesome, nothing would have given any indication that Jeanne Bertranine, *femme* Taillefer (born July 4, 1831, in Lasseubetat, Basses-Pyrénées), would join the ranks of the Commune. "Gentle and quiet, she had never before been the object of any unfavorable comment," we read in her dossier. The Commune transformed her. For two months, she followed her husband in the 118th Battalion, in a canteen worker's uniform, pistol at her waist. She was in all the sorties, and, on May 23, she went along with the armed National Guards to summon the tenants of her house to the barricade on the Place Maubert. She was arrested at Ménilmontant and sent to New Caledonia. The gentle and quiet Jeanne Bertranine, who sold fried fish, was too proud to lodge an appeal for pardon.[7]

It was also for the purpose of following her husband, a machine repairman, that Lucie-Euphrasie Boisselin, *femme* Leblanc, accompanied the 84th Battalion armed with a small rifle. She had worked at the Rue de Bussy barricade, but she tried to exonerate herself: she had not served the Commune because of political conviction. She wrote in her plea for pardon:

> under the Government of National Defense she had accepted the position of canteen worker for the 84th Battalion of the National Guard, and had had to keep this job after March 18 in view of the total lack of work, and because she had no other resources. . . . It had never entered her mind to harm the Government, but at that time seeing no other means of subsistence, and unaware of the events that were taking place and of their consequences, she believed that she was doing no wrong by keeping the insignificant job that she held during the Government of National Defense.

At L'Île-des-Pins, in New Caledonia, she worked hard to bring up her two children, and gave the penitentiary administration no cause for reproach.[8]

Other canteen workers were sentenced to one to five years in prison.

As for the women whom we saw building barricades, they too received various sentences. Marie-Augustine Gaboriaud, *femme* Chiffon, "who had always displayed the greatest sympathy for the Commune," was sentenced to twenty years at hard labor.[9] Élodie Duvert, *femme* Richoux, was sentenced to banishment to a fortress.[10]

The day-worker Marguerite Fayon appeared before the Council of War on October 16, 1871. She was a small, fragile, slightly deformed woman; only thirty-five, she appeared to be fifty. She seemed "endowed with great energy." "And the way she looked at the witnesses who came to give evidence against her makes sufficiently clear what she must have done when she found a firm support among the National Guards of the Commune, over whom she seems to have exercised a certain authority," wrote the reporter of the *Gazette des Tribunaux*. She was accused of having denounced a policeman's wife, and of having detonated Orsini bombs.* But in the end they could sustain against her only that she had handed out cartridges to the Federals during the Bloody Week fighting. She was sentenced to simple banishment.[11] The same sentence went to the hairdresser Eugénie Bruteau, née Rousseau, who had led men, women, and children to the barricades.[12] Twenty years of confinement for Joséphine Courtois, widow of Delettra, who was already called "Queen of the Barricades" in 1848, at Lyon.[13] For the others, the sentences varied from a year to five years.

The Commune had had to create its own army, courts, and police. The denunciations of Versailles agents appeared, to the Versailles government, crimes which came under civil law. It is certain that denunciations are always

---

* Mercury fulminate bombs, named after an Italian patriot, Felice Orsini, who used three such bombs in an attempt to assassinate Napoleon III, when the Emperor, the Empress Eugénie, and the imperial party were leaving the Opéra on January 14, 1858. The imperial couple was not injured, although several bystanders were killed and many wounded. Even though Orsini was wrong in assuming that an assassination attempt would provoke revolution in France—and consequently in Italy—it did galvanize Napoleon into his long-planned policy of encouraging the Italian cause.—*Trans.*

very unpleasant, even if the circumstances seem to justify them. Police tasks are repugnant to our sense of morality.

One Commune decree had compelled men from nineteen to forty years of age to enter the National Guard. The women were given the responsibility of tracking down draft dodgers, as well as Versailles agents remaining in Paris whose activities might be feared (and rightly so). The women's battalion organized in the 12th arrondissement was specifically charged with this task. And it was for having been party to an illegal arrest—illegal in the eyes of Versailles, legal in those of the Commune—that the seamstress Marie-Catherine Rogissart was sentenced. We saw her earlier speaking at the *Club Saint-Éloi*, and, wearing an armband, taking part in the women's battalion, of which she was the flagbearer. They found in her room a red poster having to do with the organization of that battalion, a kerosene lamp, and a quantity of kerosene that was so little that it was obviously only for the purpose of filling the lamp. But she had had one of her neighbors arrested.

"It is true that I had Lutz arrested, but not as a draft dodger. One day he was making noise in the house where I live. He was drunk. He had a rifle in his hand, and it went off. I had him arrested because he was disturbing the peace and quiet of the house."

And Lutz confirmed this, as the listeners burst out laughing: "One day, I came back home somewhat under the influence of . . ." But another witness testified that Marie-Catherine Rogissart had denounced him to the Central Committee as a Versailles spy. He had been released after his house was searched.

Marie-Catherine Rogissart had always given vent to opinions favorable to the Commune: "Although without education, she had a facile tongue, and misused it by talking politics," a neighbor declared. And she urged the men to fight:

"I'll make you all go, you're nothing but a bunch of chair-warmers," she said. "Me, I'm a woman, and I have more courage than any of you. Like it or not, you're going to fight the Versailles murderers. . . ."

Although she had no previous criminal record, and could scarcely be accused of anything except living "in concubinage"; although the arrest of Lutz was warranted by his drunken state; although she could be accused of no active participation in the "crimes of the Commune"— she was sentenced to seven years of hard labor.[14]

Sidonie Marie Herbelin, *femme* Letteron, was a member of the *Club de l'Église de la Villette,* which she used to call "the Black Crows' barn." She was accused of having invaded a policeman's house, of leading a battalion of women, and of looting. She had been seen with a red banner at the burial of a canteen worker. "Having done everything she could to ensure the triumph of the insurrection," Sidonie Marie Herbelin was sentenced to banishment to a fortress.[15]

Louise Elisa Keinerknecht, née Neckebecker, was also part of the women's battalion, where she held the rank of captain. She had been seen, too, at the *Club de l'Église Saint-Éloi* and the *Club de l'Église Saint-Bernard,* where she had taken up a collection; five years in prison, and ten years of surveillance by a parole board.[16]

Other women who do not seem to have participated in the 12th arrondissement battalion or in the *Union des Femmes* (their names are not to be found there) were prosecuted for denouncing policemen and their wives. For these simple women of the people—seamstresses, laundresses, cleaning women, and prostitutes too—the shameful regime was concentrated in the authority of the policeman, entirely devoted to the Versailles government by virture of the function he performed.

There was a former prostitute, Joséphine Poinboeuf, called Allix, born in Theillay, Loir-et-Cher in 1841; her lover had taken her out of a house of prostitution. Her feelings for the Commune were well known, and she had brought about the arrest of a policeman who was taken to the municipal building in the 17th arrondissement. However, he was released immediately. Fifteen years of hard labor for Allix.[17]

Ten years of hard labor to the cook Mélanie Jacques, *femme* Gauthier, born in Briare in 1820, for denouncing the wife of a policeman. "Assuming that the government of the Commune was a legal one, she believed that she was doing a patriotic deed by denouncing the Zehr woman."[18]

The same sentence went to a trousers maker, Claudine Lemaître, *femme* Garde, born in 1836 in Onlay, Nièvre; she had caused the arrest of a lady named Meyer, the wife of a former police commissioner—a stool-pigeon, Claudine said—and a Mme. Luchaire, the widow of a policeman. Luchaire's uniforms, papers, and decorations were defenestrated, to the great delight of the spectators gathered in the street. Claudine Lemaître acknowledged having taken part in these arrests, but not in the looting.[19]

Five years of hard labor for Rosalie Joséphine Delavot, *femme* Gaillardot, who pointed out a lieutenant and a policeman's wife as Versailles agents.[20] Banishment to a fortress for a concierge, Marie-Anne Dumoulin, *femme* Ajame, who chased after policemen's wives, threatening them. Apart from this, she was considered a worthy and respectable woman; but she was utterly loyal to the Commune and thought that, in so doing, she was serving it.[21]

Marie Audrain, *femme* Vincent, born in 1821 in Donges, Loire-Inférieure, was a housekeeper whose employers gave her "good references," and whose neighbors attested to her "irreproachable life and morality." But she had taken up with the Federal Colonel Laporte, who commanded the 6th sector. A staunch supporter of the Commune, she attempted to enroll men, and also women of the neighborhood "to go and avenge their husbands and brothers who were being struck down." She denounced the wives and sons of policemen. She was first arrested for seditious remarks, and then was released. But after more information, she was arrested anew, and sentenced to hard labor for life. Her trial was invalidated because of a clerical error; at the retrial Marie Audrain was sentenced to only ten years of reclusion—an adequate indication of how arbitrary were the sentences imposed upon the Commune supporters. At Auberive, Marie Audrain retained her convictions, and showed no signs of any "repentance." She was even condemned to two months of solitary confinement for insolence toward the Inspector General, the Baron de Watteville.[22]

The denunciations did not concern merely the bulwarks of the traditional order and their families, but also Versailles agents and draft dodgers.

The day-worker Thérèse Lecomte, born in Bazeilles, Ardennes, in 1836, was sentenced to five years of hard labor and twenty years' surveillance by a parole board, for having accused a neighboring woman of being in communication with Versailles. But a Federal officer did not want to take the responsibility for this arrest. The denounced woman was released after two days. Thérèse Lecomte also denounced her concierge, and it is not hard to believe that this was only a question of private vengeance. But the day when they were fighting around the barricades on the Boulevard Mazas, she pointed out to the Federals which men were taking flight.[23]

A laundress, Suzanne-Augustine Preu, *femme* Dutour, who had had a man named Costes arrested, was condemned to simple exile. The man had said that the Versailles government ought to send all the *Communards* to Cayenne. His arrest came to nothing; however, rifles and military clothing were found at the Dutours'.[24]

Simple exile, again, for the laundress Victorine Gorget,

born in 1843, in Paris, who had spoken at the *Club Saint-Michel des Batignolles* to demand a strong organization and the mobilization of all the nation's active force; and she had said to one of her neighbors that "the women ought to take up arms to guard the ramparts while the men go out on sorties against the Versailles troops." On May 23, she had stated that she was going to go back with the National Guard to "arrest the loafers who are hiding out." But she had been unable to go any farther than the command post.[25]

The same sentence for Anne Collot, *femme* Gobert, dayworker, against whom nothing could be sustained except that she had insulted "the decent folk" who stood up for Versailles, and had encouraged her husband to take up arms. But when they came to arrest her, she dared to say that they had no right to make arrests at night, and called the agents "rabble, butchers, acting in the name of a government of butchers, which lets decent people die of hunger or else shoots them."[26]

Anne Collot could scarcely be accused of anything except her remarks. By contrast, Joséphine Semblat, née Taveau, got five years in prison; on May 26, leading a group of Commune sailors, she went to arrest some draft dodgers hidden in her house.[27] Five years' imprisonment or reclusion were handed out to many others because of similar acts.

Finally, one last category included a certain number of sentences for "theft and looting." Some thefts, doubtless, can be subsumed under "civil law," although armies, on whichever side, have always had the tendency to consider abandoned or gutted houses as property that no longer belongs to anyone.

Henriette-Marie Dellière and Octavie Cornet were sentenced by the 13th Council of War to two years in prison and five years on parole, the one for having accepted jewels

from her lover, the other for having taken a sewing machine.[28] But the sentences were heavier when it came to
the Palais des Tuileries or Thiers' own private house.
Ten years of hard labor for the seamstress Alexandrine
Théodore Simon, widow of Godin; she had received a
fur coat belonging to General Trochu.[29] Twenty years of
hard labor and 5,000 francs' fine for Ernestine Garçon,
femme Coleau, at whose house they had found a New
Testament, a magnifying glass, and a paper-knife belonging to Thiers. This was rather stiff. But Ernestine Garçon
took refuge in Belgium; for the same "crime," however,
her lover was sentenced to only two years in prison.[30]

These cases are hardly political in nature. But another
affair seems much more significant. This had to do with,
not an individual theft, but a "legal" requisition, in the
context of the redistribution of property.

Marie-Joséphine Miguet, *femme* Parfond, a button
worker born in 1848 in Saint-Maurice-sur-Fessard, Loiret,
was sentenced to five years' reclusion on February 19, 1872,
for complicity in the looting of a store "in a gang, and by
open force." Some grocers on the Rue des Amandiers had
left Paris on March 18, and had abandoned their store
without a watchman. During the last days of the Commune, some members of the National Guard, led by the
Police Commissioner of the Père-Lachaise district, called
in a locksmith to get the door open. The Federals had
said that the grocer was a traitor to the Commune, and
that they were going to take away his merchandise "to
give it to poor people who don't have anything."

The ambulance worker Marie Parfond went along with
them, and voiced her approval: "Yes, that's very fair.
When I think that I have a husband who is under fire, and
that, at a time like this, there are people who run away
to get out of doing their service. . . ."

All the commodities were taken to the Ménilmontant
church to be distributed. One of the grocers, however,

later found some bottles that the Federals had not emptied, despite the reputation they have been given as drunkards. At Marie Parfond's lodgings a package was also found containing toilet articles belonging to the grocer's wife. In defending herself, Marie Parfond asserted that she had not entered the store, and that she had picked up the package from the street; she had intended to return it to its owner. Marie Parfond had no previous criminal record. But in spite of her denials before the Council of War, one can easily imagine that she had indeed participated in an operation which had no other purpose save that of distributing commodities that had been left behind by Versailles supporters.[31] This activity belongs to a social policy which the Commune conducted with the most extreme prudence (we know that the Commune did not tackle the Banque de France, and that individual property was, in general, handled with kid gloves; the demolition of Thiers' house belongs to the realm of symbols).

But like every government in time of war, the Commune effected "requisitions" of commodities, horses, and stores. The *Union des Femmes*, in the context of the reorganization of work, had the task of looking for workshops abandoned by their owners. This it did, with great attention to legality.[32] But this revolutionary legality could not, obviously, be acceptable to the Versailles government. This is why the Councils of War always subsumed under "civil crimes" those deeds which most often grew out of activity that was revolutionary, and hence political.

Victor Hugo, who understood everything, was well aware of this and had the daring to say it. Interceding for those condemned to death, he wrote:

These wretches . . . have nothing to do with politics. Everyone is in agreement on that point. They are common delinquents, guilty of the ordinary misdemeanors provided for by the penal law in any period.

Let us get this straight: it makes absolutely no difference to me that everyone is of one mind concerning the excellence of these sentences. When it comes to judging an enemy, let us guard against the raging consensus of the mob, and against the cheering of our own party. . . . Let us challenge certain phrases, such as "common misdemeanors," "civil crimes"—these phrases are pliant, and easy to stretch to excessive sentences; they have the inconvenient quality of being useful. In politics, what is useful is dangerous. To confuse Marat and Lacenaire is easy, and has far-reaching consequences. It is certain that if the *Chambre Introuvable**—that of 1815, I mean—had come twenty years earlier, and if by chance it had triumphed over the Convention, it would have found excellent reasons for declaring the Republic to be a villainous thing; 1815 would have declared 1793 subject to common jurisdiction; the September massacres, the murders of bishops and priests, the destruction of public monuments, and the seizure of private property, would certainly not have been left out of its indictment; the White Terror† would have ordered legal proceedings against the Red Terror; the Royalist Chamber would have proclaimed the members of the Convention guilty in fact and in law of ordinary misdemeanors specified in, and punishable by, the criminal code. . . . In Danton it would have seen a cutthroat, in Camille Desmoulins an inciter to murder, in Saint-Just a killer, in Robespierre a felon pure and simple. It would have cried at all of them: "You are not men of politics." And

* See note, p. 50.—*Trans.*

† A series of rebellions shortly after the restoration of Louis XVIII, committed by Catholic Royalists in southern France against former supporters of Napoleon Bonaparte and the Republic, as well as against rich Protestants.—*Trans.*

public opinion would have said: "It's the truth"—until such time as the human conscience said: "It's a lie."[33]

Now the fighters of the Commune were also "revolutionary fighters"; they, too, can be accused only of "political deeds."

We must agree that these lines, written in 1871, lack neither perspicacity nor grandeur—and both were rare at that time.

NOTES

Introduction

1. Maxime du Camp, *Les Convulsions de Paris*, II, 86–90.
2. Charles-Aimé Dauban, *Le Fond de la société*, p. 21.
3. Alexandre Dumas *fils, Lettres sur les choses de ce jour*.
4. Benoît Malon, *La Troisième Défaite du Prolétariat français*, p. 272.
5. Hippolyte-Prosper-Olivier Lissagaray, *Histoire de la Commune de 1871*, p. 209.
6. Karl Marx, *La Guerre Civile en France, 1871*, pp. 88, 98.
7. P. Robert, *Dictionnaire alphabétique et analogique de la langue française*, vol. V. "*Pétroleur, -euse.* n. (1871, derived from *pétroler*.) Person who sets fires with kerosene. See: *brûleur, incendiaire*. Note: almost never used except in the feminine. The *pétroleuses* of the Commune: "She was a strange creature. Her grey, dishevelled hair gave her, in the meetings, the aspect of a *pétroleuse*." Martin du Gard, *Les Thibaut*, VI, p. 238. "He knew what a *pétroleuse* was: a hundred times he had seen that picture from *Le Monde Illustré* of 1871, in which two women, kneeling at night near a cellar vent, were lighting a sort of fire. Locks of hair streamed out of their workingwomen's bonnets." Mauriac, *Le Sagouin*, p. 49.

Chapter 1

1. Henriette Vanier, *La mode et ses métiers*, p. 194.
2. Jules Simon, *L'Ouvrière*, p. 212.
3. Vanier, *op. cit.*, p. 219; *Journal des Demoiselles*, February, 1865.
4. Simon, *op. cit.*
5. *Ibid.*, p. 269.
6. Victorine Brochon, *Souvenirs d'une morte vivante*, pp. 62–63.
7. *Ibid.*
8. Julie Daubié, *La femme pauvre au XIXᵉ siècle*, vol. II, 2.
9. Simon, *op. cit.*, p. 298.
10. Brochon, *op. cit.*, p. 71

11. *Ibid.*
12. Maurice Dommanget, *Hommes et choses de la Commune,* pp. 194–200; A.N. BB 24, 792, 4380, S. 73; A.G. IV, 688; *Gazette des Tribunaux,* September 11, 1872.
13. A.G. Council of War III, 1416; A.N. BB 24, 852, 732, S. 79.
14. Jules Paty, *Un Rêve de femme* and *La Marguerite.*
15. Paty, *La Marguerite.*
16. *Ibid.,* p. 265.
17. Paty, *Un Rêve de femme,* preface, p. ii.
18. *Ibid.,* II, 109.
19. *Ibid.,* p. 110.
20. *Ibid.,* p. 118.
21. Simon, *op. cit.,* pp. 400 ff.
22. Victor Hugo, *Carnets intimes,* pp. 44–45.
23. On Louise Michel, consult the study by Irma Boyer, *Les Mémoires* and *La Commune* by Louise Michel. Her dossier in the Archives de la Guerre: Council of War VI, 135; her dossier of reprieve in the Archives Nationales BB 24, 822, 4922, S. 76; her dossier in the Archives de la Préfecture de Police BA 1183; also the *Gazette des Tribunaux* for December 17, 1871.
24. Louise Michel, *Mémoires,* pp. 134–139.
25. A.G. VI, 135.
26. Michel, *Mémoires,* p. 146.
27. A.P. BA 1183, The Declaration of Louise Michel in *La Marseillaise,* January 21, 1869.

Chapter 2

1. A.P. BA 1183, Louise Michel's reply to an article in *Le Figaro,* December 7, 1861, published in *Justice,* August 13, 1880.
2. Maria Deraismes, *Œuvres complètes: Nos principes et nos mœurs. L'ancien devant le nouveau.*
3. Gustave Lefrançais, *Souvenirs d'un révolutionnaire,* pp. 296–297.
4. Marc de Villiers, *Histoire des clubs de femmes et des légions d'amazones,* p. 381; A.N. BB 24, 807, 5065 and 843, 8604; Krystyna Wyczanska, *Polacy w Komuna paryskiej 1871.* . . .
5. Lefrançais, *op. cit.,* pp. 322–323.

6. A. Perrier, "Grégoire Champseix et André Léo," in *L'Actualité de l'Histoire*, January–March, 1960; A.P. BA 1008.
7. Lefrançais, *op. cit.*, p. 298.
8. *Ibid.*, p. 301.
9. *Ibid.*, p. 302.
10. Villiers, *op. cit.*, p. 381.
11. Victorine Brochon, *Souvenirs d'une morte vivante*, p. 84.
12. Jules Vallès, *L'Insurgé*, p. 120.
13. Louise Michel, *La Commune*, p. 29.
14. Karl Marx, *La Guerre Civile en France, 1871*.
15. Michel, *La Commune*, p. 14.
16. *Ibid.*, pp. 61–62; *Mémoires*, pp. 163–165.
17. Brochon, *Souvenirs d'une morte vivante*, p. 115.
18. Michel, *La Commune*, p. 68.

Chapter 3

1. Victorine Brochon, *Souvenirs d'une morte vivante*, pp. 126 ff.; *Journal Officiel*, January 18, 1871.
2. *Journal Officiel*, January 19, 1871.
3. Brochon, *op. cit.*, p. 135.
4. *Complainte et récit véridique des maux soufferts par la population parisienne pendant le siège*. Paris: published by Matt, 7 Rue des Deux-Gares (B.N., Estampes).
5. Louise Michel, *La Commune*, p. 132; A.N. BB 24, 792, 4380, S. 73; A.G. Council of War IV, 688.
6. Brochon, *op. cit.*, p. 122.
7. Michel, *op. cit.*, p. 131; A.N. BB 24, 781, 11.688, S. 72; A.G. Council of War XXVI, 101.
8. A.G. Ly 23.
9. Michel, *op. cit.*, p. 129.
10. Brochon, *op. cit.*, p. 138.
11. *Ibid.*, pp. 145, 152.
12. G. de Molinari, *Les clubs rouges pendant le siège de Paris*, pp. 173–174.
13. A.N. BB 24, 845 11.147, S. 77.
14. A.N. BB 24, 751, 5051, S. 72.
15. André Léo: article in which she gave an historical account of the situation, *La Sociale*, April 12, 1871, and *La Commune*, April 14, 1871.
16. A facsimile of the poster is in M. de Villiers' *Histoire des clubs de femmes et des légions d'Amazones*, pp. 383–385.

17. André Léo, *op. cit.*
18. Michel, *Mémoires*, p. 169.
19. A.G. Council of War XXVI, 101.
20. A.P. BA 1183, November 27, 1870.
21. Michel, *Mémoires*.
22. A.N. BB 24, 792, 4380, S. 73.
23. Molinari, *op. cit.*, pp. 74–75.
24. *Ibid.*, p. 197.
25. *Ibid.*, p. 255.
26. Michel, *La Commune*, pp. 73–75; and *Mémoires*, pp. 185–186.
27. *Ibid.*
28. Michel, *La Commune*, p. 130; *Mémoires*, pp. 186–187; Victor Hugo, *Carnets intimes*, pp. 75–76.
29. Michel, *La Commune*, pp. 97, 161; Molinari, *op. cit.*, p. 263.
30. Michel, *Ibid.*, pp. 102–103; and A.P. BA 1008.
31. Molinari, *op. cit.*, p. 266.
32. H.-P.-O. Lissagaray, *Histoire de la Commune*, p. 85.
33. *Enquête parlementaire sur l'insurrection du 18 mars*, II, 364, the statement by Denormandie.
34. Michel, *La Commune*, p. 121; Augustine Blanchecotte, *Tablettes d'une femme pendant la Commune*, p. 2.

Chapter 4
1. Louise Michel, *La Commune*, p. 139.
2. Gaston da Costa, *La Commune vécue*, I, p. 11.
3. Michel, *op. cit.*, pp. 139–140.
4. *Ibid.*
5. Da Costa, *op. cit.*, p. 11.
6. *Ibid.*, p. 12.
7. *Enquête parlementaire sur l'Insurrection du 18 mars 1871*, II, p. 434, statement of General d'Aurelles de Paladine; *ibid.*, p. 472, statement of M. Ossude.
8. *Ibid.*
9. H.-P.-O. Lissagaray, *Histoire de La Commune*, p. 99; P. Lanjalley and Paul Corriez, *Histoire de la Révolution du 18 mars*, pp. 27–31.
10. Da Costa, *op. cit.*, pp. 21–25.
11. *Ibid.*
12. *Ibid.*, pp. 152–158.
13. *Le Vengeur*, March 30, 1871.

14. Lissagaray, *op. cit.*, p. 171.
15. Lanjalley and Corriez, *op. cit.*, p. 190.
16. *L'Action* and *Le Cri du Peuple*, April 4.
17. The account by Béatrix Excoffon in Louise Michel, *Mémoires*, pp. 406 ff; A.G. IV, 57.
18. Béatrix Excoffon's account.
19. *La Commune*, April 6.
20. *La Sociale*, April 5; *Le Cri du Peuple*, April 5.
21. *Ibid.*, and April 6.
22. *Le Cri du Peuple*, April 6.
23. *L'Action*, April 6.
24. A. Blanchecotte, *Tablettes d'une femme pendant la Commune*, p. 42.
25. *Ibid.*
26. *Le Cri du Peuple*, April 6.
27. Lissagaray, *op. cit.*, pp. 296, 291–292; Benoît Malon, *Troisième défaite*, p. 330; *Enquête parlementaire . . .*, statement by M. Gerspach, II, p. 258.
28. Malon, *op. cit.*, p. 272.
29. *Journal Officiel de la Commune*, April 20.
30. *Procès-Verbaux de la Commune*, I, p. 162.
31. Arthur Arnould, *Histoire populaire et parlementaire de la Commune*, II, pp. 124–125.
32. *Journal Officiel*, April 11; *La Commune*, April 11; *La Sociale*, April 12.
33. *Journal Officiel*, April 14; *Le Cri du Peuple*, April 16.
34. Lanjalley and Corriez, *op. cit.*, p. 385.
35. *Ibid.*, pp. 410–411; *Journal Officiel*, May 8; There is a facsimile in Jean Bruhat, Jean Dautry, and Émile Tersen, *La Commune de 1871*, p. 179.

Chapter 5

1. Benoît Malon, *Troisième défaite*, p. 274.
2. *Enquête Parlementaire*, II, pp. 261, 362.
3. A.G. Council of War VI, 683.
4. Ly 23.
5. Vassili Soukholmine, "Deux femmes russes combattantes de la Commune," *Cahiers internationaux*, May, 1950; P. Tchérednitchenko, "La vie généreuse et mouvementée d'Élise Tomanovskaïa, *Études Soviétiques*, June, 1955.
6. *L'Affranchi*, April 14; *Journal Officiel*, April 17; *Le Cri du Peuple*, April 22, 23, and 28.

7. A.G. Ly 23, Report signed by Elizabeth Dmitrieff.
8. *Ibid.*; *Statuts de l'Union des Femmes*; *La Sociale*, April 20, 1871.
9. A.G. Ly 23.
10. *Ibid.*; A.S. V *bis*, 388.
11. *Ibid.*; J. Bruhat, J. Dautry, and E. Tersen, *Histoire de la Commune de 1871*, p. 180.
12. *Le Réveil du Peuple*, May 1.
13. A.G. Ly 23.
14. *La Montagne*, April 16.
15. Maxime Vuillaume, *Mes Cahiers rouges*, II, p. 56.
16. H.-P.-O. Lissagaray, *Les huit journées de mai*, p. 292.
17. P. Fontoulieu, *Les Églises de Paris sous la Commune*, p. 48.
18. *Rapport sur la délégation de Levy-Lazare et Evette à l'habillement militaire et les conclusions de Léo Frankel* in *Journal Officiel*, May 13; Dauban, *Le fond de la société*, pp. 250–252.
19. A.G. Ly 23.
20. *Journal Officiel*, May 7.
21. A.G. Ly 23.
22. A.G. Ly 23, *Adresse du Comité central de l'Union des Femmes à la Commission du travail et d'échange*, signed by Elizabeth Dmitrieff.
23. Ly 23, Central Committee of the *Union des Femmes*.
24. A.G. Ly 23, Commune. Organizational plan for the Ministry of Public Works, Labor and Exchange.
25. *Le Cri du Peuple*, May 18.
26. *Le Vengeur*, May 14.
27. *La Sociale*, May 11; *Journal Officiel*, May 17.
28. A.G. Ly 23.
29. *Ibid.*, text written by Elizabeth Dmitrieff; *Journal Officiel*, May 18.
30. *Le Cri du Peuple*, May 22.

Chapter 6
1. Vassili Soukholmine, "Deux femmes russes . . ."; A.P. BA 1123.
2. A.G. Ly 23.
3. *Le Cri du Peuple*, April 26.
4. *Le Cri du Peuple*, May 2.
5. Account by Béatrix Excoffon in *La Commune* by Louise Michel, p. 407.

6. *La Révolution politique et sociale*, May 16.
7. Maxime du Camp, *Convulsions de Paris*, IV, pp. 250–251.
8. *Journal Officiel*, May 5.
9. Benoît Malon, *Troisième défaite*, pp. 269–271.
10. Lissagaray, *Histoire de la Commune*, pp. 297–299.
11. Article in *The Times*, dateline May 4, 1871; reprinted in *L'Étoile*, May 10.
12. P. Fontoulieu, *Les Églises de Paris sous la Commune*, p. 288.
13. *Les Femmes célèbres*, I, p. 307.
14. Fontoulieu, *op. cit.*, pp. 254–256.
15. A.N. BB 24, 861, 4567; Krystyna Wyczanska, *Polacy w Komuna paryskiej 1871*. . . .
16. *La Sociale*, May 6; *Journal Officiel*, May 6.
17. Fontoulieu, *op. cit.*, pp. 163–165.
18. A. Blanchecotte, *Tablettes d'une femme pendant la Commune*, p. 202.
19. *La Vérité*, April 28.
20. *Ibid.*, April 29.
21. *Ibid.*, May 2.
22. Fontoulieu, *op. cit.*, p. 160.
23. A.N. BB 24, 746, 4082, S. 72.
24. A.N. BB 24, 756, 5761, S. 72.
25. A.N. BB 24, 799, 981, S. 74.
26. *Journal Officiel*, May 16; *Le Populaire*, May 17.
27. Abbé Coullié, *Saint-Eustache pendant la Commune*, pp. 46, 79–80.
28. *Ibid.*
29. *Le Vengeur*, May 12.
30. Fontoulieu, *op. cit.*, p. 13.
31. *Ibid.*, pp. 182–184.
32. *Gazette des Tribunaux*, September 11, 1872.
33. *Le Cri du Peuple*, May 10.
34. A.G. Ly 22.
35. Fontoulieu, *op. cit.*, p. 63.
36. A.N. BB 24, 781, 11568, S. 72; A.G. XX, 528.
37. Fontoulieu, *op. cit.*, pp. 270–275; Marc de Villiers, *Histoire des Clubs des Femmes*, p. 397.
38. Fontoulieu, *op. cit.*, p. 111.
39. *Ibid.*, p. 175.
40. A.N. BB 24, 761, 6809, S. 72; A.G. XXVI, 212.
41. Fontoulieu, *op. cit.*, p. 80; Da Costa, *La Commune vécue*, pp. 213–220; A.G. VI, 135.

42. *La Commune*, May 7.
43. Fontoulieu, *op. cit.*, p. 224; A.G. Ly 22.
44. A.N. BB 24, 768, 8345, S. 72.
45. BB 24, 760, 6427, S. 72 and 4826, S. 76; A.G. XV, 419.
46. A.G. Ly. 22.
47. Fontoulieu, *op. cit.*, pp. 228–229.
48. A.G. IV, 57.
49. *Ibid.*; A.N. BB 24, 736, 1046, S. 72.

Chapter 7

1. Louis Barron, *Sous le drapeau rouge*, quoted in H. d'Alméras, *La Vie parisienne pendant le Siège et sous la Commune*, p. 489.
2. *Journal Officiel*, May 5.
3. *La Sociale*, May 9.
4. P. Fontoulieu, *Les Églises de Paris sous la Commune*, p. 217.
5. *L'Étoile*, May 10.
6. A.G. Ly 22.
7. *Enquête Parlementaire*, III, p. 204.
8. *Le Cri du Peuple*, May 20.
9. *Journal Officiel*, May 19.
10. *Ibid.*, May 18.
11. *Procès-Verbaux de la Commune de 1871*, II, pp. 446.
12. Louise Michel, *La Commune*, p. 248; Maurice Dommanget, *Hommes et Choses de la Commune*, pp. 200–205.
13. A.G. Ly 22, *Club Saint-Ambroise*.
14. A.G. Ly 22, *Club des Prolétaires*.
15. *La Sociale*, April 5.
16. *Le Cri du Peuple*, April 7.
17. C.-A. Dauban, *Le fond de la société sous la Commune*, p. 205.
18. Benoît Malon, *Troisième défaite*, p. 209.
19. A.G. Council of War XX, 528; A.N. BB 24, 781, 11.568, S. 72.
20. A.N. BB 27, 107–109.
21. A.N. BB 24, 773, 9263, S. 72.
22. A.N. BB 24, 745, 3884, S. 72.
23. A.N. BB 24, 744, 3375, S. 72.
24. A.N. BB 24, 748, 4425, S. 72.
25. A.N. BB 24, 772, 9167, S. 72.
26. A.N. BB 24, 781, 11.470, S. 72.
27. A.G. Ly 22, *Club Saint-Ambroise*.

28. A.G. Ly 22, *Club Révolutionnaire.*
29. *Le Cri du Peuple,* April 25.
30. *Les Misérables,* III, pp. 284–286, 289–290.
31. *Spiridion.*
32. *Le Cri du Peuple,* May 19.

Chapter 8
1. *Journal Officiel,* April 2; *La Sociale,* April 5.
2. *Le Réveil du Peuple,* April 23; *L'Affranchi,* April 24.
3. *Journal Officiel,* April 14; *La Sociale,* April 28; *Le Réveil du Peuple,* April 29.
4. *Journal Officiel,* April 30.
5. A.G. Council of War VI, 135.
6. A.G. Ly 23.
7. *Journal Officiel,* May 15–17.
8. *Journal Officiel,* April 20.
9. *Journal Officiel,* April 30.
10. *Ibid.*
11. P. Fontoulieu, *Les Églises de Paris,* p. 49.
12. *Journal Officiel,* May 12.
13. *Gazette des Tribunaux,* December 16, 1871.
14. A.G. Council of War III, 1416; A.N. BB 24, 852, 732, S. 79.
15. A.G. Ly 23, Schools.
16. Jean Allemane, *Mémoires d'un Communard,* p. 73.
17. *Journal Officiel,* May 16.
18. *Le Vengeur,* April 3.
19. *Journal Officiel,* May 8.
20. *Journal Officiel,* May 13.
21. *Le Cri du Peuple,* May 21.
22. *Journal Officiel,* May 22; A.P. BA 1123.

Chapter 9
1. Benoît Malon, *Troisième défaite,* pp. 273–274.
2. *La Sociale,* April 9.
3. *La Commune,* April 10; *La Sociale,* May 3; Malon, *op. cit.,* pp. 169–173.
4. *La Commune,* April 22; *La Sociale,* April 23.
5. *La Sociale,* May 16.
6. *La Sociale,* April 18.
7. *La Sociale,* April 21.
8. *La Sociale,* April 22.

9. Louis-Nathaniel Rossel, *Mémoires, Procès, et Correspondance*, pp. 250–252.
10. *La Sociale*, May 14.
11. *La Sociale*, May 15.
12. *La Sociale*, April 28.
13. *La Sociale*, April 30.
14. *La Sociale*, May 6, May 8, May 9.
15. *Le Vengeur*, May 8; *L'Étoile*, No. 4.
16. A. Blanchecotte, *Tablettes d'une femme pendant la Commune*, p. 181.
17. Maxime Vuillaume, *Mes Cahiers rouges*, III, p. 234; *L'Avant-Garde*, May 5.
18. *Le Vengeur*, May 8; *L'Étoile*, No. 4.
19. *La Vérité*, May 22.
20. Vuillaume, *op. cit.*, II, p. 129; Gustave Labarthe, *Le Théâtre pendant les jours du Siège et de la Commune*, pp. 127–130.

Chapter 10
1. Louise Michel, *La Commune*, pp. 188–189.
2. *Journal Officiel*, April 14.
3. *Le Cri du Peuple*, April 26; A.G. Ly 23.
4. *Le Cri du Peuple*, April 28.
5. *Le Cri du Peuple*, April 30.
6. *Journal Officiel*, May 12.
7. Jean Allemane, *Mémoires d'un Communard*, p. 81.
8. *La Vérité*, May 13; *Journal Officiel*, May 22.
9. *La Sociale*, April 25.
10. *La Sociale*, April 22.
11. Michel, *op. cit.*
12. *Ibid.*
13. A.G. Ly 23.
14. Account by Béatrix Excoffon in Louise Michel's *La Commune*, pp. 404–407.
15. *Ibid.*
16. Vuillaume, *Mes Cahiers rouges*, IV, p. 113.
17. Victorine Brochon, *Souvenirs d'une morte vivante*, pp. 122–127.
18. *Les Milliet: La Commune et le second Siège de Paris. Alix Payen ambulancière*, pp. 67–99.
19. *La Sociale*, May 13; *Le Cri du Peuple*, May 21.
20. *Procès-Verbaux de la Commune*, II, p. 380.

21. *La Sociale,* May 6.
22. *La Sociale,* May 7.
23. *La Sociale,* May 9. The first woman to receive an M.D. degree was an Englishwoman, Miss Garrett, in 1870; the second was an American, Miss Putnam, in 1871. Lipinska, *Les Femmes et le progrès des sciences médicales.*
24. *La Sociale,* May 8.
25. *Le Cri du Peuple,* May 20.
26. A. Blanchecotte, *Tablettes d'une femme,* p. 186.
27. B. Malon, *Troisième défaite,* p. 279; A.N. BB 24, 756, 5805, S. 72.
28. *La Justice,* May 15; *La Discussion,* May 15.
29. *Ibid.*
30. Gaston da Costa, *La Commune vécue,* I, p. 373.
31. *L'Affranchi,* April 13, *Le Vengeur,* April 12.
32. *Le Vengeur,* April 12.
33. *La Commune,* April 14.
34. *Le Cri du Peuple* and *La Vérité,* May 18.
35. *Le Vengeur,* April 12.
36. *La Commune,* April 20.
37. *Le Cri du Peuple,* April 8.
38. *La Commune,* April 18; *L'Avant-Garde,* April 19.
39. *Le Cri du Peuple,* May 22.
40. *Journal Officiel,* May 17.
41. A.N. BB 24, 759, 6263, S. 72.
42. *Journal Officiel,* April 9.
43. *La Commune,* April 12–13.
44. Louise Michel, *Mémoires,* p. 70.
45. Jules Clère, *Les Hommes de la Commune,* pp. 88–89.
46. A. J. Dalsème, *Histoire des Conspirations sous la Commune,* p. 127; Maxime du Camp, *Les Convulsions de Paris,* II, p. 102.
47. Louise Michel, *La Commune,* p. 192.
48. *La Montagne,* April 16; *Journal Officiel,* April 20.
49. Michel, *La Commune,* pp. 161–162.
50. *Ibid.,* p. 189.
51. *Journal Officiel,* April 10.
52. Michel, *La Commune,* pp. 192–193, 219.

Chapter 11

1. *La Sociale,* April 20.
2. H.-P.-O. Lissagaray, *Huit Journées,* pp. 29–30.

3. *Bulletin Communal,* 3 Prairial, 79. [As the days of the Commune drew to a close, the French Revolutionary Calendar came increasingly into vogue. This was May 23.—*Trans.*]
4. Jules Vallès, *L'Insurgé,* p. 255.
5. Lissagaray, *op. cit.,* p. 50.
6. *Ibid.*
7. A. Blanchecotte, *Tablettes d'une femme,* pp. 257–258.
8. A.N. BB 24, 765, 7603, S. 72.
9. A.N. BB 24, 746, 3960, S. 72.
10. A.N. BB 24, 787, 779, S. 73.
11. A.N. BB 24, 735, 837, S. 72.
12. A.N. BB 24, 753, 5271, S. 72.
13. A.N. BB 24, 798, 62, S. 74.
14. A.N. BB 24, 782, 12096, S. 72.
15. A.N. BB 24, 748, 4540, S. 72.
16. A.N. BB 24, 778, 11072, S. 72.
17. A.N. BB 24, 758, 6120, S. 72.
18. A.N. BB 24, 799, 981, S. 74.
19. A.N. BB 24, 798, 60, S. 74.
20. A.N. BB 24, 738, 1493, S. 72; A.G. IV, 62.
21. A.N. BB 24, 775, 10096, S. 72.
22. A.N. BB 24, 737, 1149, S. 72; BB 27, 107–109.
23. A. Clémence, *L'Amnistie au Parlement,* p. 74.
24. A.G. IV 688.
25. Lissagaray, *Huit Journées,* p. 61.
26. *Ibid.,* p. 63.
27. A.G. VI, 683.
28. Louise Michel, *La Commune,* p. 266.
29. Camille Pelletan, *Le Comité central,* pp. 162–166, quoted in Georges Bourgin, *La Commune,* p. 174, note 3.
30. B. Malon, *Troisième, défaite,* p. 410; Karl Marx, *La Guerre Civile,* p. 65.
31. Malon, *op. cit.,* p. 432.
32. Lissagaray, *Huit Journées,* p. 93.
33. Lissagaray, *Histoire de la Commune,* p. 340.
34. J. Allemane, *Mémoires d'un Communard,* pp. 130–131.
35. A. Blanchecotte, *Tablettes d'une femme,* p. 274.
36. Malon, *Troisième Défaite,* p. 461.
37. *Ibid.;* Lissagaray, *Huit Journées,* May 27.
38. Arsène Houssaye, *Les Comédiens sans le savoir,* quoted in Henri Alméras, *La Vie Parisienne pendant le Siège et sous la Commune,* pp. 519–522.

39. M. Vuillaume, *Mes Cahiers rouges,* I, 78, note 1.
40. Lissagaray, *Histoire de la Commune,* p. 382.
41. Lissagaray, *Huit Journées,* p. 170.
42. *Ibid.,* pp. 297–298, note 5; *Histoire de la Commune,* pp. 526–527.
43. *The Times,* May 29.
44. Maxime du Camp, *Les Convulsions de Paris,* II, 419.
45. Lissagaray, *Huit Journées,* p. 202.
46. Michel, *La Commune,* pp. 295–300.
47. *Ibid.,* Béatrix Excoffon's account, p. 407.
48. *Ibid.,* p. 306.
49. *Ibid.,* p. 409.
50. Mme. C. Hardouin, schoolteacher, *La détenue de Versailles en 1871.*
51. Lissagaray, *Histoire de la Commune,* p. 401.

Chapter 12

1. *L'Avant-Garde,* May 27, 1871.
2. H.-P.-O. Lissagaray, *Huit Journées,* pp. 248–253; *Histoire de la Commune,* p. 392.
3. Gustave Lefrançais, *Souvenirs,* p. 568.
4. Lissagaray, *Huit Journées,* p. 253.
5. *Ibid.,* p. 97.
6. Maxime du Camp, *Convulsions de Paris,* II, pp. 401–403.
7. Louise Michel, *La Commune,* p. 274.
8. Lissagaray, *Histoire de la Commune,* pp. 533–534.
9. M. Rubel, "Deux interviews de Karl Marx sur la Commune," *Le Mouvement Social,* March, 1962.
10. *La Sociale,* April 20; A.G. Ly 23.
11. Lissagaray, *Histoire de la Commune,* p. 286.
12. *Enquête Parlementaire sur l'insurrection du 18 mars 1871,* II, pp. 362–364.
13. A.N. BB 24, 731, 5412, S. 71.
14. A.N. BB 24, 748, 4503, S. 72, and 733, 89, S. 72. *Gazette des Tribunaux,* October 1.
15. A.N. BB 24, 780, 11441, S. 72; A.G. IV, 639.
16. A.G. IV, 21.
17. *Ibid.*
18. A.N. BB 24, 730, 3975, S. 71.
19. A.G. IV, 21, evidence of her landlord, Verry.
20. *Gazette des Tribunaux,* September 4–5, 1871.
21. *Ibid.*
22. *Ibid.*

23. *Ibid.*
24. A.N. BB 24, 730, 3975, S. 71.
25. A.G. IV, 21; A.N. BB 24, 764, 7519, S. 72.
26. *Ibid.*
27. A.G. IV, 21; A.N. BB 24, 730, 3975, S. 71.
28. *Gazette des Tribunaux,* September 4–5, 1871.
29. A.G. IV, 21.
30. *Gazette des Tribunaux,* September 6.
31. *Ibid.*
32. *Ibid.*
33. Victor Hugo, *Depuis l'exil, 1871–1876,* pp. 17–18.
34. *Ibid.,* p. 16.
35. *Gazette des Tribunaux,* December 15; A.N. BB 24, 730, 3975, S. 71.
36. Du Camp, *Convulsions de Paris,* III, pp. 113–114.
37. *Ibid.,* pp. 122, 481.
38. A.G. IV, 439, Evidence of Ignace Langlet.
39. A.G. IV, 439; A.N. BB 24, 762, 6976, S. 72.
40. *Ibid.*
41. A.G. IV, 439.
42. *Ibid.*
43. Du Camp, *Convulsions de Paris,* III, pp. 113–114.
44. A.G. IV, 439; A.N. BB 24, 744, 3312, S. 72.
45. *Gazette des Tribunaux,* April 17, 1872.
46. A.N. BB 24, 746, 4082, S. 72.
47. A.N. BB 24, 762, 6976, S. 72.

Chapter 13

1. *Journal Officiel,* April 6.
2. *Procès-Verbaux de la Commune de 1871,* II, p. 388.
3. Lissagaray, *Histoire de la Commune,* p. 325.
4. A.N. AB XIX, 3353, dossier 10.
5. Pierre Lévêque, "Le nombre des victimes de la Commune," *L'Information Historique,* November–December, 1960.
6. Maxime du Camp, *Convulsions de Paris,* IV, p. 209; Gaston da Costa, *La Commune vécue,* p. 474.
7. A.N. BB 24, 761, 6771, S. 72; A.G. VI, 549. *Gazette des Tribunaux,* July 3, 1872.
8. Lissagaray, *Histoire de la Commune,* pp. 338, 532.
9. A.N. BB 24, 759, 6263, S. 72; *Gazette des Tribunaux,* January 10–11, 1872; Da Costa, *op. cit.,* II, p. 2.

10. Du Camp, *op. cit.*, I, 299.
11. *Gazette des Tribunaux*, February 14–18, 1872.
12. *Gazette des Tribunaux*, March 13, 1872.
13. Jules Vallès, *L'Insurgé*, pp. 285–287.
14. A.N. BB 24, 782, 11788, S. 72.
15. A.N. BB 24, 759, 6314, S. 72; 747, 4186, S. 72.
16. *Gazette des Tribunaux*, April 24, 1872.
17. *Ibid.*
18. A.N. BB 24, 759, 6314, S. 72; 747, 4186, S. 72.

Chapter 14
1. *Gazette des Tribunaux*, December 17; A.G. VI, 135; A.N. BB 24, 882, 4922, S. 76.
2. *Gazette des Tribunaux*, December 18, 1871.
3. A.N. BB 24, 781, 11688, S. 72.
4. A.G. IV, 57; A.N. BB 24, 736, 1046, S. 72.
5. *Ibid.*
6. *Ibid.*
7. *Ibid.*
8. *Ibid.*
9. *Ibid.*
10. A.N. BB 24, 862, 5156, S. 79.
11. *La Sociale*, May 12.
12. V. Soukholmine, "Deux femmes russes combattantes de la Commune," *Cahiers Internationaux*, XVI (May, 1950), p. 62; A.P. BA 1008.
13. André Léo, *La guerre sociale*, Neuchâtel, 1871; AP BA 1008.
14. *Gazette des Tribunaux*, September 11, 1872; A.G. IV 688; A.N. BB 24, 792, S. 73.
15. A.N. BB 24, 856, 2832; A.G. VI, 683.
16. H.-P.-O. Lissagaray, *Huit Journées*, p. 115.
17. Lissagaray, *Histoire de la Commune*, p. 534, Appendix.
18. P. Tchérednitchenko, "La vie généreuse et mouvementée d'Élise Tomanovskaiia," *Études Soviétiques*, June 1955.
19. A.N. BB 24, 862, 5738, S. 79.
20. A.N. BB 24, 852, 732, S. 79; A.G. III, 1416.
21. A.N. BB 24, 852, 732, S. 79.
22. *Gazette des Tribunaux*, December 16.
23. A.G. XV, 419; BB 24, 760, 6427, S. 72, and 4826, S. 76.
24. A.N. BB 27, 107–109.
25. A.N. BB 24, 745, 3885.

26. A.G. XXVI, 155.
27. A.N. BB 24, 749, 5742, S. 72.
28. A.G. XV, 478; BB 24, 745, 3837, S. 72.

Chapter 15

1. Louise Michel, *La Commune*, p. 344; *Mémoires*, p. 205.
2. Michel, *Mémoires*, p. 343.
3. Michel, *La Commune*, p. 353.
4. Henri Rochefort, *Les Aventures de ma vie*, III, pp. 254 ff.
5. Michel, *La Commune*, pp. 354, 355; *Mémoires*, pp. 283–287.
6. Michel, *La Commune*, p. 440.
7. Michel, *Mémoires*, p. 306.
8. Michel, *La Commune*, p. 373.
9. Michel, *Mémoires*, p. 307.
10. Michel, *La Commune*, p. 387.
11. Michel, *La Commune*, p. 376.
12. A.N. BB 24, 786, 70, S. 73.
13. A.N. BB 24, 838, 2814, S. 77.
14. A.N. BB 24, 776, 10384, S. 72, and F 7, 12695–12696.
15. A.N. BB 24, 775, 10096, S. 72; BB 24, 732, 5705, S. 71.
16. A.N. BB 24, 768, 8345, S. 72.
17. A.N. BB 24, 760, 6407, S. 72.
18. A.N. BB 24, 781, 11470, S. 72.
19. A.N. BB 24, 747, 4186, S. 72.
20. A.N. BB 24, 747, 4183, S. 72.
21. A.N. BB 24, 773, 9289, S. 72.
22. Da Costa, *La Commune vécue*, I, pp. 402–403.
23. A.N. BB 24, 759, 6263, S. 72.
24. *Enquête Parlementaire sur l'Insurrection du 18 Mars*, III, p. 309.
25. *Les Poètes de la Commune*, p. 68.
26. *Ibid.*, p. 154.
27. *Ibid.*, pp. 41–43.
28. *Ibid.*, pp. 64–65.
29. Victor Hugo, *L'Année Terrible*, pp. 222–223.
30. Hugo, *Toute la Lyre*, I, 39. "Victor Hugo à Louise Michel: Viro Major."
31. Paul Verlaine, *Oeuvres poétiques complètes*. Bibliothèque de la Pléiade. "Ballade en honneur de Louise Michel," p. 299.

32. Arthur Rimbaud, *Oeuvres complètes.* Bibliothéque de la Pléiade, p. 83.

Appendix

1. A.N. BB 27, 107–109.
2. A.N. BB 24, 773, 9289, S. 72.
3. A.N. BB 24, 747, 4183, S. 72.
4. A.N. BB 24, 836, 2440, S. 77.
5. A.N. BB 24, 775, 10.287, S. 72.
6. A.N. BB 24, 822, 4512, S. 76; BB 27, 107–109, supplement.
7. A.N. BB 24, 838, 2812, S. 77.
8. A.N. BB 24, 786, 70, S. 73.
9. A.N. BB 24, 775, 10096, S. 72; BB 24, 732, 5705, S. 71; A.G. IV, 142.
10. A.N. BB 24, 753, 5271, S. 72.
11. A.N. BB 24, 738, 1493, S. 72; A.G. IV, 62. *Gazette des Tribunaux,* October 16–17.
12. A.N. BB 24, 737, 1149, S. 72.
13. A.N. BB 24, 778, 11072, S. 72.
14. A.N. BB 24, 781, 11568, S. 72; A.G. XX, 528; *Gazette des Tribunaux,* August 7, 1872.
15. A.N. BB 24, 761, 6809, S. 72; A.G. XXVI, 212.
16. A.N. BB 24, 756, 5805, S. 72; A.G. XXVI, 94.
17. A.N. BB 24, 762, 6961, S. 72.
18. A.N. BB 24, 744, 3375, S. 72.
19. A.N. BB 24, 748, 4425, S. 72.
20. A.N. BB 24, 773, 9209, S. 72.
21. A.N. BB 24, 755, 5676, S. 72.
22. A.N. BB 24, 773, 9263, S. 72.
23. A.N. BB 24, 780, 11297, S. 72.
24. A.N. BB 24, 781, 11470, S. 72.
25. A.N. BB 24, 768, 8345, S. 72.
26. A.N. BB 24, 776, 10384, S. 72.
27. A.N. BB 24, 771, 9112, S. 72.
28. *Gazette des Tribunaux,* May 16–19, 1872.
29. A.N. BB 24, 783, 12217, S. 72.
30. A.N. BB 24, 856 B, 2793, S. 79.
31. A.N. BB 24, 756, 5756, S. 72.
32. *Gazette des Tribunaux,* January 18, 1872; A.G. Ly 23.
33. Victor Hugo, *Depuis l'Exil,* II, p. 17.

MANUSCRIPT SOURCES

National Archives (A.N.) : Index cards on the reprieved of the Commune: BB 27, 107–109. Reprieve dossiers: BB 24. Documents concerning the deported and exiled: F 7, 12695–12698. Drawings with captions portraying the women of the Commune: AB XIX 3353, Dossier #10.

Archives of the Seine (A.S.) : Municipal buildings of Paris: V bis 388.

Archives of the Ministry of War (A.G.): Dossiers from the Councils of War of 1871. Documents concerning the Clubs and the Women's Committees: Ly 22 and Ly 23.

Archives of the Prefecture of Police (A.P.) : BA 1008, 1123, 1183.

NEWSPAPERS CONSULTED

L'Action.
L'Affranchi.
L'Avant-Garde.
La Commune.
Le Cri du Peuple.
La Discussion.
L'Étoile.
Le Figaro.
Gazette des Tribunaux.
Journal Officiel de la République Française (La Commune).
La Justice.
Le Moniteur des Citoyennes, 1870.
La Montagne.
La Patrie.
Le Père Duchêne.
Le Réveil du Peuple.
La Révolution politique et sociale.
Le Rouge, journal des Jeunes.
La Sociale.
The Times [of London].
Le Vengeur.
La Vérité.

BIBLIOGRAPHY

Adam, Mme. Edmond. *Idées anti-proudhoniennes sur l'amour, la femme et le mariage.* Mme. Juliette La Messine. Paris: A. Taride, 1858.

Allemane, Jean. *Mémoires d'un Communard. Des Barricades au Bagne.* Paris: Librairie socialiste, 1910.

Alméras, Henri. *La Vie parisienne pendant le Siège et sous la Commune.* Paris: Albin Michel, 1925.

Amodru, Abbé Laurent. *Annales de Notre-Dame des Victoires . . . publiées en 1871 et 1872 par . . . avec un supplément renfermant des documents inédits sur le Siège et la Commune.* Paris: Le Coffre, 1891.

Arnould, Arthur. *Histoire populaire et parlementaire de la Commune de Paris.* 3 vols. Brussels: Librairie Socialiste H. Kistemaeckers, 1878.

Audebrand, Philibert. *Histoire intime de la Révolution du 18 mars.* Paris: Dentu, 1871.

Audouard, Olympe. *Guerre aux hommes.* Paris: Dentu, 1866.

————. *Le luxe effréné des hommes.* Paris: Dentu, 1865.

B . . . (Victorine Brochon). *Souvenirs d'une morte vivante. 1848–1851, 1870–1871.* Preface by Lucien Descaves. Lausanne: Librairie A. Lapie, 1909.

Barron, Louis. *Sous le drapeau rouge.* Paris: A. Savine, 1889.

Bellessort, André. *La société française sous Napoléon III.* Paris: 1960.

Blanchecotte, Augustine-Malvine. *Tablettes d'une femme pendant la Commune.* Paris: Didier, 1872.

Bourgin, Georges. *Histoire de la Commune.* Paris: Publications de la Société Nouvelle, E. Cornely et Cie, 1907.

————. *La Commune.* Paris: Presses Universitaires Françaises, 1953.

Boyer, Irma. *Louise Michel, la vierge rouge.* Preface by Henri Barbusse. Paris: Delpuech, 1927.

Bruhat, Jean; Dautry, Jean; and Tersen, Émile; eds. (with the collaboration of Pierre Angrand, Jean Bouvier, Henri Dubief, Jeanne Gaillard, and Claude Perrot). *La Commune de 1871.* Paris: Éditions sociales, 1960.

Chevalier, Louis. *Classes laborieuses, classes dangereuses à Paris pendant la première moitié du XIXᵉ siècle.* Paris: Plon, 1958.

Clère, Jules. *Les Hommes de la Commune. Biographie complète de tous ses membres.* Paris: Dentu, 1871.

Cluseret, General Gustave-Paul. *Mémoires.* 3 vols. Paris: L. Lévy, 1887–1888.

Cobb, Robert. "Mentalité révolutionnaire," *La Revue d'histoire moderne et contemporaine,* April–June, 1959.

Coullié, Abbé. *Saint-Eustache pendant la Commune, mars, avril, mai, 1871.* Paris: Imprimerie et Librairie administratives, 1871.

Da Costa, Gaston. *La Commune vécue, 18 mars–28 mai 1871.* 3 vols. Paris: Ancienne Maison Quantin, Librairie-Imprimerie réunies, 1903–1905.

Dalsème, Achille. *Histoire des Conspirations sous la Commune.* Paris: Dentu, 1872.

Dauban, Charles-Aimé. *Le fond de la société sous la Commune décrit d'après les documents qui constituent les Archives de la justice militaire avec des considérations critiques sur les moeurs du temps et sur les événements qui ont précédé la Commune.* Paris: Plon, 1873.

Daubié, Julie. *La femme pauvre au XIXᵉ siècle.* Paris: Guillaumin, 1866.

Dautry, Jean and Scheler, Lucien, eds. *Le Comité central républicain des vingt arrondissements de Paris (septembre 1870–mai 1871) d'après les papiers inédits de Constant Martin et les sources imprimées.* Paris: Éditions sociales, 1960.

Dayot, Armand. *L'Invasion, le Siège, la Commune 1870–1871, d'après des peintures, gravures, photographies, sculptures, médailles, autographes, objets du temps.* Paris: Flammarion, n.d.

Delmas, Abbé. *La Terreur dans l'Église en 1871.* Paris: Dentu, 1871.

Deraismes, Maria. *Œuvres complètes.* 4 vols. Paris: Alcan, 1895–1898.

Dommanget, Maurice. *Blanqui et l'opposition révolutionnaire à la fin du Second Empire.* Paris: Colin, 1960.

———. *Hommes et choses de la Commune.* Marseille: Éditions de la Coopérative des Amis de l'École émancipée, 1937.

Du Camp, Maxime. *Les Convulsions de Paris*. 4 vols. Paris: Hachette, 1878–1880. (Copy annotated by the author in the Library of the Archives Nationales.)

Duveau, Georges. *La vie ouvrière en France sous le Second Empire*. Preface by Édouard Dolléans. Paris: Gallimard, 1946.

Enquête Parlementaire sur l'insurrection du 18 mars 1871. 3 vols. Versailles: Cerf, Imprimerie de l'Assemblée Nationale, 1872.

Esquiros, Adèle. *L'amour*. Paris, 1860.

————. *Les amours étranges*. Paris: A. Courcier, 1853.

————. *Histoire d'une sous-maîtresse*. Paris: E. Pick, 1861.

————. *Un vieux bas-bleu*. *L'amour au couvent*, in *Les Veillées Littéraires illustrées*. Paris: J. Bry aîné, 1849.

Excoffon, Béatrix. *Récit* in *La Commune* by Louise Michel.

Femmes célebrès (Les). 2 vols. Paris: Éd. Mazenod, 1960–61.

Fontoulieu, Paul. *Les Églises de Paris sous la Commune*. Preface by A. de Pontmartin. Paris: Dentu, 1873.

Grousset, Paschal, and Jourde, Francis. *Les condamnés politiques en Nouvelle-Calédonie. Récit de deux évadés*. Geneva: Ziegler, 1876.

Hardouin, Mme. C., Schoolteacher. *La détenue de Versailles en 1871*. Paris: published by the author, 1879.

Hemday. *Bibliographie de Louise Michel, 1830–1905*. Brussels-Paris: Pensée et Action, 1959.

Héricourt, Jenny d'. *La femme affranchie, réponse à MM. Michelet, Proudhon, E. de Girardin, A. Comte et aux autres novateurs modernes*. 2 vols. Brussels: A. Lacroix, Van Meenen et Cie, 1860.

Houssaye, Arsène. *Les Comédiens sans le savoir*. Paris: Librairie illustrée, 1886.

Hugo, Victor. *L'Année Terrible*.

————. *Toute la Lyre*.

————. *Depuis l'Exil, 1871–1876*.

————. *Carnets intimes. 1870–1871*.

Jeloubovskaïa, E. *La chute du Second Empire et la naissance de la Troisième République en France*. Moscow: Foreign Language Editions, 1959.

Labarthe, Gustave. *Le Théâtre pendant les jours du Siège et de la Commune*. Paris: Librairie Fischbacher, 1910.

Lanjalley, Paul, and Corriez, Paul. *Histoire de la Révolution du 18 mars.* Paris-Brussels: A. Lacroix, Verboeckhoven et Cie, 1871.

Lecour, Charles-Jérôme. *La prostitution à Paris et à Londres, 1789–1871, augmenté des chapitres sur la prostitution à Paris pendant le Siège et la Commune.* . . . Paris: Asselin, 1872.

Lefrançais, Gustave. *Souvenirs d'un révolutionnaire.* Preface by Lucien Descaves. Brussels: Les Temps Nouveaux, 1902.

Lenin, Nikolai. *The Paris Commune.* Moscow: Foreign Language Editions, n.d.

Léo, André. *Une divorce.* Paris: Librarie Internationale, 1866.

———. *La femme et les moeurs, Liberté ou Monarchie.* Paris: Le Droit des Femmes, 1869.

———. *La Guerre sociale. Discours prononcé au Congrès de la Paix à Lausanne, 1871.* Neuchâtel: Imprimerie G. Guillaume fils, 1871.

———. *Un mariage scandaleux.* Paris: Hachette, 1862.

———. *La vieille fille. Articles de divers journaux sur un mariage scandaleux.* Paris: Achille Faure, 1864.

Lepelletier, Edmond. *Histoire de la Commune de 1871.* 3 vols. Paris: Mercure de France, 1911–1913.

Levêque, Pierre. "Le nombre des victimes de la Commune," *L'Information historique,* November–December, 1960.

L'Huillier, Fernand. *La lutte ouvrière à la fin du Second Empire.* Paris: A. Colin, 1957.

Lipinska, Dr. Melina. *Les Femmes et le Progrès des Sciences médicales.* Paris: Masson, 1930.

Lissagaray, Hippolyte-Prosper-Olivier. *Histoire de la Commune de Paris. Nouvelle édition précédée d'une notice sur Lissagaray par Amédée Dunois.* Paris: Librairie du Travail, 1929.

———. *Les huit journées de mai derrière les barricades.* Brussels: Bureau du Petit Journal, 1871.

Malon, Benoît. *La Troisième Défaite du Prolétariat français.* Neuchâtel: G. Guillaume fils, 1871.

Marx, Karl. *La Guerre Civile en France, 1871.* Paris: Bureau d'Édition, 1933.

———. "Deux Interviews de Karl Marx sur la Commune," (ed. M. Rubel). *Le Mouvement social,* January–March, 1962.

Michel, Louise. *La Commune.* "Bibliothèque Sociologique," #22. Paris: P.V. Stock, 1898.

————. *Mémoires.* Paris: F. Roy, 1886. Vol. I.

————. *A travers la vie, avec illustrations de l'auteur.* Paris: Librarie des Publications à cinq centimes, n.d.

Milliet (Les). Une famille de républicains fouriéristes. Paris: Cahiers de la Quinzaine. Vol. X.

Molinari, G. de. *Les clubs rouges pendant le siège de Paris.* Paris: Garnier frères, 1871.

Parent-Duchâtelet, Dr. Alexandre Jean-Baptiste. *De la Prostitution dans la ville de Paris.* 2 vols. Paris: J.-B. Baillière et fils, 1857.

Paty, Jules [Marguerite Tinayre]. *Un Rêve de femme.* 2 vols. Paris: l'éditeur 53 Rue Sainte-Anne, 1865.

————. *La Marguerite.*

Pelletan, Camille. *Question d'histoire. Le Comité central de la Commune.* Paris: M. Dreyfous, 1879.

————. *La Semaine de Mai.* Paris: M. Dreyfous, 1880.

Perrier, A. "Grégoire Champseix et André Léo," *L'Actualité de l'Histoire,* January–March, 1960.

Planche, Fernand. *La vie ardente et intrépide de Louise Michel, avec des documents inédits et de nombreux portraits.* Paris: Imprimerie La Slim, 1946.

Poètes de la Commune, Les. With a preface by Jean Varloot for the eightieth anniversary of the Paris Commune. Paris: Éditeurs Français Réunis, 1951.

Procès-Verbaux de la Commune de 1871. Critical edition by Georges Bourgin and Gabriel Henroit. 2 vols. Paris: A. Leroux and E. Lahure, 1924–1945.

Proudhon, Pierre-Joseph. *Amour et Mariage.* Paris: A. Lacroix, 1876.

————. *La Pornocratie ou les femmes dans les temps modernes.* Paris: A. Lacroix, 1875.

Ravailhe, Chanoine Romain Pierre. *Une semaine de la Commune de Paris.* Paris: V. Palmé, 1883.

Reclus, Élie. *La Commune au jour le jour. 1871, 19 mars–28 mai.* Paris: Reinwald-Schleicher, 1908.

Rimbaud, Arthur. *Oeuvres complètes.* "Bibliothèque de la Pléiade." Paris: Gallimard, 1946.

Rochefort, Henri. *Les Aventures de ma vie.* 5 vols. Paris: Dupont, 1896–1898.

Rossel, Louis-Nathaniel. *Mémoires, Procès et correspondance, présentés par Roger Stéphane.* Paris: J.-J. Pauvert, 1960.

Sarcey, Francisque. *Le siège de Paris. Impressions et souvenirs.* Paris: E. Lachaud, 1871.

Schulkind, Eugène W. "Le rôle des femmes dans la Commune de 1871," *1848, revue des révolutions contemporaines,* Vol. XLII, February, 1950.

Simon, Jules. *L'ouvrière.* Paris: L. Hachette, 1861.

Soukholmine, Vassili. "Deux femmes russes combattantes de la Commune," *Cahiers Internationaux,* XVI, May, 1950.

Tchérednitchenko, P. "La vie généreuse et mouvementée d'Elisa Tomanovskaïa . . . ," *Études Soviétiques,* LXXXVII, June, 1955.

Tchernoff, Iouda. *Le parti républicain au Coup d'État et sous le Second Empire, d'après des documents et des souvenirs inédits.* Paris: A. Pédone, 1906.

Vallès, Jules. *L'Insurgé.* Paris: Nouvelle Librairie de France, 1950.

Vanier, Henriette. *La mode et ses métiers. Frivolités et Lutte des classes, 1830–1870. Les Faits, la Presse, l'Opinion.* Paris: A. Colin, 1960.

Verlaine, Paul. *Œuvres poétiques complètes.* "Bibliothèque de la Pléiade." Paris: Gallimard, 1954.

Vermersch, Eugène. *Les Incendiaires.* London: 29 Frith Street (Soho), 1872.

Vésinier, Pierre. *Histoire de la Commune de Paris.* London: Chapmann and Hall, 1871.

Villiers, Baron Marc de. *Histoire des clubs de femmes et des légions d'Amazones: 1793–1848–1871.* Paris: Plon-Nourrit, 1910.

Vuillaume, Maxime. *Mes Cahiers Rouges.* 10 vols. Paris: Cahiers de la Quinzaine.

Weill, Georges. *Histoire du parti républicain en France de 1814 à 1870.* Paris: 1900.

Wyczanska, Krystyna. *Polacy w Kommune Paryskiej 1871.* Warszawa.

INDEX

Allix, Jules, 40, 71, 74, 77, 89, 91, 113, 115, 117, 177, 178
Amodru, Abbé, 94
André, Agathe, 215
André, Françoise, 109
Arnould, Arthur, 64
Arzelier, Louise, 109
Audouard, Olympe, 33
Audrain, Marie, 109, 238–39
Aurevilly, Barbey d', 27

Babick, Jules, 10
Bakunin, Mikhail, 73, 120
Barbier, Auguste, 131
Beaufort, Comte de, 191–94
Bellanger, Marguerite, 3
Belly, Félix, 42–44
Béra, Léonide, see Léo, André
Bernard, Claude, 19, 220
Bertranine, Jeanne, 233–34
Billault, Madeleine, 154
Blanqui, Louis Auguste, 101, 110, 146, 201
Blanquists, 34, 35, 90, 92
Bocquin, Lucie, see Maris, Lucie
Boidard, Constance, 42
Boisselin, Lucie-Euphrasie, 222, 234
Bonaparte, Pierre, 34
Bordas, Rosalie, 130, 131
Bouquet, Marie-Jeanne, 98, 187
Bourroit, Julie, 97
Braun, Marie, 222
Briot, Captain, 223, 224
Brochon, Victorine, 6–7, 9, 34, 36, 39–40, 41, 137
Brunel, Antoine, 171, 182–83
Bruteau, Eugénie, 217, 235

Cailleux, Marie, 196, 220, 222

Camp, Maxime du, ix–x, 93, 146, 147, 161, 167, 169, 172, 182, 185, 187, 191, 210, 225
Cartier, Marie, 114, 154
Champseix, Grégoire, 30
Chartrus, Célina, 153
Chiffon, Jules, 154, 222
Chiffon, Marie, see Gaboriaud, Marie-Augustine
Chilly, Eugénie, 171–72
Clariot, Amélie Célestine, 191, 192
Clemenceau, Georges, 40, 53, 202
Club de Belleville, 49–50
Club de la Boule Noire, 201, 202
Club de la Révolution Sociale, 142, 143
Club de l'Église Saint-Bernard, 237
Club de l'Église Saint-Éloi, 237
Club des Prolétaries, 107
Club Saint-Michel, 215, 240
Club Saint-Nicolas-des-Champs, 187
Clubs, 45, 48, 49–50, 88–103, 104, 105–11, 134, 135, 147, 224
Cluseret, General, 108, 129
Colleville, Henri, 71
Colleville, Noémie, 67
Collot, Anne, 215, 222, 240
Comédie Française, 131–32
Comité des Femmes, 40, 70–71, 91
Commune Sociale de Paris, La, 113
Comte, Auguste, 21, 24
Cornelly de la Perrière, Jeanne Blanche, 28
Cornet, Octavie, 240–41
Coullié, Abbé, 98
Courtois, Joséphine, 153, 235

Da Costa, Gaston, 56, 191
Daubié, Julie, 7–8, 15

Decroix, Antoinette, 107
Deguy, Élizabeth, 99, 222
Delavot, Rosalie Joséphine, 238
Delescluze, Charles, 34, 126, 192, 193
Dellière, Henriette-Marie, 240–41
Delmas, Abbé, 94
Delorme, Emmanuel, 226
Delvainquier, Aimée, 67
Delvainquier, Celine, 67
Demahis, Charles-Étienne, 16
Demar, Claire, viii
Denis, Anne, 116, 213–14
Deraismes, Maria, 27, 28, 33
Deroin, Jeanne, viii, 10, 140
Desfossés, Adèle, 231–32
Desfossés, Louise, 222
Desmoulins, Camille, 243
Dmitrieff, Elizabeth, 41, 67, 89, 90, 91, 95, 156, 209–11, 225
  and Union des Femmes, 70–75, 77, 82–83, 87, 170, 208
Dombrowski, General, 139, 141, 155
Dostoyevsky, Feodor, 72, 90
Dubois, Marcelin, 175
Ducoudray, Félix and Élie, 114
Dulimbert, Joséphine, 99
Dumas fils, Alexandre, xi, 144
Dumay, Edmond, 114
Dumoulin, Marie-Anne, 238
Duvert, Élodie, 153, 235

Esquiros, Adèle, 35
Esquiros, Alphonse, 35
Eudes, General, 35, 36, 133, 146, 172
Euvrie, Ange, 58
Excoffon, Béatrix, 48, 58–59, 89, 102, 133, 135, 136–37, 162, 163, 202–204, 217
Excoffon, Francois, 58, 103, 203
Expilly, Marceline, 191–92, 223

Fayon, Marguerite, 154, 235
Fédération des Sociétés Ouvrières, 11
Fernandez, Mariani, 133, 136

Ferré, Théophile, 47, 147, 166, 181, 198, 218
Flourens, Gustave, 34, 144
Frankel, Léo, 80, 81
Freye, Alphonse, 138

Gaboriaud, Marie-Augustine, 154, 217, 222, 234
Gaillard, Rosalie, 152
Gallois, Célestine, 232–33
Garçon, Ernestine, 241
Garoste, Henriette, 112
Girardin, Émile de, 21, 24, 27
Gorget, Victorine, 102, 163, 222, 239–40
Graix, Sophie, 67
Guerrier, Antoine Ambroise, 10, 211–12
Guerrier, Jean, 11
Guinder, Marguerite, 145–46

Hachette, Jeanne, 95, 147
Haussmann, Georges Eugène, 4, 151, 158, 181, 197
Herbelin, Sidonie Marie, 101, 237
Héricourt, Jenny d', 24–25, 31
Houssaye, Arsène, 160
Hugo, Victor, 17, 41, 47, 111, 131, 181–82, 226, 227, 228, 230, 242

Idées napoléoniennes, 33

Jaclard, Anna, 89–91, 105–106, 118, 134, 135, 141, 204–205, 225
Jaclard, Victor, 90–91, 141, 204
Jacques, Mélanie, 109, 238
Jacquier, Aline, 75, 87
Jarry, Algaé, 75
Jobst, Jeanne-Marie, 98
Jouenne, Captain, 178–80
Justice, La, 143

Kawecka, Lodoyska, 96, 99, 100
Keinerknecht, Louise Elisa, 237
Kovalevsky, Sophie, 89–90, 205

Kovalevsky, Vladimir, 90, 205, 211
Krukovskaya, Anna V. K., see Jac-
   lard, Anna
Krukovskaya, Sophie, see Kovalev-
   sky, Sophie
Krukovsky, Vassily Korvine, 89, 205

Lachaise, Marguerite, 134, 145, 192–
   94, 223
Lafitte, Louise, 112
Lamber, Juliette, 25–26
Lavigne, Anna, 97
Laymet, Jeanne-Victorine, 171
Lecomte, General, 53, 54, 147, 190,
   198, 200
Lefebvre, Blanche, 75, 87, 102, 156,
   211
Lefrançais, Gustave, 31–33
Lemaître, Claudine, 109, 238
Lemel, Nathalie, 9, 10, 39, 45, 74,
   75, 87, 99, 101, 105, 156, 170,
   207–209, 219, 220
Léo, André, 28–31, 33, 34, 35, 74,
   89, 91, 92, 100, 105, 118, 134,
   141, 205–207, 225
   as journalist, 119–30, 139, 140
   and Siege of Paris, 41, 42, 46, 48
Leroux, Pierre, 29, 30
Leroy, Louise, 107
Leroy, Marie, 139, 169, 190, 222
Lissagaray, Hippolyte-Prosper-Olivier, xi–xii, 79, 94, 156, 158,
   167, 209–10, 211
Louvet, Victorine, 146–47

Machu, Aurore, 182, 183, 187
Mains de Jeanne-Marie, Les, 229
Malon, Benoît, xi, 81, 94, 119, 158
Marchais, Joséphine, 172, 175–76,
   180, 181, 187, 223
Marguerite, La, 11–12
Mariage scandaleux, Un, 28–29
Marie Caroline, Queen of Naples,
   96
Maris, Lucie, 172, 175, 181
Marmite, La, 9–10, 39, 207–208

Marx, Karl, viii, xii, 8, 70, 72, 73,
   120, 157, 168, 211
Mason, Amélie, see Wandeval, Florence
Mekarska, Paulina, see Minck, Paule
Mekarski, Jean Népomucène, 28
Mekarski, Jules, 28
Menand, Anne-Marie, 182, 183,
   185–86, 187, 223
Menans, Marie, 99
Méricourt, Théroigne de, 71
Michel, Louise, 26–27, 33, 34, 35,
   36, 52–53, 71, 88, 101, 105, 107,
   124, 129, 146–49, 154, 156, 161,
   162, 163, 167, 205, 207, 209, 211,
   225
   as ambulance nurse, 133–34, 136,
   137, 140
   background of, 15–20
   as prisoner, 217–21
   and Siege of Paris, 39, 41, 44–49
   trial of, 197–201
   tributes to, 227–30
Michel, Marianne, 16, 33, 53
Michelet, Jules, 21, 24, 26–27, 35
Miguet, Marie-Joséphine, 241–42
Mincke, Paule, 28, 96, 101, 116, 205
Montaud, Barral de, 70, 139, 169,
   190
Mont-de-Piété, 7, 12, 57, 63, 80, 101,
   173
Moreau, Édouard, 106
Moreau, Hégésippe, 131
Mortier, Marie, 215–16
Moussu, Marie-Jeanne, 170–71, 223
Musset, Jeanne, 75

Napoleon III, 18, 33
Neckebecker, Louise, 143
Noël, Louise-Frédérique, 171
Noir, Victor, 34, 130, 163

Orlowsky, Jean-Édouard, 102, 214

Papavoine, Eulalie, 163, 172–75,
   181, 187, 226

Parfond, Marie, *see* Miguet, Marie-
 Joséphine
Paris, Archbishop of, 191, 201
Paris, Siege of, 37–51
Paty, Jules, *see* Tinayre, Marguerite
Peace Congress (Lausanne), 205–
 207
Pearl, Cora, 3
Peru, Suzanne, 109
Petit, Jeanne, 215, 222
"*Pétroleuses*," xii, xiv
Piesvaux, Victorine, 75
Pisan, Christine de, *vii*, 15
Poinboeuf, Joséphine, 237–38
Poirier, Sophie (Doctrinal), 40, 44,
 48, 89, 91, 102, 105, 114, 134,
 135, 201–202, 217
Pottier, Eugène, 226–27
Poulain, Malvina, 133, 136, 162
Prat, Joséphine, 67
Preu, Suzanne-Augustine, 222, 239
Proudhon, Pierre Joseph, 9, 21–23,
 24, 26, 28
Pyat, Félix, 98

Quérat, Jeanne-Marie, 154

Ravailhe, Abbé, 94
Reclus, Élisée, 144
Reclus, Noémie, 33, 118
Rétiffe, Élizabeth, 172, 173, 177–78,
 180, 181, 187, 223, 226
Reve de femme, Un, 12, 13
Revolution (1848), *viii,* 14, 25
Revolution (1789), *viii, xi,* 16, 25,
 59, 95
Rigault, Raoul, 147
Rimbaud, Arthur, 226, 227, 229, 230
Rochebrune, Mme. de, 129, 146
Rochefort, Henri, 34, 218, 219
Rogissart, Marie-Catherine, 100,
 109, 236–37
Roland, Pauline, *viii, ix,* 31, 113
Rossel, Louis-Nathaniel, 119, 125–
 26, 140–41, 181
Rouchy, Victorine, 134, 145

Rousseau, Élisa, 231
Rousseau, Éugenie, 154
Rousseau, Jean Jacques, 16, 221

Saint-Hilaire, Geoffroy, 24
Saint-Simon, Comte de, *vii,* 21
Saint-Simonians, *vii,* 10, 21
Sand, George, *viii, ix,* 11, 25, 28, 29,
 111
Schmitt, Marie, 134, 220, 222, 232
Ségaud, Marie, 102, 214–15
Semblat, Joséphine, 240
Séret, Pauline Lise, 194
Siméon, Honorine, 145
Simon, Alexandrine Théodore, 241
Simon, Jules, 5, 6, 7
Simon, Mme. Jules, 33
Sociale, La, 120, 125, 139, 143
*Société de la Revendication du
 Droit de Femmes,* 33
*Société Democratique de Moralisa-
 tion, La,* 19–20
Société des Amis de l'Enseignement,
 114
Société des Droits des Femmes, 30
Société des équitable de Paris, 10
Society for New Education, 112,
 113–14
Stael, Mme. de, *vii, ix*
Stern, Daniel, *vii,* 11
Sue, Eugène, 111
Suétens, Eugénie, 172, 175, 176–77,
 180, 181, 187, 223, 226

Tardif, Octavie, 80, 107
Taveau, Joséphine, 109
Temps des Cerises, Le, 226
Thierry, Palmyre, 42
Thiers, Adolphe, 50, 52, 77, 107,
 124, 139, 147, 198, 200, 241
Thomas, Clément, 55, 147, 190, 198,
 200
Tinayre (Paty), Marguerite, 10, 15,
 116–17, 160, 211–13, 225
 as novelist, 11–14
Tomanovskaya, Elizabeth, *see*

Dmitrieff, Elizabeth
Tristan, Flora, *viii, ix*, 23
Trochu, General, 35, 41, 44, 45, 47, 48, 241

Union des Femmes Pour la Defense de Paris, 66–69, 70–87, 88, 89, 91–92, 102, 107, 110, 136, 155–56, 169, 170, 177, 188, 198, 207, 208, 224, 225, 237, 242
Urbain, Raoul, 139, 169, 190

Vaillant, Édouard, 117, 126
Valentin, Adélaïde, 67, 143
Vallès, Jules, 34, 61, 151, 185, 194
Vallet, Clotilde, 98

Vataire, Octavie, 75, 77
Verdure, Maria, 112, 114
Verlaine, Paul, 226, 227, 229, 230
Vésuviennes, 143
Vigilance committees, 45, 47, 48, 89, 91, 92, 102, 110, 114, 135, 147, 154, 202
Vinoy, General, 48, 53, 55
Vivien, Geneviève, 41
Vrecq, Marie-Virginie, 233
Vuillaume, Maxime, 79, 131, 137, 185

Wandeval, Florence, 182, 183, 184–85, 186–87
Wolff, Marie, 195–96